"An intimate portrait of the surreal terror of growing up in an abusive house-hold, *The Best Girl* takes you on a journey that will ground you in the reality of the fear that many victims of domestic violence face—often in silence. *The Best Girl* is engaging, vulnerable and captivating from beginning to end. Rays of light pierce through the cascade of unceasing torment, shedding light on moments of genuine human joy and contentment providing the reader with insight into the full scope of the author's experiences."

—HUNTER E. CANTRELL

"A compelling emotional journey brimming with strength, survival, tears and even smiles. Told with poetic soul, *The Best Girl* reminds you that hope cannot be stopped."

—RENITA FISHER

The Best Girl

by Joan Hicks Boone

© Copyright 2018 Joan Hicks Boone

ISBN 978-1-63393-582-2

Published by

 köehlerbooks™

210 60th Street
Virginia Beach, VA 23451
800-435-4811
www.koehlerbooks.com

Patricia /
Always
Hold onto
Hope
Joan Hicks Boone

THE
BEST
GIRL

Joan Hicks Boone

VIRGINIA BEACH
CAPE CHARLES

SCHOOL PRAYER

Diane Ackerman

In the name of the daybreak
and the eyelids of the morning
and the wayfaring moon
and the night when it departs,

I swear I will not dishonor
my soul with hatred,
but offer myself humbly
as a guardian of nature,
as a healer of misery,
as a messenger of wonder,
as an architect of peace.

In the name of the sun and its mirrors
and the day that embraces it
and the cloud veils drawn over it
and the uttermost night
and the male and the female
and the plants bursting with seed
and the crowning seasons
of the firefly and the apple,

I will honor all life
—wherever and whatever form
it may dwell—on Earth my home,
and in the mansions of the stars.

For my brother, Mark
You are my idol, my rock star.

For my sister, Gloria
You are the wind beneath my wings.

For my husband, John
My love for you grows stronger every day.

For my sons, Greg and Tony
I am proud to be your mom.

For Donald Hoffman
Thank you for listening.

For child survivors of trauma
Whether you witnessed it or were a target—
I hope The Best Girl *speaks to your truth*
and gives you hope.

IN MEMORIAM

LYLA TIGHE HICKS, AKA "MOM"
FEBRUARY 28, 1929—SEPTEMBER 21, 2012

BERNICE AND LAWRENCE YOUNGBAUER

KAY KEWATT

ANNIE SAWCHUCK

EARLY YEARS

WITNESS

DAD'S IN A VERY bad mood. He's been yelling loudly at Mom almost all day. He keeps yelling louder and louder. I don't want to be in the family room with him. I think we should run away from him! Dad is lying on his back on the white floor, and he's listening to his favorite song, "Your Cheatin' Heart." Dad taught me the words, but I don't feel like singing along today—I only want to do that when he's happy and he says, "How's my best girl today?" Then I know I can sing with him, but not today.

It's just me, Mom, and Dad in the house today. My brother Mark is ten years old, which is way older than me, so he gets to go outside and play with his friends whenever he wants to. Mom and I are sitting at our table—she calls it a Duncan Phyfe. I hate our table because it's very tipsy and always makes me spill my milk, which makes Mom's angry face come alive. That's when she presses her lips together so they go into a very straight line, and her eyes become kind of squinty. I try super hard not to spill, but sometimes it just happens. So anyways, that's why I hate our Duncan Phyfe.

When Dad's in a bad mood, everyone must be silent. If I ask for a glass of milk, Dad might yell at me. I don't want to leave the family room right now because if I did, I would have to tiptoe on my highest of tippy-toes, because if he heard me would roar like a lion, or maybe a bear. Whichever one roars the loudest. But what I worry most about is that he might get mad at Mom. That's when he gets meaner than the ugliest, greenest monster I can think of. So right now, I'm trying to sit still and not make a single sound.

Dad has his favorite things right by him: his can of Hamm's beer, a scrunched-up pack of Camels (his ashtray is full, but I don't want to empty it right now) and his special records. As soon as he finishes one can of the icy-cold beer, he orders Mom to bring him another one. Mom takes a beer for herself, too. I don't know how many cold ones Dad is going to drink today.

Oh no! Mom made Dad roar like a lion! She was supposed to pull the tab off the top of the Hamm's, but she forgot! Mom is trying to back away from him and get to her spot at the table. Dad is screaming at her. Uh oh. Mom just stepped on one of Dad's records! That is another rule in our house—don't ruin any of Dad's records!

"For God's sake, Lyla! How can you be so stupid? Can't you do anything right? How am I supposed to drink this?! How?" Dad yells. He's on fire now, yelling bad words at Mom because she doesn't know how to follow orders. I try to help Mom now. I send her a message with my mind. *Mom, remember to take the top off. Don't stand on Dad's special records.*

Mom brings Dad another beer and I'm so happy because she opened it right this time! But now he's shouting at her, because she put it next to his Camel cigarettes instead of by his hand. I try sending a mind message to Dad: *Tell Mom what you want.*

Dad's "Your Cheatin' Heart" record ended, and he hates it when there isn't any music playing—he hates the scratchy sound the needle makes on the record even more. He orders Mom to make it play again. Did she do it right? I'm only four years old and I know how to do it, but I don't want to right now. Oh, good, she did it right. Now the music is playing again.

I don't know why Dad's still mad, but he is. I'm afraid he's going to turn into the ugly green monster type of Dad. Oh no! Dad's getting up! He wants Mom to come over to him.

"Get over here, Lyla! Front and center," Dad demands. I watch as Mom gets up from her chair and takes a couple steps towards him, then I close my eyes as tight as I can and plug my ears with my fingers, because he's yelling so loud it hurts my ears, and I don't want to see what he does to Mom. But wait—I guess I do want to see. I open my eyes. Dad is standing up now, his hands are on Mom's shoulders, and he's shaking her. Oh no! Now he's holding Mom by her hair; I haven't seen him do that before! I want to close my eyes again, but I can't.

"Dad, no!" I cry. But he doesn't hear me. I watch as he lifts Mom into the air and then throws her down onto the white floor.

Now he's dragging her through the kitchen by her hair. I guess he wants her to be in the living room. She can't get away because her arms can't reach the floor. I wonder if Mom's hair will come out? I get off my chair and follow them. My stomach hurts. What if I throw up? My eyes are burning. *Don't cry, Joanie,* I tell myself, *just be a big girl.* Should I yell at Dad again? I don't think that would help. Now Mom is screaming, "Let me go, John! Let me GO!" But he doesn't. It's getting hard for me to walk because my legs are shaky.

We are in the living room and Dad is dragging Mom back and forth on the scratchy carpet. Why does this room have to have that stupid carpet anyway?

I look out the front window. It looks so nice outside—Mom would call it a beautiful, sunny day. I want to say to Mom: *Do you want to go for a walk around the block? Or do you want to sit out on the step and watch the neighbors? Maybe we could do that instead?* But I can see it's no use, because Dad isn't done with Mom's punishment.

"Sit right here!" Dad yells at Mom, making her sit on the floor by the couch. Mom is crying and screaming; I can't understand her. She sounds like she is underwater. Mom's knees are bloody, and the red blood is dripping down her legs. I hope it doesn't leak onto her pretty white socks! Oh, good, Dad went back in the family room, maybe he's done now.

Oh no—he's back—grabbing her again! I can't believe her hair hasn't come out! He's pulling her back towards me. She is crying so hard. Poor Mom. Now he is dragging her to the couch again, making her sit up. There is lots of blood on her legs, and on her face! What happened to her face?

Dad is back in the family room now. I sure hope he's done with Mom's punishment. I want to go sit with Mom, but I can't move. My bare feet are stuck, like when I step on bubblegum outside. I give my feet a mind message to make them work. I take a few steps and bend over to look at Mom's face. I want to help her feel better. "Mom, are you okay? Those are big owies," I say as I fit myself into her lap. She isn't answering me, but that's okay, sometimes I can't talk when I am crying either.

I look up at her and see that her hair is sticking up on top. It looks funny, like my doll's hair when it gets wet, but I decide not to tell her. I send her a mind message: *We can work on your hair later. I will hand you the rollers, and you can put the curls back the way they should be.* I look at her face. She has a whole bunch of blood on her face. Maybe there's an owie by her eye? I'm not sure.

If Mom could talk, she would say that her knees are in "bad shape." They need a cool cloth and a bunch of Band-Aids. I watch the blood make lines down Mom's legs and think she might need some new skin, too.

Mom is still crying. It isn't fake-crying, it's real.

"Ssshhh," Mom says to me. She wants to listen for Dad. We can hear him trying to make "Your Cheatin' Heart" play again, but he can't do it. He's yelling at his record player! We hear other noises—crashing, crushing—maybe he threw something? I wonder if Dad is mad at himself now?

Oh no! He must think it's still Mom's fault. He is coming back into the living room! He grabbed Mom's hair again! I jump out of Mom's lap and run over to the corner by the front door. He's dragging her again, and she looks like a big doll! I think he's done, because he told her to sit by the couch again. Oh, good, he went back to the family room.

I'm really scared now. I want to go back in Mom's lap, but what if Dad comes in again? What if he pulls my hair? I make a plan: every time Dad comes into the living room, I'll hop like a bunny back into the corner, pull my knees up, and put my head down. That way he won't see me. I tell myself not to cry. I know it's important to be the best girl for Mom.

Even though I am sitting in her lap, it isn't helping. Mom is still crying. "Are you going to die, Mom?" I ask. Mom whispers in my ear, but she doesn't answer my question. She wants us to go into the bathroom together so she can tell me a secret! When we stand up to go into the bathroom, I see that one of her eyes is all purply, and I think that must be why she has blood all over her face.

Mom and I go into the bathroom. I am a little bit excited, because I like secrets! Mom is sitting on the toilet, but she doesn't have to go potty. She wants to tell me the secret right away. "We're going to leave the house, Joanie. I need you to listen very carefully. When we leave the bathroom, we are going to be very quiet and walk as fast as we possibly can, straight out the front door. No talking. I don't want you to even whisper. After I close the front door, we are going to run like the wind down the street to Mrs. Stedman's house. Can you do that, Joanie? Can you run like the wind? Run really, really fast?"

I think this will be easy! "I can, Mom! I can run real fast! Can we race each other, Mom?"

"Ssshhh . . . we have to be very quiet," Mom whispers in my ear. "No talking, no more whispering—go out the door quietly—and then RUN." Mom and I tiptoe on our way to the door. Dad's music stops, and so do we. As soon as Mom hears the singer's voice start again, we creep a little closer to the door. When we reach the door, Mom opens it slowly—she doesn't want it to make any sound. Once she has it open, we step outside. We can't run yet, because Mom is closing the squeaky screen door very carefully, so it doesn't slam shut.

We are running now, but it isn't like a race, because I'm holding Mom's hand. But wait, why are we turning here? This isn't Mrs. Stedman's house! Mom is making a mistake. This is Annie Sawchuck's house. My brother is friends with two of the brothers that live here, but I don't know their names. Why are we going here instead of to Mrs. Stedman's?

We run up to the side door, and before Mom even knocks, Mrs. Sawchuck opens the door.

"Annie . . . I . . . " Mom's voice sounds wobbly, and when I look up at her, I see that she's crying real hard.

"My goodness, Lyla—come in, please, come in," Annie says. She smiles at me, seems glad to see me, even. How can she be glad to see me when I don't even know her? "Joanie, what a pretty little outfit you have on today. Would you like to meet my daughter? Maybe the two of you can play together."

"Okay," I say.

"Jeannie, can you come out here?" Annie calls into the living room. Annie puts a hand on one of Mom's arms and tells her to sit down at the kitchen table.

"What's up, Mom?" Jeannie says, stopping in the entryway. She is taller than me and has long, blonde hair.

"Jeannie, this is Joanie." I think our names sound funny together, but I don't laugh. "Her mom, Lyla, is here with me in the kitchen. Take Joanie into your room for a while. I want the two of you to stay in your room. Don't come out until I tell you, okay? Maybe you could play a game with Joanie, or get out your old dolls? Lyla and I need some time to ourselves."

Jeannie reaches down, takes my hand. "Joanie, let's go in my room. I have some candy we can share."

"I love candy! But I better ask my mom."

"This time you don't have to ask your mom," Jeannie tells me, "You and I are going to have a party, just the two of us! Today you can have all of the candy you want."

৫৯

Shoot! My party with Jeannie is over. Mom says it's time to go back home now. "Come back again sometime, Joanie!" Jeannie tells me.

Mom says we don't need to run this time. It's a little dark out, so I'm glad Mom is holding my hand. I think it was a good idea to go to Mrs. Sawchuck's. I can see that she took good care of Mom—the blood isn't dripping on her face anymore, and her knees have Band-Aids on them.

As we go in our front door, Mom gives my hand a tight squeeze and tells me to be quiet. I decide to tiptoe.

It's very quiet in here. There are no lights on. My head feels kind of spinny, like when I am on a ride at a carnival. My tummy is shaking a little. I decide not to tell Mom—I probably ate too much candy, and she might get mad.

I follow Mom through the living room and into the family room. I don't think Dad is home; he's not in the family room, and I don't hear him yelling or screaming.

Mom turns a light on, and we see that Dad left a big mess. Stupid Dad! He should have cleaned it up before he left. I see his "Your Cheatin' Heart" record on the floor. The table and chairs are upside down and not in the places they are supposed to be. He didn't even wipe up his spilled beer! What a mess he made! His ashtray tipped over and spilled into a little pool of beer, making it look gray. I look over at Mom. She's looking at the wall by the refrigerator. There is a hole in the wall. Did Dad make that hole?

Mom looks down at me. Her eye is still purply, and I can see the scratches from the carpet on her forehead. "Dad is gone for now, Joanie. Let's get this place cleaned up."

ை

I didn't really sleep last night, because I was afraid Dad might come home to hurt Mom again. I'm feeling too tired to go to church, but Mom says it is Sunday and I have to go.

Our church is called St. John the Baptist, and we have to go there every Sunday, or else God won't love us. I follow Mom into the big building, but she turns a different way than normal. We are going to sit in a different place today! From this spot, I can see the whole church.

I think Mom is sad, because of her owies. Her face scrunches up when she kneels. She's trying to hold one hand on her eye so other people won't see how big of an owie it is.

I love to look around in church. I think that's my job when I'm here and usually it makes me happy. Especially when I see a lot of babies! But, today, nothing can make me happy, because I'm sad about what happened to Mom yesterday.

DULUTH

WHY IS DAD WAKING everyone up in middle of the night? Is he yelling? He was in a good mood when I went to bed. I wonder what happened to make him angry?

I cover my ears with my pillow, but I can still hear him yelling. Suddenly, my bedroom door opens, and Dad comes flying in. He turns on my light, but it's hard for me to see because the bright white light hurts my eyes.

"Get up, Joanie. We're going on a trip! Get ready fast! We're leaving in five minutes!" Dad yells as he turns to go back into the hallway. My eyes are blinking fast, trying to get used to the bright light.

"John, we are NOT going anywhere," I hear Mom scream. "What are you thinking? I don't understand! Why do we have to leave right now?" I can hear in Mom's voice that she is scared, like the time she told me the secret in the bathroom and we went to Mrs. Sawchuck's house.

"I'm in charge here, Lyla, and what I say goes. Now get yourself together!"

"I need to call my mother, John. We can't go anywhere; Mark is coming home today," Mom says. Then I remember that my brother has been at Grandma and Grandpa Tighe's farmhouse in Madelia, and we are supposed to go to the bus station today to pick him up. "We have to be at the bus station this afternoon. I have to call my mother!" Mom continues.

I'm not sure what is going on, so I decide to stay in my room. I move from my bed to the wall by the family room and press my ear next to the vent so I can hear better. No one else knows it, but this is my spying spot. Mom wants to call Grandma Tighe, but Dad won't let her.

"Give me that goddamned phone!" Dad shouts. "Sit down and shut up! I will call your parents and get this straightened out. Better yet, I want you out of this house right now! Go get in the car and wait for me and Joanie. We have got to get going! I have a meeting set up with a man in Duluth, and if we don't get on the road soon, I'll be late!" Dad screams as he dials the phone number.

"Lyle, this is John. There's been a change in plans for today. I need you to put Mark on a bus to Duluth, instead of to Minneapolis, as soon as possible. We'll have to meet him there," Dad explains to Grandpa Tighe.

Grandpa is talking now, so Dad is quiet for a minute. I wonder where Duluth is?

"For God's sake, Lyle. Are you even listening to me? I don't give a crap if he is only ten years old, get him on a bus to Duluth immediately!" Dad yells. "Oh, you want to talk to Lyla, do you? Your precious daughter, ha? Well, no, you won't be talking to her. And if you don't put Mark on that bus, I will come down to that godforsaken farmhouse of yours and destroy you!" I hear Dad slam the phone into its holder on the wall. Dad is going to destroy Grandpa Tighe? I don't want him to!

"Joanie, where are you? We have to leave right now!" Dad screams as he comes running back into my bedroom. I'm still huddled next to the wall. "Get dressed! Now, Joanie! Now!"

I don't move. I'm afraid. What if he pounces on me like a ferocious tiger? His blue eyes are scaring me—they're kind of wild looking. Little bits of hair on Dad's head are sticking up towards my ceiling. His hands are shaking.

"Move it!" Dad yells as he turns and heads out of my room.

I am four now, and I know how to dress myself, but today, I wish Mom could help me. When I'm all dressed grab my little stuffed puppy, go to the bathroom and then slowly walk to the side door.

"You're finally ready. It's about time," Dad says. He grabs my hand and pulls me out the door and into the dark night.

We hurry down the sidewalk and get into the car. My eyes still feel like they want to sleep. I'm trying to wake up my whole body so I can walk as fast as Dad. I'm cold, but I don't have a coat on. It's probably cold out, because the sun is still sleeping. When we get to the car, I can see Mom inside. She hops out and helps me into the car.

"It's going to be a long drive, Joanie. Why don't you lay down and get a little more sleep?" Mom says. I climb into the back seat, curl up like a little bear, and tuck my stuffed puppy under my head for a pillow.

When I wake up, I'm very cold. I look out the car window. It isn't dark anymore; I can see the sun has woken up now. But other than the sun, all I can see is land and grass. There are no buildings, hardly any trees. I look for cows or horses, but there aren't any. Mom and Dad are both smoking cigarettes, but they're not talking. It is silent in the car.

I have to go to the bathroom, but I don't think it would be a good idea to tell Dad. He isn't yelling right now, and I don't want him to start. I wonder how much longer it will take to get to Duluth? I don't think I have ever been on such a long car ride.

"We're here!" Dad suddenly announces. "Welcome to Duluth, Joanie!" I catch him smiling at me in his driving mirror. When I look at his blue eyes in the mirror now, they look cold, like the ice cubes in our freezer. His icy eyes don't match his smile and his happy voice. I turn away and look back out the window. I can see lots of buildings all right next to each other, and sidewalks, too.

"Have I been here before?" I ask.

"No, Joanie, you haven't been here before. This is a winner of a city! Your dear old Dad has some business to take care of here today," he tells me, still looking at me in the mirror. His eyes are still icy, but he sure is happy that we finally made it to Duluth.

"And Mark is coming?"

"No idea about Mark, Joanie. Can't help you there. That is all up to your Grandpa Tighe," Dad says. Mom isn't saying anything, and I can't see her face in a mirror, so I don't know if she likes Duluth or not. I don't know anything about buses, but I hope Mark will make it to Duluth okay. I think it will take him a long time to get here, though, because Madelia must be far away from here.

Dad is pulling the car over to the curb now. I can see people out walking on the sidewalks. Someone has a cute dog on a leash. There is a bench near the curb where an older man is sitting, reading the paper. My mom never reads her newspaper outside!

"Okay, out with you two," Dad says.

"John, what?" Mom asks. "You want us to get out here?"

"Yes, O-U-T—OUT! I can't take you with me. If the two of you are with me, it will ruin the whole thing. OUT!" His smile is gone; his eyes look more frozen and they aren't light blue anymore—they are darker. I wonder if my eyes change color when I get mad?

"But you are the one who said we had to come along! I don't have any money, John. What are we supposed to do? When are you coming back?" Mom tries to ask, but Dad is not listening because he has gotten out of the car. He opens my door and tells me to get out and wait for Mom on the sidewalk.

"Aren't we going to stay together, Dad? I'll be on my best behavior, I promise!" He probably doesn't want a naughty girl like me to ruin his meeting. "Shouldn't we all be together when Mark gets here?" But he has already made his decision.

"Get out of the car, Lyla! I have an important meeting with a very important guy, and the two of you will ruin everything!" Mom gets out of the car and comes and stands by me. Together we watch Dad get back in the car. "And furthermore," Dad yells out the open window, "I will not be coming back to get you. Good luck, Lyla!" I jump a little as the car makes a loud sound and then zooms off. Mom and I watch Dad and our car disappear, swallowed up by this place called Duluth.

Mom reaches down and takes my hand. I look up at her. Her forehead is all wrinkled, so I know she's worried. We stand on the sidewalk for a bit, and then she gives my hand a little squeeze, and we start walking. I am not going to cry, because I know it is important to be brave when you are scared. Crying doesn't help anything; that is for sure.

"I'm sorry, Joanie. I'm not sure where to go around here," Mom says quietly. She turns her head and looks around. I guess she is trying to figure out where we are.

"Are we having an adventure, Mom?" I ask.

Mom nods her head.

I have never seen so many sidewalks! I try skipping while I walk, but it's too hard to skip with Mom holding my hand so tight. I try to be nice and quiet: I don't want to cause trouble for Mom. I look up at all the old buildings. They are connected to each other, and almost all of them are brown. If you ask me, it's kind of a boring city. A big grey bus passes by us, and I wonder if my brother is on it. I wonder if kids can ride a big bus like that? We walk by a park, kind of like Hansen Park in New Brighton, and I see some people laying down, sleeping. That seems kind of silly. No one sleeps at Hansen Park!

I have to go to the bathroom so bad I think my pee might leak out, but I don't know if I should say anything to Mom. It doesn't seem like this would be a good time to find a bathroom. I look up at her face, and she looks like she is going to cry.

"It'll be okay," I tell Mom. "I'm sure everything will work out."

"I sure hope so, Joanie," she says.

We climb up a hill, and suddenly, Mom stops in front of a tall, brown building. The door is hidden: you go through a little tunnel to get to it. I look up and see there are a lot of windows, kind of like my bedroom window, but taller. The building is made of brown bricks, kind of like the brick house on our street. It is an old building, older than Mom, even.

"Is this where we're headed?" I ask. But Mom doesn't answer me. She stares and stares at the building. I see her mouth is in a straight line, so I guess she's angry. Finally, she pulls me through the tunnel and opens the door.

Just inside the door is a living room with a couch and a chair. A man is standing behind a tall desk. It seems like he was waiting for us to come. Maybe this is where we find Mark? Mom tells me to sit in the big chair while she talks to the man. A few minutes later, we are headed for the elevator.

"We're going to stay in a room in this building for a while," Mom says. She opens the door with a key, and suddenly, I realize this is a hotel! We have stayed in hotels a few times, and I remember two great things: there is usually a swimming pool and yummy food at the restaurant! After I go to the bathroom, I hop up onto the big bed and let out a little squeal. Then I run over to look out the window. Way down below is the street we were walking on. This is going to be a fun adventure after all!

"Is this where Mark is coming, Mom?" I ask. "Can we go swimming? Go get something to eat? Can I have a can of pop?"

"Joanie, no. There is no swimming pool here. And even if there was, we don't have our swimsuits. And I don't have any money, so we can't have anything to eat. Do you understand? I'm going to make some phone calls to try to figure out how to get us back to New Brighton. I want you to lay down on the bed and be quiet. Can you do that?"

"Yes, I can," I say. But what I truly think is that this isn't fair. I already had to be the best girl for practically the whole day, and I want to have some fun. I try to lay quietly on the bed, but it's almost impossible. I'm not tired at all! But I am hungry. Mom has a very important job at the bank, and I wish she would've brought some of her bank money with us so we could get some lunch.

When Mom is done with her phone calls, she tells me some good news. First, my Uncle Lee is coming to get us! He is my Aunt Sharon's husband and is super nice and super funny. Second, Mark is safe and sound with Grandma and Grandpa in Madelia. We don't have to worry about what bus he is on anymore. Mom starts to cry, but I think she is crying happy tears because Mark is safe and because of my Uncle Lee. But then, I think, maybe she is crying sad tears because Dad is gone and we don't know where he is.

I can see out the window that it is starting to get dark now, and Mom thinks it would be a good idea for us to try to sleep until Uncle Lee gets here.

"It will take him a long time to get here—he has to drive the same way we did this morning," she tells me.

We pull down the covers on the bed, take off our shoes and climb into bed together. I bet at home the streetlights are coming on, which means all my friends are going in for the night. I snuggle my stuffed puppy and drift off to sleep.

The phone in our room is ringing—it's Uncle Lee. Mom tells me to hurry up and get ready, and we hop back on the elevator. When the elevator door opens, Uncle Lee is standing there waiting for us. Mom is so glad to see him! But I'm not so sure he is glad to see us. He doesn't pick me up and swing me onto his shoulders like he usually does. His eyes are watery. Maybe he is tired?

"I've got some money here from your parents," he says to Mom. "We can use that to pay your bill and get you something to eat. Then we need to get on the road." I wait in the big chair while they pay the man at the desk.

It is real dark out now, and my uncle tells me to settle in for the long ride. I curl up in the back seat, but I think I slept too much today, because I don't feel tired at all. I try to listen to Uncle Lee and Mom talk, but they are whispering, and I can't make sense of their words.

The next thing I know, Uncle Lee is waking me up.

"Here we are, Joanie. Back at home, right here at 509," he tells me as Mom scoops me up. She carries me into the house and, after I go to the bathroom, tucks me into bed. What a boring day this was. All I did was ride in a car and sleep.

When I wake up, Mom tells me that Grandma and Grandpa are bringing Mark home from Madelia today. They are supposed to get here after lunch. She doesn't know when Dad is coming home.

When I see Grandma and Grandpa's car, I realize that I missed Mark and am super excited to see him!

"I thought you were going to get stuck on a bus trying to find Duluth," I tell him when he comes through the door. But he doesn't seem to know what I'm talking about.

"Yeah, for some reason, Grandpa and Grandma kept me on the farm for another day," he says. "I guess you guys went to Duluth without me, ha?"

"Thank you, Mother," Mom says to Grandma. "I'm sorry you had to bring him home. I couldn't figure out any other way right now."

"Is John here?" Grandpa asks.

"No, he isn't. I don't know where he is or when he will be

back," Mom reports. Her lips aren't straight right now, but she's talking in her worried voice.

"Well, this is the last time, Lyla. We can't help you again; it's too dangerous. We can't take the chance," Grandpa tells her.

"You will need to figure this out on your own from now on," says Grandma, as they turn to leave.

"Goodbye, Grandma and Grandpa! Have a safe trip!" I yell out the front door.

Grandma turns and waves, then she gets in the car. As they pull away from the curb, I see her handkerchief, the one with the little flowers on it. I watch as she brings it up to her face to dab her eyes: my grandma is crying.

BRENDA'S BIRTHDAY

I DON'T HAVE A babysitter this summer, so I'm trying to be on my best behavior. Most of the time I'm by myself, because Mark is eleven years old and can go anywhere he wants with his friends. Mom works at the bank, which is a super important place in downtown New Brighton. My Dad kind of works, but mostly he sleeps on the couch. I don't know why he's so tired, but I do know that when I'm inside the house, I must be real quiet. He doesn't like it if I wake him up—even when I open the fridge, I can't make any noise. Most days, I play with my best friend, Brenda.

I don't know why I don't go to Aunt Sharlene's house for babysitting like I did when I was four. Aunt Sharlene is one of my mom's sisters. She lives in a whole different part of New Brighton with her husband, Uncle Allen, and my cousin Debbie. Whenever I see my cousin, she tells me about all the fun we had at her house, but I don't remember it. Debbie likes to play school, and I guess I was her best student! In fact, that's where I learned my ABC's! I'm not sure, but I think we don't go there anymore, because my brother scared Aunt Sharlene half to death. I don't think my brother meant to scare our aunt so badly that she almost died, but when he lighted a whole pack of firecrackers in her garage, there was an awfully loud BANG! Aunt Sharlene almost fainted when she heard the BANG! sound, which is what happens when someone gets scared half to death.

Brenda's mom doesn't work at the bank, like my mom does, or anywhere. Brenda knows my dad is kind of mean, and since her mom never lets us play in the house, we pretty much stay outside all the time. Brenda has long hair, like me, but she's real little. I'm sitting out on our front step right now, eating my breakfast. I hope Brenda comes out soon—today is her fifth birthday, and I'm ready to celebrate!

One thing I think it would be fun to do is have a birthday party with our dolls! We could build a fort over the fence with some of our old blankets, and I'll sing the "Happy Birthday" song to her. I bet her big brown eyes will twinkle when I sing to her! After that, I'll sneak into my house and get us some cold hot dogs and Kool-Aid for lunch. I don't have any birthday cake for her, though.

"Hi, Brenda!" I shout as I see Brenda come running across the street.

"Hi, Joanie! Want to do something fun today?" Brenda is talking fast and trying to catch her breath from her short run.

"Sure!" I say as she sits down on the step and takes a sip of my milk. I guess we won't make a fort after all, because Brenda already has a plan!

Her eyes are twinkling as she tells me her idea. "Here is what I want to do . . . it's my birthday and . . . "

Brenda has a great plan! We're going to walk up to Super Valu to get some treats for her birthday. I've never been to the store without Mom, but we both know how to get there. We're going to hold hands the whole way there—and we're going to skip instead of walk!

"I'm going to sing 'Happy Birthday' to you!" I tell Brenda as we skip our way to Super Valu.

"Finally, we're here!" Brenda says as we walk through the magic doors—all you do is step on the black sidewalk and the doors open!

"Over here!" Brenda says, heading to where the men bag your groceries. Brenda grabs two little paper bags from a shelf, and we head over to the candy rack by the cash register. Brenda and I are huddled together, putting all our favorites (Necco Wafers, Topps BubbleGum, Whoppers, JawBreakers, and Bit-O-Honeys) into our bags. "Fill your bag up, Joanie! We don't have to pay today because it's my birthday! Follow me!" Brenda says. I didn't know that people don't have to pay on their birthday!

Wait—why is Brenda's mom here? She's running, maybe flying, towards us. "Mrs. Peterson, calm down. I know I called you but—" the Super Valu lady is trying to talk, but Mrs. Peterson is not listening. Boy, is she mad!

"What in the world do you two think you are doing?! You didn't even have permission to come here! I can't believe this! I'm sitting at home, having my coffee, and then I get a call from the store that you two are in here stealing a bunch of candy!" Her hair is whirling as if she is running through a windstorm. "You dump that candy out on the belt right now, do you hear me? Tell the lady you're sorry and that you will never do this again!"

There are other moms waiting to check out, and they watch as we pour our candy out. Brenda is crying, but I decide to stay brave.

Brenda's mom will not stop yelling. My ears are starting to hurt! We follow her out the magic doors and climb into the back seat of her station wagon. Mrs. Peterson gets in her seat, slams her door shut and starts driving us back to Eleventh Avenue.

She's driving so fast that it feels like we are in a race.

"Your parents will be hearing about this!" Mrs. Peterson yells at me. "What were you thinking, coming up with such a stupid idea to steal candy from Super Valu?"

"Please don't tell my dad," I beg. "He's sleeping, and you can't wake him up!" But she can't hear me because she's yelling too loudly. I don't feel so brave anymore. When I get out of the car and stand on the sidewalk for a minute before going in the house.

I turn the doorknob carefully, trying hard not to wake Dad up. I close the door without making any noise. But what if Brenda's mom comes over here and bangs on the door? Dad will wake up for sure—

I know! I will make it look like we aren't home! I shut all the windows and close all the curtains. If Brenda's mom looks over here, she will see how dark it is and decide that we aren't home.

Just in case Dad does wake up, I'm going to hide. I climb up on the corner section of the living room couch, hop over it, and hide behind its curved back. The brown, wiry fabric is scratchy, so I sit close to the wall so it doesn't touch me. I'm going to wait here until Mom gets home from work. I know Mom will help figure this whole thing out.

But now, the phone starts to ring. My plan isn't working, because I forgot to take the phone off the hook. "Yes, Mrs. Peterson," I hear Dad say.

My stomach is hurting now. I'm so scared. I've really done it this time. *Be quiet,* I tell myself, *quieter than you have ever been.* Oh no! I'm starting to cry! That will be too noisy! *BE QUIET,* I tell myself again.

Wait—how did Dad find me so fast?

"Don't you know I need my sleep? I can't have the phone ringing when I am trying to sleep!" Dad yells. Then he pulls me out from behind the couch and slaps me on my face. I feel my cheek start to burn. Now he turns me over and spanks my tiny bottom! I start to cry. What if he hurts me like he hurts Mom?

"I thought you were my best girl! You ruined everything!" Dad yells as he hits me. "Go to your room and stay there until your mother gets home!"

"I do want to be your best girl," I scream from my bed. A whole bunch of tears are running down my cheeks, and my nose is running. I want Mom to come home. She'll be so mad when she finds out what Dad did to me!

Finally, I hear Mom's high heels clicking on the sidewalk outside my window. I'm not crying big tears anymore, just little ones that drip out every once in a while. I move over to my listening spot by the vent and listen as Dad tells Mom what happened. He's still hopping mad. "She ruined my sleep, Lyla!"

"Come over here, Joanie," Mom says as she comes into my room. I get up and go stand by her. My nose is running and my eyes feel wet and I'm afraid the giant tears are going to start coming again. I try to tell Mom what happened, but it's hard to get my words out. When I look at her, I see her straight lips and her squinty eyes, and I wonder if she's listening to me.

"Mom!" I yell. "Did you hear me? Dad spanked me real hard!"

But Mom does not say a word, just stands there staring at me. Then, quick as a wink, she grabs my hands, spins me around, and pulls down my pants and panties. She lands her big hand on my bottom and gives me a spanking that hurts more than Dad's did.

"Stop being such a naughty girl when I'm at work! You need to act like a young lady and not cause any trouble from now on! You are going to stay in this room for the rest of the night. You can go to the bathroom, but that's all. Is that clear?" I nod my head as she turns and leaves my room.

"I didn't mean to be a naughty girl!" I scream. Then I lay down on my bed again, crying so hard that my body starts to shake and my chest hurts. "Why doesn't anyone in this family love me?"

I'm trying to fall asleep, I have my stuffed puppy and everything, but I can't make my eyes close. Why don't my parents love me? I think I know why. I think Mom and Dad have me because no one else wanted me. I don't even think Mark is my real brother. I'm not exactly sure how Mom and Dad got me; they probably found me at church or something. Father Paul probably told them he had a baby no one wanted. But it's just not working out. I'm going to run away and try to find a new family that doesn't mind having a naughty girl like me.

ALL MIXED UP

SOMETHING SAD HAPPENED a few days after Brenda and I stole the candy. Brenda moved. Mom says she doesn't know where they moved to and that I probably won't see her again in my whole life. It's been about one hundred days since she moved, and I still miss her.

On Saturday and Sunday mornings, I must be extra quiet, because those are the only days that Mom doesn't have to go to work at the bank and she likes to sleep in. The rule is that I'm not supposed to wake her up until 11:00 a.m.—that's when the big hand is on the twelve and the little hand is only on the eleven. Today is a Saturday, and the little hand is on the nine, so I head outside to play.

Rhonda and Connie are my brand-new friends. Rhonda lives on my side of the street, next to Sawchuck's house, and Connie lives across the street from her. I'm lucky that Rhonda and Connie are my new friends because they are both older than me and super smart!

"Hi, guys! What are you doing?"

"We're going for a walk! Want to come with?" Rhonda and Connie are too old to make forts or play with dolls, so we usually go for walks instead.

"Are we going around the block?" I ask.

"Nope, today we are going to walk through the trailer court to see if we know anyone who lives there," Rhonda says.

"Okay," I say. I'm excited, because even though the trailer park is only one block away, I have never been there.

Rhonda and Connie talk the whole time we walk—they are into boys, and since I'm not, I don't have much to say. I look around and skip a little. The sun is making my shoulders warm, and I can feel it tickling my cheeks. It is so cool to be on this adventure with my new friends!

As we stroll through the trailer park, I think it is more like a different kind of neighborhood, not like a park at all. The trailers are on small streets, and the street signs are teeny-tiny, much smaller than ours. There aren't any garages or driveways, so cars are parked right by each trailer door. We walked through the whole park but Rhonda and Connie didn't find anyone they knew, so now we're heading home.

We are back on Eleventh Avenue now, and I can see Mom and Dad in our front yard. It must be after 11:00! I'm glad, because I can't wait to tell Mom about our walk.

"My God, Joanie, where have you been?!" Mom yells as I run up to her. Her face tells me I'm in big trouble.

"I went for a walk with Rhonda and Connie," I say. Why is Mom so mad? I go for walks all the time! And I followed the rules and didn't wake her up before 11:00. And then, Mom grabs me and slaps me on my bottom—right in front of Rhonda and Connie!

"Get in the goddamned car, Joanie," Dad yells. "We are going to be late because of you!"

"And you two," Mom says, looking at Rhonda and Connie. "You should know better! Who do you think you are, taking a little girl on a walk!"

"But Mom, we go for walks all the time," I try to explain.

"Don't argue with me, young lady! Do you know we had to call the police to try to find you? We have someplace to be today! And we had no idea where you were. We're going to be late, and it's all your fault! Now get into that car before I spank you again!'

I get in the car and watch as my new friends run down the street towards their houses. I feel bad they got in trouble for taking me on a walk. They probably won't want to play with me again. I wonder why the police didn't find me? I guess they didn't think to look at the trailer park.

৩৯

I never go anywhere on Saturday mornings now, because I don't want to get in trouble again. But today is Saturday and Rhonda wants to take me to Long Lake Beach with her! Rhonda's going to ride her bike and will give me a ride on her handlebars. I know it isn't 11:00 yet, but I don't want to miss my chance to go to the beach.

"I have to go in and ask my mom," I tell Rhonda. "I'll be right back."

"Mom? Mom? I have to ask you something!" I yell as I run through the living room to Mom and Dad's bedroom. As I swing the door open, I hear yelling.

"No, John, NO!" I hear Mom yell.

"Hold still, God damn it," Dad yells at Mom. Dad is getting ready to hit Mom. He is standing next to the bed, and one of his hands is up in the air. Mom is laying on the edge of the bed. Her legs are hanging over the edge, but her bare feet can't quite reach the floor. Her favorite nightgown, the one with the pretty flowers all over it, is pulled up so that her underpants are showing.

I want to run out of the bedroom, but—

"Don't hit her, Dad! Don't do it!" I scream.

"Joanie, what the hell are you doing in here? Get out of here NOW! This is between your mother and me. Go!" Dad yells.

"But I am supposed to ask permission if I want to—" I start to say.

"Get out of here! Do you hear me! OUT!"

I run to the back door and head back outside. The door slams shut behind me, but I don't care.

"Can you go?" Rhonda is asking. I look up at her, and she sees that I am crying. "What's wrong, Joanie?" she asks. I squeeze my eyes shut to try to stop the tears, but they drip down my cheeks anyway.

"I can't go to the beach," I say. "I think you should go home."

"Okay, Joanie," Rhonda says, turning to head back to her house. "Maybe we can go another time."

Why do I have to be so dumb? Why did I go in Mom's bedroom before 11:00? I know the rules. Why can't I do anything right? Now Mom and Dad probably hate me even more than ever before.

I want to run. Fast. Head down to Hansen Park, or anywhere. I'll be gone so long Mom and Dad will have to call the New Brighton Police and the Fire Department to find me.

And I do. I run all the way down the Fifth Street hill, through the park and over to the swamp side. When I think I'm running as fast as I can, I run even faster. I cross the wobbly bridge and go through the creepy woods. And then I stop. It felt good while I was running: I didn't think about Mom or Dad or anything. But now that I've stopped, my head feels funny, like I just got off the Tilt-a-Whirl at the Super Valu carnival. There is a whirring noise in my ears that sounds like a toy top that's spinning real fast. There is a pain deep inside my stomach, and a bass drum is beating a loud message in my chest.

"Make it stop!" I scream as I fall into a mess of tangled weeds. Maybe a swarm of gnats or mosquitos will attack me, and I'll die right here, by this icky swamp. Finally, I get up. I don't know where to go now, except back to good old 509.

NIGHTMARES AND HAIRCUTS

I'M AWAKE. I'M SCARED. My eyes are opened as far as I can make them, but it's so dark in my room I can't see anything, which makes me even more scared. I can't go back to sleep knowing that the creepy, scary lady is going to come back to visit me. Mom says it's a nightmare, a bad dream, which means it's not real. But I'm not so sure. Why do I have to have a nightmare every night? I have my sheet pulled up to my chin and my whole body covered in case that witchy lady with the black dress and cape is real. I'm so scared, my skin is shaky and there are little cold bumps on my arms. Why can't she go and bother some other little girl? Maybe she should go bother a boy, because boys aren't scared of anything.

What happens in the nightmare is that the witch lady, who is taller than Mom, finds me playing by a huge rock on a nice, sunny day. As soon as she finds me, thunder starts to crack through the sky and lightning strikes the ground right by where I'm playing. I try to hide behind one side of the rock so that she won't see me, but it doesn't work. As soon as she finds me, she screams something I don't understand, and I try to run away. I run as fast as I can, but she can run just as fast, maybe even faster, so I'm sure she's going to catch me. Right when I think I can't breathe, and I'm sure her claws are going to catch me, I wake up. The first night I had the nightmare, I woke up so scared. I was sure the lady was in the house somewhere. I decided to go and wake Mom up to tell her about it, because I didn't want the scary lady to hurt me, or anyone else in my family. I crept out of bed, tiptoed past Mark's room, and went into Mom and Dad's room. I tried to be brave and quiet, and I hoped that if the lady was in the house, she wouldn't hear me crying. When I got to Mom's side of the bed, I tried to wake her up. She snores loudly, so I had to shout "Mom!" a bunch of times before she woke up. Mom let me snuggle in her bed with her for a few minutes and told me there was absolutely nothing to be afraid of. She said I was perfectly safe and we would talk about it the next day, and then she sent me back to bed. I'm not allowed to go into Mom's room anymore, because she says she can't be woken up during the night or she won't be able to do good work at the bank the next day. I decide there is only one way to make the nightmare stop.

"I'm not going to go to bed ever again," I tell Mom. "If I don't go to bed, then I won't fall asleep, and then I won't have the nightmare about the creepy witch lady."

"Oh, I don't think that's the right answer," Mom says. "How about if we try to make the nightmare go away?"

"How do we do that? She's been scaring me for like a hundred nights now!" Mom doesn't understand how scary it is.

"Well, how about this. We'll write a letter to the Good Dream Angel. We can tell her about your bad dream and ask her to make the bad lady go away. You can put your letter under your pillow. What do you think of that?"

"I didn't know there was a Good Dream Angel! Are you sure she'll read the letter?" Maybe Mom does understand?

"Oh, yes! That's her only job, to read notes from children who are having nightmares. Let's get your hair wash done, and then we'll write the letter."

I love it when Mom washes my hair. First, she gets all the supplies ready—baby shampoo, a towel, and the special vinegar rinse. Then, she moves one of our chairs so that it is right by the kitchen sink. I kneel on the chair and lean my head over the edge. My hair is so long that it touches the bottom of the big white sink! Mom gets the water nice and warm and then starts getting my hair wet. When she adds the shampoo, my whole head gets covered in big, soapy bubbles, and Mom starts singing, which always makes me giggle.

"Tiny bubbles . . . in your hair . . . make me feel happy . . . make me feel fine . . . "

"Sing it again!" I request.

"Nope, now it's time for the rinser dinser," Mom says. "You have to stop your giggling, though!"

But I can tell Mom likes it when I laugh. She doesn't care if I keep giggling. After she rinses all the bubbles out, she pours the vinegar into my hair and moves her fingers all around my head to make sure every bit of my hair gets some.

"Okay, little lady! Time to stand up! Let's see if your hair is squeaky clean!" Mom wraps the huge towel around my head and then scoops me up into her arms. As she sits in the chair, I settle into her lap. She rubs the towel all around my head to dry my hair, and then it's time to check for the squeaky sound that super clean hair makes. Mom takes a piece of my long, wet hair that is right in front of my eyes, and puts it in between her thumb and first finger. When she pulls her fingers down it, I hear a squeak!

"It worked, Mom! It worked!" I squeal.

"Yes, it did! That vinegar always does the trick, don't you think?" Mom asks me. When we stand up, she lifts me practically all the way to the ceiling, and it feels like I could fly! As she brings me down for a landing, she tickles my back, and I start to giggle again. Mom is laughing, too, and I am so glad that she is having a happy night. "Okay, enough goofing—sit nice and tall on the chair now so I can comb your hair out. I want to tell you something—on Saturday you're going to get a haircut," Mom says as she combs my hair and puts the curlers in. "We're going to walk up to Mrs. P.'s house. She gives little girls fantastic haircuts!"

"Mom, what are you talking about? Am I going to be bald like Dad? Am I going to have ugly boy hair like Mark?" I cry out.

"No, calm down now. It'll be great! You'll have nice short hair, but you won't be bald, and you won't look like a boy. Lots of girls have short hair, and I think you'll look cute!"

"No!" I shout. "I don't want a haircut. I like it just the way it is! I don't even know Mrs. P.! What if she is the mean lady from my nightmare?" I'm crying now. How can this be happening? I don't want a haircut, not now and probably not in my whole life!

"Mrs. P. is most definitely not the lady from your nightmare. She happens to be a very nice lady. She's a customer at the bank, and lives right down the street."

"She lives on Eleventh Avenue?" I ask.

"Yes, right by the cemetery."

Oh great, the lady who is going to cut my hair is a cemetery lady! So she probably is the creepy one from my nightmare! I can't believe Mom wants me to get my hair cut, especially by a cemetery lady!

But now Mom wants to know what I want to tell the Good Dream Angel. I tell Mom what to write on the paper, and I truly hope it works.

Dear Good Dream Angel,

My name is Joanie Hicks, but you probably know that already. I keep having a dream about a creepy, scary lady chasing me around a big rock. Can you please make it go away?

Love, Joanie

Mom says I did a good job on my note and tells me to fold it in half. We go in my room, and Mom watches as I put it under my pillow.

"Okay, now hop in and say your prayers," Mom says.

"Should I pray for the Good Dream Angel to come?" I ask. Mom tells me she thinks that would be a good idea, so I add that to my prayers. "Mom, will you tuck me in like a log?"

"I suppose," Mom says. I lay on my back, and she tucks the sheets in tightly all around me. It's so tight I can't even pull my arms out! As she turns to leave, I ask her about the haircut.

"Mom, why do I have to get a haircut? I like my hair exactly the way it is."

"Joanie, your hair is too long—I don't have the time to keep it brushed and looking nice—half the time you look like a ragamuffin! Now, I don't want to hear another word about it. Tomorrow is Friday. The next day will be Saturday, and after I wake up, we're going to Mrs. P.'s house. Now, go to sleep, and I hope you have only the sweetest of dreams tonight!" Mom says as she heads out my door.

I try to fall asleep fast so the Good Dream Angel can come right away and save me from my nightmare. It seems like I'm still trying to fall asleep when I wake up and find out it's morning! I didn't have the nightmare! I'm so happy, but I'm wondering why I didn't have a good dream instead? I think maybe the Angel was extra busy and didn't have time to put a good dream inside of me.

When I wake up on Saturday morning, I'm both happy and sad. Even though Mom said I didn't need to, I put my note under my pillow again last night, just to be safe, and it worked! No nightmare. That's what makes me happy. What makes me sad is when Mom wakes up, we're going to Mrs. P.'s cemetery house. I'm watching cartoons when Mom finally wakes up and comes into the family room.

"Okay, are you ready?" she asks me. "I'm going to have my toast and coffee, and then we'll start our walk."

On the way to Mrs. P.'s house, I try once again to get Mom to understand that I don't need a haircut.

"I'll take care of my hair myself! I promise. I won't look like a ragamuffin ever again!" I don't think she even hears me; she just keeps walking along, holding my hand. "Mom, did you hear me? Plus, what if Mrs. P. doesn't even like me? She might be a mean person and cut it all off, and then I will be bald even though you said I wouldn't be! Huh, Mom? What if that happens?"

She doesn't answer me, and before I know it, we're walking up Mrs. P.'s sidewalk. I look across the street and see the edge of the cemetery and get a funny feeling in my stomach. I don't think this is going to work out at all.

"Well, hello, Lyla. And you must be Joanie!" Mrs. P. says as we come through the door. Are you all set for your first haircut?" I look up at Mrs. P., and of course, Mom was right. She isn't creepy or scary, and she isn't the witchy lady from my nightmare. But even though she seems nice, I still don't want her to give me a haircut.

"No, I think I'll do it a different day," I say. "C'mon, Mom, let's go, okay?" I try pulling on Mom's hand, to get her to turn around.

"Oh, Joanie," Mrs. P. says. "It's always a little scary the first time, but I can see that you are a big, brave girl and I think you're going to be fine. Why don't you come into the kitchen with me, okay?" I know she's trying to be nice to me, but I start to cry anyway.

"I don't want to get my hair cut!" I cry, while she leads me into the kitchen.

"How about if we put your hair into a ponytail, and then I can trim that off. You can even keep your ponytail if you want to," she suggests.

"Okay," I mumble. She puts a plastic shirt on me and then gets out the longest scissors I have ever seen! I feel her pulling my hair into a ponytail. She touches me in the middle of my back and tells me that is how long my ponytail is now. Then she points to the back of my neck and tells me that is how much she's going to trim off. "Is it going to hurt?" I ask. I feel all trembly, and my tummy is shaky inside. This is the worst idea Mom has ever had.

"No, it won't hurt a bit, and it will be all over in . . . There we go! I trimmed off your ponytail! Do you want to see it?" I nod my head, and she puts my old ponytail in my lap. I'm bald, I'm sure of it. There is so much hair in my lap there can't be any left on my head! "Are you okay?" she asks.

"I don't want to be bald!" I cry.

"Now, now. You're not bald! I wouldn't do that to a pretty girl like you! Why don't you peek in the mirror while I touch up the rest of your hair? You are going to be so cute!" Mrs. P. says happily.

I look in the mirror, and I don't even know it's me. I barely have enough hair to cover my ears. My shoulders have no hair on them at all! I look down at my ponytail, and start to cry. "There we are! All done! My goodness, you look adorable, don't you think? You can touch it if you want to. I'm going to have your mom come and take a look."

After Mom and Mrs. P. get done with their chatting and everything, Mom and I walk back to our house. Mrs. P. let me keep my ponytail, but I'm having a hard time holding onto it, because it's kind of slickery. I'd probably drop it if it didn't have a rubber band around it. I know one thing: I'm never talking to Mom again! She is the meanest mom ever!

"Your hair looks cute, Joanie. Mrs. P. did a good job, just like I knew she would. Now it'll be so much easier to take care of!" Why is Mom so happy? She must not have had long hair when she was a little girl, or she would never have made me get my ponytail cut off!

Dad and Mark are home when we walk in the door. They both want to see my new hair, but I don't want them to. They might laugh at me now that I have short hair. But Dad says it looks good, and Mark tells me that some of the girls at his school have short hair and it's totally cool. That surprises me, because every girl I know has long hair.

"They do?" I ask him.

"Oh yeah, lots of 'em. There are probably twenty girls at my school with short hair! You look great!" I guess that since Mark thinks it's okay, it must be. I ask him if he wants to see my old ponytail, and he does. "Wow, that's a lot! But you know what's cool about hair? It grows back! So maybe someday you can have a ponytail again."

When Mom tucks me into bed that night, I tell her I think my short hair is going to be okay, but I'm still mad about getting a haircut.

"Can I still have a special hair wash? With the vinegar rinse? And make sure it's squeaky clean? And get my back tickled?" I ask as she tucks the sheets in around my legs.

"Yes, to all of that," Mom answers. "And occasionally, I might tickle your back just for the fun of it!" And then she rolls me over and tickles my back! I guess I shouldn't be so mad at

Mom after all, and if Dad and Mark think I look adorable, then I think I will be okay.

"Do you want to put the note to the Good Dream Angel under your pillow again tonight?" Mom asks.

"No, I think I'm only going to have happy dreams now," I say.

"Sounds good," Mom says, and then gives me a kiss on my forehead. "Love you lots and lots, Joanie!"

Before I close my eyes, I run my hands through my new hair. It's short—but it does feel slickery and shiny. "I love you, too, Mom!" I tell her as she closes my door.

ARE YOU MY MOTHER?

SUMMER IS OVER NOW, and since I am five and one-half years old, I have to go to school. Mom told me that is what all kids do when they are five years old. It is called kindergarten.

"Will I go to school with Mark?" I ask.

"No, Mark goes to St. John's. You will be going to New Brighton Elementary, because they don't have kindergarten at St. John's," Mom says. "When you start first grade, you'll go to St. John's."

Then I find out about another change happening. I am not going to stay at home by myself anymore—I have a babysitter, and her name is Bernice. She is my mom's best friend and lives real close to us—to get to her house, you go through our backyard and cross over the alley.

"Does Bernice know I'm coming to her house? What if she doesn't like having a little girl at her house?" I ask.

"Yes, I have it all arranged. It will be fine. I think you are going to like Bernice, and school," Mom says. But I am not so sure.

෨

Today is the first day of kindergarten, and when I woke up this morning, my tummy was all fluttery. Mom bought me a new outfit, and I'm already dressed when she gets up. I tell her about my tummy, but she says it will be fine. Before we go to Bernice's, she pins a card on my sweater that has my name on it. Out on the back sidewalk, she takes my picture and tells me to head on over to Bernice's house.

"Well, look at you!" Bernice exclaims as I walk in her back door. "The prettiest little kindergartener that has ever walked the Earth! How about some Froot Loops for breakfast, Joanie?"

"How long before the bus comes?" I ask.

"The bus will come right after lunch, sweet pea," Bernice tells me. When it stops at my house, I'll walk down the sidewalk with you. And when it brings you back, I will be here waiting for you. How does that sound?"

"That sounds okay," I say. But I am still not so sure about this school thing.

Bernice sure makes fancy lunches! She made a sandwich and chips and gave me freshly-baked chocolate chip cookies for dessert! I finish my lunch just in time; when we go outside, the bus is coming down the street.

"Good-bye, pretty girl!" Bernice shouts as I climb the stairs.

When we get to school, our teacher is waiting for us. She walks us down the hall to our room, and we sit in a circle while she tells us all about school. Then she tells us all to line up because we are going to take a tour of the school.

First, we meet the principal. He is the boss of the whole school, so we must be on our best behavior while we visit him. Next, we visit the first graders. They have a smaller room than us and have desks they sit at. Now we go and see a room that has a piano. It's kind of like ours at home, but taller. The teacher in this room is going to have us learn a whole bunch of songs.

"Okay, children," our teacher says. "Now we are going to go to the library. You can each take one book home today! Once everyone has a book, we will head back to our classroom."

I have never seen a room like this! It is full of books—there are at least a hundred books in here! I can't imagine where they got all of them. There are a few of us who don't know what to do, so we stand back for a few minutes and watch other kids take books off the shelves and look at them.

"Go ahead, everyone," my teacher says. "Choose a book and take it up to the desk."

I pick out a book that has a picture of a bird sitting on a dog's head on the front and take it to the desk.

"I don't have any money," I tell the lady behind the desk. But she writes down my name and gives the book back to me!

"There you go!" she says.

When we get back to our classroom, our teacher says it is time to take a nap. When we wake up, she gives us a carton of milk and reads us a story, and then it's already time to go home.

"Grab your library books," she tells us. "Line up right by the door and I will walk you to the bus. I can't wait to see all of you tomorrow!"

On the way home, I start to worry. I don't think I know where Bernice's house is anymore! How am I going to find it? What if Bernice forgot about me and she isn't home when I get there? I guess I didn't have to worry, because the bus driver knows exactly where Bernice lives. As I hop off the bus, Bernice is right there waiting for me.

Bernice gives me a big squeeze. "Guess what!" I say. "They have a room full of books at school, and we all got to bring one home. When I bring it back in one week, I can trade it for a different book! Do you want to see it, Bernice?"

"Oh, yes I do! I can't wait! Let's have a snack and then we'll look at it together," she says.

After my cookies and milk, Bernice sits in her chair in the living room, and I climb up in her lap with my book. She has kind of a big tummy, but I am small, so I snuggle between her tummy and the side of the chair. "Oh, this one," Bernice says.

"Do you know about this book?" I ask. "I love the picture on the front! Isn't the bird so cute, sitting on the dog like that?"

"Yes, I used to read this one to Jim and David," Bernice tells me. "It's called *Are You My Mother*? This book was one of their favorites, and I bet it will be one of yours, too!" Bernice says. "A mother bird sat on her egg. The egg jumped," Bernice begins.

When the baby bird finally chips its way out of the shell, the mom bird is not there. The baby bird doesn't even know what its Mom looks like.

"That would be sad if a baby couldn't find its mom," I say to Bernice after the little bird asks a dog if she's his mother.

"Yes, it would be," Bernice agrees. "But you keep listening, I have a feeling baby bird is going to find his mother."

"Bernice, can I tell you something?"

"Yes, sweet pea, you can tell me anything. What is it?"

"Did you know that my parents are not my real parents?"

Bernice sets the book down in her lap, takes my face in her hands and looks at me. She looks right into my eyes, and I notice she has brown eyes like me!

"Now, why would you think that, Joanie? Of course they're your real parents," she says.

"Well, I think they found me at church and they felt sorry for me, so they took me home," I tell her. "That's why Mom and Dad don't love me and tell me to leave them alone all the time. I'm such a bad girl they don't know what to do with me." A few tears start down my cheeks, but I squish my eyes shut to stop them, because Bernice has never seen me cry and I want her to think I'm a big girl.

"Oh, Joanie. I don't think that is true at all. I am your mom's best friend, and I can tell you that you are her real little girl, for sure! You were not found at church. I can even remember the day you were born!" she tells me.

"Really?" I ask.

"Really," she says as she wipes my tears. "Now let's find out what happens to the baby bird, okay?"

"Okay, Bernice," I say, with a big smile on my face. And when she reads the page with SNORT on it, we both giggle real loud!

"Did you have a good day, Joanie?" Bernice asks when she finishes the book.

"I think it was my best day ever!" I tell her, and she gives me a kiss right on my nose!

IT'S MIDNIGHT

DAD BROUGHT SOMETHING HOME for me and Mark! I can't believe it! A super cute, very tiny puppy! A girl! She gives Mark a little lick, then comes over to me. I'm pretty sure she likes me better. Soon, she's running all over the house, jumping from me to my brother. I can't believe how much energy she has! She has a long tail that wags constantly! My brother says she reminds him of a dog he had a long time ago, before I was born. That dog's name was Blackie. Mark says this dog is darker than Blackie was; her coat reminds him of the sky at midnight. So guess what? We decide to name her Midnight!

Dad is giving us the rules for Midnight, and I am listening carefully. I hope I can remember them all, because Dad says we will be in big trouble if we don't follow them exactly.

"Number one," Dad starts. "Midnight can't go potty in the house. If you see her going potty, yell at her and take her outside. If she does it again, spank her on her bottom before you take her out." I nod my head and look at Mark. He's thinking the same thing I am—neither of us will hit Midnight, no matter what.

"Number two. The two of you are in charge of picking up her poop in the yard. Your mother has too much to do right now, and she will get upset if she has to do it," Dad continues. "Are we clear on that?" he asks us. We both nod, though I don't want to even think about picking up her poop.

"Number three. Midnight has to be on a chain when she is outside. Otherwise, she might run off." This rule seems like the easiest one to follow.

Midnight and I are best friends now. She is just adorable. She sleeps in my bed with me, cuddling right up next to me! I never spank her, and she never goes potty inside the house. When I tell her what a good girl she is, I get a great big kiss from her! I take her for walks around the neighborhood, even down to Hansen Park. The whole neighborhood knows her now. If someone asks how old she is, I tell them she is six months old, and I am six years old!

I'm trying to follow all the rules, but sometimes it is hard. Mark is busy with his friends, so I pick up the poop most of the time. Sometimes I forget, and Dad was right, Mom does not have time to do it. She also gets hopping mad if she steps in poop—"Get out there and pick that up!"

One thing is for sure: Midnight doesn't like to be put on her chain. I have to make my hands work fast to hook the chain to her collar, and sometimes she takes off before I can get it on. Her favorite thing to do when this happens is to run to Hansen Park. She can run faster than me, because she has four legs and I only have two, so I can't catch her. When she takes off, I grab her leash and a bunch of treats and run as fast as a rabbit down the hill to the park. If Mark is home, he will go with me, but most of the time I go by myself. I call her name over and over when I get to the park, and as soon as Midnight sees me, she comes running up to get her treats. Then, I quickly grab her collar to put her leash on and walk her back home.

☙

Today is Sunday, and we are all getting ready to go to St. John's for church. Mom is telling us to hurry or we'll be late. I tried to convince Mom and Dad that I should stay home from church today. Midnight had surgery at Doctor Caldwell's office, and even though she's back to normal, I don't want to leave her home alone. But my parents told me not to worry; she'll be fine for one hour.

But when Dad opens the door, he accidentally lets Midnight out! Watching out the front window, I see her run out of the yard as quick as she can. She's headed to the park! I grab her leash and some treats and head out the door to go get her.

"Oh, no. We're going to church. There's no time to go look for the damn dog right now," Dad announces.

"Joanie and I can run down to the park real fast, Dad. We can get her and bring her home. We've done it before," my brother tells him.

"Mark, I am telling you to get in the car. NOW! We are not going to look for that dog. Your mother is ready to go, and church starts in five minutes. You can look for her when we get home." Dad has made his decision.

"We have to leave now. I don't want to be late for Mass," Mom adds.

"Can't we skip church so Mark and I can go get her?" I ask.

"Absolutely not. You kids have to get better at getting her hooked up on the chain when you let her out so that things like this won't happen," Dad yells. But he is the one who let her out!

Mark and I look at each other. We both want to go get Midnight. She has never stayed at the park for a whole hour! I hope someone will find her and keep her for us while we're at church.

At church, I sit next to Mark in the pew, and we whisper about how we are going to find Midnight right away when we get home. Mark tells me not to worry: he is sure she will be okay.

In the car on the way home from church Mark and I make our plans. He is going to hop on his bike right away and head down to the park while I grab Midnight's leash and some treats. If he finds her before I get to the park, he will hold on to her until I get there.

As Dad pulls our car onto Eleventh Avenue, Mark and I see our friends, and some of their parents, standing at the corner. "Oh, my God," Mom says.

"What?" Mark asks.

I look out the car window at the group of people. Some of the neighbors turn toward us, and I see some of the kids are crying. Dad parks the car, and Mark and I jump out and run to the corner. As our friends step away, we see Midnight in the center of the circle. She is not moving.

"Midnight!" I cry as I run to her. But Mark grabs me and holds me back.

"No, Joanie, you can't go to her now," he tells me.

"Joanie, get in the house. Right now! I mean it," Mom is yelling at me as she and Dad come closer. But I don't go in. The kids have moved a bit, and through the opening, I can see what my taller brother has already seen—she has a lot of blood on her, and she is not moving.

"Hey man, Hicks, geez. I'm sorry about your dog," one of Mark's friends is saying.

"Okay, okay, everybody. The show's over, you can all head home now," my Dad says. Some of the kids hop on their bikes and take off. As Mom leads me into the house, I watch Dad scoop Midnight off the ground and lay her in the back seat of the car.

"Where is Dad going to take her?' I ask Mom as we enter the house.

"Up to Dr. Caldwell's clinic," Mom tells me. Then I remember the time Lassie got real sick on television and the doctor fixed her right up! Maybe Dr. Caldwell can save Midnight!

Dad is back from Dr. Caldwell's clinic now, but Midnight did not get saved. Dr. Caldwell wasn't even there.

"Dr. Caldwell doesn't work on Sundays, Joanie. He'll bury Midnight when he gets to work tomorrow. I left her right by the steps," Dad says.

I think about Midnight laying outside on Dr. Caldwell's steps, her black coat glistening in the sun as the blood gets all crusty. She has never slept outside before; she has never seen the sky at midnight like Mark has.

Once I climb into bed, I try to stay up until it is as dark as Midnight. I open my curtain so I can see the sky out of my window. "Goodbye, Midnight," I say when the first stars start to twinkle. "I will miss you."

HONOR

NORMALLY, I LOVE HOLIDAYS, because Mark and I don't have to go to school and Mom doesn't have to go to the bank—we get to sleep in and do whatever we want. But every year, on the holiday called Memorial Day, we get up super early and walk up to St. John's Cemetery for church.

"Get up, Joanie! No lazy-bag-of-bones for you today! We have to get going so we're on time for the service at the cemetery," Mom is in my room, trying to wake me up.

"I don't want to go! I'm seven years old now and I don't have to!" I try, knowing it won't work.

"Come on, get up now. Let's pick out a dress—and you can wear your fancy shoes today, too!"

"Aren't Dad and Mark going?" I ask, as Mom and I head out the side door.

"Nope, they're both still sleeping. It's just me and you this year."

"No fair! How come Mark doesn't have to go, but I do? I don't want to go!" I know I am whining, but this is so unfair!

"Oh, well, your brother is almost thirteen now, so I told him he didn't have to go if he didn't want to. I told him it was up to him."

"So when I'm thirteen, I won't have to go, right?" I ask, hoping for fairness.

"How about if we talk about it when the time comes? Come on, let's start our walk—no more complaining, okay?"

To get to the cemetery, you walk down Eleventh Avenue for two blocks, then cross over a busy road called Seventh Street, and you are there. It has a high fence around it, and inside is an oval-shaped path that goes all around the cemetery. I have never walked on the path, because it is too creepy, and I'm glad that our house isn't on that part of Eleventh Avenue, because I would probably be scared all the time.

I wish there were other kids here—usually, Mark and I are the only ones, and now, without him, I am the only one. Of course, just like regular church, we got here way too early, which makes it even more boring. Finally, I see the priest and all his helpers arrive through the gate. I stand quietly by Mom as all the old people gather around to listen. After what seems like a hundred hours, the service ends. But then Mom announces she wants us to take a walk around the cemetery.

"Mom, I'm bored out of my skin! I want to go home. We can walk around the cemetery any old time. I've been here long enough with all these old folks!"

But Mom doesn't give in to my protest. "Old folks, ha? Are you counting me in as an old person?" she says, as she takes my hand and leads me down the path.

"Well, your hair is gray, so, yeah, I guess you're pretty old."

"Hmm. Well, for your information, young lady, I'm only forty, which is NOT considered old."

"Oh, well, sorry if I hurt your feelings," I say. But I'm still upset that I have to do this walk thing. Why can't we just go home already?

"Let's go over here, onto the grass," Mom says as we round the far corner of the trail, and I wonder if this misery will ever end. "Kneel down right here, Joanie. I want you to look at one of these stones, the one right under the pine tree. Do you see it? Can you read what it says?" Mom asks as she kneels on the grass.

"Well, the last name is Hicks," I say. The first name is long and starts with a C, but I can't pronounce it.

"Her first name is Cecelia. She would have been your older sister. She was born in 1959, and you were born in 1962."

"Mom, what? I don't understand. I had a sister? Did she look like me? Did she love me? Did she . . . "

"Okay, hold your horses. I need you to listen carefully. This is kind of hard to explain. Cecelia was born dead, so she never met you, and you never met her. Do you understand?"

"So—she was in your tummy, but when she came out she was dead? I thought only old people died? Babies can't die!" I start to cry, and Mom moves closer, puts her arm around me.

"It's called stillborn—it's two words put together. *Still* means they aren't alive—they don't breathe, they don't cry, they don't move. *Born*, because the baby has to come out of the mom's tummy. Does that help explain it?" It does help, but I can't talk to Mom right now, because I can't stop crying for my poor, dead sister. I want to dig up the dirt covering Cecelia so that I can hold her and touch her. I can't imagine a baby being dead. On television, every baby is alive and snuggled up in their Mother's arms.

"But—that's so sad, Mom. That's so sad for you to have a stillborn baby," I say, trying out the new word. "Did you cry when it happened?"

"Oh, yes, I cried for a very long time. I want to tell you something else," Mom says. "There was another baby, a boy that was also stillborn. He would have been the oldest child; I had him before Mark. We named him Stephen, but he isn't buried at this cemetery," Mom is holding me, tightly, but I can't stop crying. Two stillborn babies? If they had lived, there would be four kids in the family instead of two? Suddenly, I have a lot of questions—I break away from Mom's embrace.

"What did they look like, Mom? Did the boy baby look like Mark? Did Cecelia look like me? Were they pudgy babies or skinny babies?"

"I don't know what they looked like, Joanie. I didn't get to see them," Mom says softly. Her voice is cracking, so I know she's going to cry. "When a mom has a stillborn baby, they don't let her see the baby, because they think it will make her sadder than she already is. The doctor took the babies away, and your dad figured out where to have them buried."

"But on television, they always give the new baby to the mom right away," I say, in protest.

"Yes, well, television doesn't show real life," Mom says. I feel a zap hit my chest, right by my heartbeat, like when I shock myself on the outlets at home, and I think my heart is breaking for my mom, for Cecelia, for Stephen. Even for Dad, I guess.

"Do you miss them? Even though you didn't get to see them?" I ask.

"Every day, Joanie. I think about them every day of my life."

"Are they in Heaven, with God?"

"Well, I don't know for sure about that. Your dad didn't think to get Stephen baptized, so Father Paul told me he's in what the church calls Limbo. That's where people's souls go if they haven't been baptized," she explains. She tells me that Cecelia was baptized, so she's in Heaven.

"So even though Stephen and Cecelia are brother and sister, they can't see each other?" I ask, thinking that is the stupidest thing I have ever heard. Why wouldn't God want them to be together?

"I never thought about it that way, but I guess you're right."

"I think I better get baptized," I say. "If I die I want my soul to go to Heaven, not to that Limbo place."

"Oh, you and Mark are already baptized—you had that done when you were a tiny baby, so you don't remember it. Uncle Earle and Aunt Sharon are your godparents."

"Does Mark know about Stephen and Cecelia?" I ask. Mom tells me he does, she told him when he was about my age.

"Can we visit Stephen, too?" I ask Mom.

"Well, no. I don't know what cemetery he's in," Mom says. "So anyway, that's why we come to the service on Memorial Day. It's a day for people to honor loved ones that have died. We can honor, and pray, for Cecelia," Mom explains. "Should we say a prayer for her?"

"I think we should pray the Hail Mary. Would that be okay?" I ask. Mom nods her head. Kneeling right next to each other, we fold our hands to pray. The words mix with our tears.

HAIL MARY,
FULL OF GRACE,
OUR LORD IS WITH THEE;
BLESSED ART THOU AMONG
WOMEN,
AND BLESSED IS THE FRUIT OF
THY WOMB, JESUS
HOLY MARY,
MOTHER OF GOD,
PRAY FOR US SINNERS,
NOW AND AT THE HOUR
OF OUR DEATH.

AMEN

When we get home from the cemetery, I decide I don't want to ride my bike after all. Mom and I make lunch and a pitcher of Kool-Aid and sit out on the front step to have a little picnic.

After supper, we sit on the couch to watch television and snuggle. Soon, it's time for bed. The Memorial Day holiday is over. I have one more question to ask Mom as she tucks me in for the night.

"Mom? Do we have to wait until next Memorial Day to visit Cecelia?" I ask.

"No, we can visit her anytime we want. But Memorial Day is the only time there's a church service at the cemetery," Mom explains.

"Oh. Do you think it would be okay if I visited Cecelia once in a while?"

"Yes, I think she would like that very much," Mom says, smiling. "But now, it's time for you to get some sleep. Don't forget to say your prayers, Joanie."

I add Stephen and Cecelia to my nightly prayer. And at the end of my prayer, I ask God if he would honor my brother Stephen by moving him from Limbo over to Heaven, even if he isn't baptized, so that he can be with Cecelia. That way they can be together—like me and Mark.

ICE CREAM

DAD IS IN A super good mood today! He has a surprise for the whole family. Something he bought at Coast to Coast. "I know you are going to love it! We'll open it up as soon as your mother gets home," Dad says.

When Mom walks in, Dad grabs the box on the table and opens it up—revealing his treasure. Mark and Mom figure out what it is right away—an ice cream maker!

"Folks, you are about to taste the best ice cream you have ever had!" Dad exclaims as he empties out the parts and sets them on them on the table.

"Better than Dairy Queen?" I ask.

"Way better than the old DQ," Dad says. "You won't ever want to go back to the DQ once you taste your Dad's homemade ice cream."

The machine has several pieces, and Dad explains each one to us.

"This is the outer can, the one the salt and ice will go in."

"Salt?" I ask. "I don't think the DQ uses salt!"

"Oh, well now, I don't know about that. But for the homemade stuff, you need salt, ice, cream, and sugar. The salt is a special kind, called rock salt, and it helps the ice get the cream cold fast! Soon we will all have a delicious dish of ice cream, just perfect for this hot summer day, don't you think?"

Dad goes on to explain the other parts: the inner canister, the paddlewheel, and the crank. I am so lucky to have a Dad that is smart enough to know how to make us a homemade treat.

"We'll all take turns with the crank. Joanie, you will go first, then your mother, then Mark, and then myself. It'll get a lot harder as we go."

Dad takes us all out on the back steps and starts assembling the machine and the ingredients. Mark and I help by putting the ice and salt just inside the big can, which is black and smooth-looking. Once Dad has the inner can nestled into the icy salt mixture, he opens the cardboard carton of cream and pours it in. Next, he sprinkles in a full cup of sugar. Once all the ingredients are taken care of, Dad puts the paddlewheel into the cream. He pops the lid on, and now it is time to turn the crank.

"Okay, Joanie, let's see what you've got! Put some muscle into it now!" Dad says as I put my hand on the handle. As I turn the crank, a tiny trickle of water comes out the bottom of the machine and pools on the sidewalk near my foot. It is super cold! Soon it is too hard for me, and Mom takes over.

"Mark, you're next up," Dad says when Mom's arms get tired. "It's starting to get nice and thick! " Dad says, excitedly. "We need to get it to the point where we can hardly move the paddlewheel— then we will know it is ready."

Mark is way stronger than me! He has one hand on the wooden handle, and the other on the edge of the ice cream maker to hold it still. He cranks for a long time.

"Can we try some now, Dad? Can we?" I ask, knowing I am being a little impatient. But it isn't quite ready, and soon it is my turn again. When I try to turn the handle, I can't do it.

"That's okay, Joanie, you can be done," Dad says. "Let's skip over your turn, Lyla, and go straight to Mark's. We're almost there!"

"I think it might be ready, Dad. It feels pretty thick, I can't turn it anymore," Mark reports after a few more turns of the crank.

"Well, let me take one more crack at it," Dad says. He grabs the handle and starts cranking. He has to push hard to make the handle go around, not at all like when we first started.

"Okay, everyone, I think it is ready for tasting!" Dad finally announces. "Lyla, can you go get us some bowls and spoons? Mark, go in and grab the Hershey's chocolate syrup off the counter."

We all stand by and watch as Dad ever so slowly pulls the paddlewheel out. The paddles are coated with the softest-looking ice cream I've ever seen! I can't believe it! With a long metal spoon, he scrapes the frozen mixture off the metal paddles and into our bowls. Then, he takes the long spoon and sinks it into the middle of the canister, scooping out the luscious-looking cream. By the time the canister is empty, my mouth is watering, and I can hardly wait to taste it.

"Let's take our first bites all at the same time," Dad says. "Lyla, do you want to start the chocolate syrup?"

Mom pours the syrup, one of my favorite things, onto our ice cream. Oh, it looks so good! She passes a bowl to each of us, and Dad tells us to dig in!

"John, this is the best ice cream I have ever had!" Mom says with a big smile.

"I love it, Dad! No more DQ for me! I want you to make the homemade stuff every day from now on!" I giggle. And although it is melting fast, because it's so hot out, I try to make it last as long as I can.

Mark, scraping the last of the ice cream out of his bowl, is also enjoying it. "Pretty good, Dad, pretty good. All that work was definitely worth it!"

THE PIANO

"PIANO NIGHT TONIGHT!" MOM announces after supper. "Mark, you're going to play, too!"

Way before I was born, when Mom first started working at the bank, she opened a special savings account so she could buy a piano. The musical instrument is the most beautiful piece of furniture in our house, and Mom is extremely proud of it. I love piano nights. I wish Mom would have them more often. Mark takes piano lessons from Mrs. Day, and sometimes we go to concerts where her students play for an audience. Mark has an extra gift—it's called playing by ear. Even Mom is amazed at how he can sit at the piano and work out a song, without looking at any music.

Guests are not allowed to play or even touch the piano. If one of our friends taps a key or slides a hand along the wood when Mom's home, she immediately yells at them. My friends are always amazed that she knows the piano has been touched, even when she isn't in the room.

I'm the first one in the living room tonight, and while I wait, I run my hand over the top of the piano, freshly polished with Pledge. The wood is the color of Mom's coffee when she adds a little milk to it. Under my hand, the wood is smooth—it feels a lot like the silky lining in Mom's winter coat. When no one is playing it, the black and white keys are hidden behind a rolling door. As I slide the door back, I watch it magically disappear inside the piano. When it settles into its hiding place, it makes a slight squeaking sound, which alerts my mom.

"Are you getting everything ready, Joanie?" Mom asks from the kitchen.

"Yes! Are you playing Christmas first, or requests?" I cross my fingers and hope for requests first—I already know what mine will be.

"Christmas first!" Mom shouts. "I'm almost ready, just finishing up the dishes."

Mom stores her music inside the matching piano bench, and when I open it tonight, I find my favorite songbook. I open it to page 111, and then carefully place it on the top of the piano. I search through the bench until I find Mom's Christmas music. I know she will want to play "Silent Night," "Away in a Manger," and "Deck the Halls," but I also enjoy "Frosty the Snowman" and "Rudolph the Red-Nosed Reindeer," so I get those out, too.

"Okay, everything's ready!" I announce. "Who's going to be your page turner tonight, Mom?" I ask. But I already know the answer. Mark doesn't like to be the page turner anymore, so it will be me.

"Hmm . . . " Mom says. "I wonder."

The reason I like to be the page turner is I get to see Mom's elegant, long fingers slide and zoom up and down the keys, and be the first to hear the music soar out of the piano before it fills the living room. I can't believe that something made of wood, felt, and strings can produce such joyful, lively music.

While I wait for Mom, Dad, and Mark to come in the living room, I push a key down softly and slowly, listening for the quiet sound of the felt hammer striking the string. Then, I do the opposite and press my finger down hard, so I can hear the sound full blast.

Everyone finally comes into the living room, and Mom gets started. We all sing our hearts out as Mom plays one Christmas song after the other. Our "Fa La La La La's" on "Deck the Halls" are the best we've ever done!

Behind the piano bench is the Christmas tree, with all our presents under it. Well, except the ones from Santa—those are in Mom's closet. I know they are, because I found them there. Not only did I find them, but I opened them all. I didn't take all the wrapping off, just enough to see that I'm getting an EZ Bake Oven. And some mixes for it. And a Lite Brite. I didn't mean to peek at every single present, but once I got started, I couldn't stop. When I was done, I taped the paper back up the best I could. I guess I'll have to pretend to be surprised when Santa comes this year.

When Mom finishes playing almost every Christmas song ever invented, Mark plays one of the songs he is working on with his piano teacher. I would never say it out loud, but I think Mark might play the piano better than Mom!

"Okay, time for requests," Mom announces.

"I'll go last! Mark, you and Dad can go before me," I say.

"'Hey, Good Lookin'" is my request!" Dad says, with a big smile on his face. He's lying on the floor, between the bench and the Christmas tree. His arms are folded behind his head, his eyes are twinkling, and he has a dreamy smile on his face. This is another thing I love about piano nights—Dad is always in a good mood. I don't worry, not even a little bit, that he will start shouting, yelling, or hitting. When Mom plays the chorus, we all join in—and we start to laugh when we sing the last line—"How's about cookin' somethin' up with me?"

"Hey, Mom—can you play 'The Old Lamplighter?'" Mark asks.

"One of my favorites!" Mom's smile spreads across her face as she plays and sings about the little old man with white hair brightening up the night sky in his town.

"Is it my turn?!" I ask as soon as Mom plays the last notes of "The Old Lamplighter". "I bet you can't guess what I'm thinking of!"

"Oh, Joanie!" Mom says, with a little giggle. "Let's see, can anyone guess what Joanie wants to hear?"

"It can't be . . . wait, is it . . . 'Oh, Susanna?'" Mark teases. And then we all laugh, because "Oh, Susanna" is my favorite song of all time.

"You guessed it! Page 111 in *The Little Brown Book of Songs*, Mom!" I say.

"I sure hope you come up with a new favorite when you turn eight in February!" Mark says.

As Mom plays, I make sure we all sing along. While we sing, I see a picture in my mind of a young man, a cowboy I suppose, traveling around with a banjo on his knee, trying to find his one true love. I try to figure out how there could be dry weather and rain at the same time, how it could be so hot that you could freeze to death. And I picture Susanna, wearing a long dress—not a wedding dress, but a long purple one with flowers on it—sitting on her porch watching for him and then running out to meet him as he finds his way to her.

At the end of the night, Dad gets out his Polaroid camera. "Let's take a few pictures before we hit the hay," he says. After we've all had our picture taken, he hands the camera to Mark.

"Take a picture of your old man, will you, Mark?" Dad requests. Mark snaps the photo, and once Dad has put the backing on and spread the liquid on the top of the picture, he takes a pen and writes something on the back.

"Thanks for a great night," he says to Mom. He hands her the photo and then leans over and gives her a peck on the cheek. Mom looks at the photo, then turns it over and reads the back. She gives Dad a peck on his cheek and then sets the photo on the top of the piano.

"Yeah, thanks, Mom!" Mark says.

"It was the best!" I say. "How about one more round of 'Oh, Susanna?'" I ask, hopefully.

"I don't think so, little lady! Nice try, but it's off to bed for you!" Mom says. I try to read her face, because once in a great while, even though she says no, she will still play it one more time. But then I see her pull the wood cover over the keys, and I know it's not going to happen.

After I put on my nightie, I head to the family room to say goodnight to Mom and Dad. As I walk through the living room, I pick up Dad's photo. He didn't get the back stuck on straight, and the liquid stuff smeared his picture a little, but he's smiling, and the lights on the tree are sparkling bright behind him. I turn it over to read what he wrote. It takes me a minute, because it is part printing and part cursive, but finally, I make out the words: *To Lyla, my sweetheart. Love, John.*

RUNAWAY

TODAY IS THE PERFECT day to run away, because Mark and Dad aren't home, and Mom is at work. I've done it before, back when I was just a kid. The last time I ran away, I was so little that I couldn't walk very far, but now that I'm eight years old I'm positive I can make it at least one hundred miles a day. Once I make it five hundred miles, like the song on the radio, then I'll know I'm far enough away from 509 that no one will ever find me. I know Dad won't miss me, because he's always gone or sleeping. And I don't think Mom will miss me too much, either.

Even though Bernice told me that I'm Mom's real daughter, I don't believe it, because almost everything about me makes her mad. I think most daughters make their moms happy so that they say, "I love you!" with a nice voice instead of "Why'd you do that?!" or "Leave me alone!" in a crabby voice like mine does. Even when I'm on my best behavior and I try to do everything right, Mom tells me she's too busy or too tired to play with me. Plus, with me out of her hair, Mom can pay more attention to the bank.

The last time I ran away from home, I packed silly things into a paper bag: a Barbie doll, my old stuffed puppy, and one pair of underwear. But this time, I'm using a real suitcase—the brown one with white stripes that we keep in the basement. And this time I packed only useful things. I could hardly get it closed after I filled it up with a blanket, clothes, peanut butter and jelly sandwiches and chocolate-chip cookies (those are tucked into the blanket so that they won't get crushed).

I'm not sure where I am exactly, but I know I've walked far enough that Eleventh Avenue is WAY behind me. I'm keeping my eyes open, watching for other kids that are running away. I'm pretty sure, but not all the way sure, that it's mostly girls that run away. I'm not sure how long it'll take to find the other girls, but the first thing I'm going to tell them is that I'm sorry their parents don't love them. The girls I meet will probably say the same thing to me—and then we'll become good friends! If we like each other, we can be each other's moms and take care of each other. I'm super good at cooking and cleaning, so I guess I can do those things. The girls that don't like to cook and clean can get jobs to pay for our food and stuff.

It's true that I have a new friend—her name is Nancy, and she is exactly my age. She and her family moved into the house right across the street from ours. Her parents, Mr. and Mrs. Kewatt, are nice, and so is her sister, Patti Jo. I wonder if Nancy will notice that I don't live at 509 anymore. I'm sure she'll be able to make friends with Rhonda and Connie, so she probably won't miss me too much.

I wasn't planning on this suitcase being so heavy! Maybe I packed a little too much in it. I guess I could carry it with my right arm for a while and let my left arm rest. I wonder how I'll know when I'm in the next town? As soon as I get there, I'm going to stop for lunch, because I'm getting super hungry!

It feels like I've been walking for about a hundred hours now, and my tummy is rumbling. I wish I was at a park or something, but I guess I'll rest on the side of the road and have my lunch. The suitcase isn't that comfortable to sit on, but it'll be okay for a few minutes. I wonder what town I'm in now? UGGHH. It's kind of hard to swallow peanut butter without milk! I wonder where I could get one of those little cartons like they have at school?

I should probably find a place to go to the bathroom. What kind of bathrooms do people who are running away use? I don't see any houses around here, just one incredibly long road. Wait— is that a woman calling my name? Where did she come from? I didn't even notice her station wagon, but there it is, parked on the side of the road.

"Joanie Hicks? Is that you?" The lady is wearing a dress, and her high-heels are clickety-clacking as she walks towards me. How could this strange woman possibly know who I am? Is she from New Brighton?

"Yes, I'm Joanie," I mumble.

"What are you doing way out here?" she asks. "It's so hot out today. My goodness! Is that a suitcase you have there?"

I don't like her; I can tell she's going to ruin all my plans. I can't believe this stranger has caught me! Whoever she is, I need to convince her to leave me alone.

"I'm just out for a walk, enjoying the beautiful day," I try, hoping she will head back to her car. Instead, she comes right up to me, stands in front of me. She's got her hands on her hips, so I'm guessing she means business. The sun is shining on her blonde hair, making it sparkle. She might be pretty and nice, but I still don't like her.

"Oh, hmmm. Well, I wonder if you know who I am?" She tells me her name, Mrs. Somebody, but I still don't know who she is. "I have a son your age; I think you know him? I can't imagine you being out here all by yourself. I think you might be a little sunburned. I know you said you're out for a walk, but I wonder, do you think you might be lost?" She puts one of her hands up to her forehead to keep the sun out of her eyes while she looks right at me.

"No, I'm not lost," I say, hoping she doesn't ask me if I know my way home, because I'm not sure I do. The whole point was to get away from 509, not go back to it. Might as well tell her the truth, maybe Mrs. Somebody will leave me alone once she knows. "I'm running away from home. I am trying to get to one hundred miles today, but I'm not sure how many I've gone so far."

"Running away! Oh, goodness," Mrs. Somebody says, her smiling face turning into a slight frown. "Well, hmm. You're a bit young to run away, don't you think? I'm sure your mom would miss you! She works at the bank, right?"

I'm doomed. This strange lady with her friendly smile and her light blonde hair sparkling in the sunlight not only knows who I am, but she knows Mom. My eyes brim with tears at the prospect of another failed runaway mission, but at this point, there isn't much I can do.

"I don't think she will miss me. I'm trying to help her, so she doesn't have to put up with me anymore. You can go back to your house now. I need to keep moving," I tell her. I want to convince her that I know what I'm doing, but I'm having a hard time keeping the shakiness out of my words. By the look on her face, I'm guessing she's not going to let me continue with my plan.

"How about this? You hop in my car, and I'll drive you to the bank," Mrs. Somebody says. "We'll talk to your mom and get this all straightened out. I bet after you see your mom, you will feel a lot better. How about it?" She sounds excited; she wants me to like this idea of hers.

I don't say anything, because the tears behind my eyes will fall out if I try to talk. Why is this lady being so kind to me? Why would she care about someone like me? Why can't she understand that I've got to get away?

The next thing I know, Mrs. Somebody picks up my suitcase, takes my hand, and walks me to her car. So much for running away.

I watch out the side window as she turns her car around and we drive down the road. Mrs. Somebody is talking and talking, but I've stopped listening, because I'm worried about what Mom is going to think when we show up at the bank. I've only been inside the bank for Santa Day—that's when Santa comes all the way from the North Pole to the bank so that all the kids from New Brighton can sit on his lap and tell him what we want for Christmas.

"Mom's working hard at the bank and I'm not supposed to interrupt her, so you can just take me home. I live on Eleventh," I tell Mrs. Somebody.

"Oh, well, I see what you mean. But don't worry, I think in this case, it will be okay. I think your mom is going to be glad to see you today!"

A few minutes later she turns into the parking lot. The bank is right next door to Clark Pharmacy. On the other side of Clark's is Coast to Coast. I've been to both of those places plenty of times, and I think I wouldn't mind if Mrs. Somebody wants to take me to the counter at Clark's for an ice cream treat. But I'm guessing that's not going to happen. As she pulls the car into a parking spot, I decide I'm not going in. If Mrs. Somebody wants to talk to Mom, she'll have to do it by herself.

"I'll wait in the car. You can wave out the window if Mom wants me to come in."

She turns around and looks at me. Her lips are coated in bright-red lipstick, and are drooping down; I made Mrs. Somebody feel sad. "Oh, Joanie. I think you should come in with me. I guess I can go in and talk to your mom myself first if that's what you want."

"Okay," I say, as she gets out and heads into the bank. I could open the car door and run away again—I still have my suitcase, cookies, and sandwiches. But I don't know how long Mrs. Somebody is going to be inside the bank, so I'm pretty sure

I'd get caught again.

Mrs. Somebody is already stepping out of the bank—she didn't wave at me, so I guess I'm not going in. Once she's all settled in the driving spot of her car, she turns and looks right at me. Her pretty smile is gone, and her eyes are real big. I hope she doesn't cry. We stare at each other for a few minutes. It's kind of like a staring contest, but not like a fun one. "Well," she says. "Your Mom told me to bring you home. When you get in the house, you're supposed to spend the rest of the day in your room, until she gets home from the bank."

"Okay," I say, quietly. I thought Mom might come out and talk to me, but I'm guessing she's super busy. I don't care.

Mrs. Somebody finally starts her car up, backs out of the parking spot. "My house number is 509. On Eleventh Avenue," I say.

After she pulls up in front of my house, we both get out of the car. I stand on the sidewalk while Mrs. Somebody hands me my suitcase. Then she kneels in front of me, right on the hard cement, so that she is almost my size. "Joanie, it's lunchtime. Do you think you can make your own lunch today?" I tell her that I already ate, because I was hungry, and I didn't know what time it was.

"I packed sandwiches and cookies for my trip," I explain. I don't know why, but I think I should do something nice for Mrs. Somebody. "Do you want some cookies for your family?" I ask. "I won't need them now that I'm not running away."

"No, Joanie, you keep those for yourself. I think you are a very brave little girl and you deserve every single one of those cookies!"

In my room, I'm not sure what to do. I don't want to play with my Barbie or anything. But I am kind of hungry. And I still want some milk. I don't think Mark or Dad are home yet, but I sit near the vent and listen to be sure. Would they even know I'm in trouble? I don't think Mom could've told them yet. If I run out to the kitchen and pour my milk fast, I should be able to get back to my room even if someone starts to come in the door.

It worked! And I even stopped in the bathroom, too. Now I can stay in my room without any worries. I guess I'll take a little nap—I might've gotten up a little too early today, because, suddenly, I'm tired . . .

"Joanie, wake up!" Mom yells. "Wake up!" When I blink open my eyes, Mom tells me what I already know. "Do you have any idea what you put me through today? I can't be interrupted at the bank. You know that!"

"I'm sorry, Mom. I was trying to get out of your hair, so you wouldn't have to worry about me anymore," I explain.

"From now on, your brother is in charge! You are not to leave this house without his permission! Do you understand?"

Mark's going to be in charge of me? He's going to be as mad as Mom is! He doesn't want to hang out with his dumb little sister! Great, just great. Now Mark is going to be mad at me, too.

DYNAMITE

I GUESS IT'S A good thing that I didn't run away, because Dad brought home a new dog today. He thinks this will be a good replacement for Midnight, but I'm not so sure. One weird thing is that he already has a name: TNT.

"Stands for dynamite, one of the best explosives in the world! You can blow up a building with it!" Dad explains. Who would name a dog with letters that stand for something dangerous? I can't figure that one out.

"This dog is not a mutt like Midnight was, no siree," Dad continues. "TNT is a cocker spaniel, purebred. He's got papers and everything. He was going to be a show dog, but his teeth are crooked. If there's one thing a show dog must have, it's straight teeth!" Dad exclaims, and I wonder how he knows so much about show dogs.

"How old is he?" I ask as Dad and I examine our new addition. TNT is not the size of a puppy, so I figure he is an older dog. He does not have a black velvet coat like Midnight did, more like a curly mixture of black and gray hair. His hair curls all over his body, even over the tops of his eyes. I check under his lips, and it's true: his teeth are crooked.

"Two years old, Joanie. That means he's fourteen years old in human years. So he's a teenager like your brother! Ha, well, let's review the rules for having a dog again . . . " As Dad reviews the rules (same ones I had for Midnight), I get down on the floor and try to make friends with TNT. He seems a little shy, not quite as spunky as Midnight was.

"Shake!" I command, and he does. "Good boy!" I say, impressed that he would already know a trick. Maybe this dog with the strange name and crooked teeth won't be so bad after all.

Dad isn't around when Mom gets home from work, and I guess he forgot to tell her we were getting another dog.

"Where in the world did he come from, Joanie? Did you find him at the park?" she asks me.

"He belongs to us, Mom," I tell her. "His name is TNT, and he was going to be a show dog, but he has bad teeth, so Dad brought him home for us." Mom sits down in her chair at the table, and TNT immediately jumps up into her lap! I think he likes her!

"A dog. Really? A dog? I can't believe this," Mom says. I don't think Mom is falling in love with TNT like I am.

ᏩᎥ

TNT and I are best friends now. He loves to go for walks, and I take him all over the neighborhood and down to Hansen Park. I tell the neighbors that I am eight years old and that TNT is two in dog years, fourteen in human. TNT isn't a fan of strangers, though, and sometimes when people stop to pet him, he growls and shows them his crooked teeth.

It's true that TNT's teeth are crooked. But mine are too, so it's no big deal. He loves me, and that is what matters most. And though it's also true he barks and growls at just about everyone, he truly loves me. When I come home from school, I call his name as I open the door and he comes running—jumps right up on me and gives me the biggest kisses. And guess what? He knows how to smile! After I let him outside, he climbs up on the couch with me while I have a snack and tell him about my day. As it turns out, he's a very good listener.

Even though Dad is the one who brought TNT to our house, he doesn't seem to like him. Whenever TNT does something bad, like bark at the front window, Dad kicks him and tells him "Bad dog!" I don't know if all dogs know how to cry, but TNT does. When Dad is mad at him, I go into my bedroom and yell "TNT!" as loudly as I can. After he comes running in, I close my door, and we snuggle on my bed.

"Don't worry, TNT," I say to him. "Dad shouldn't kick you like that. I'll try to protect you, okay?"

A BUNDLE

TODAY'S THE BIG DAY! I've been waiting and waiting for this day to come, and now here it is. It's December 20, 1970—and I think it will quite possibly be the best day of my life! Why? Because today I'm going to become a big sister! I suppose some eight-year-olds wouldn't want to have a little sister or brother, but I can't wait!

I'll never forget the hot summer day that I found out that Mom was going to have a baby—my friend Rhonda told me, and I didn't believe her. I called Rhonda a liar, because I was sure that if Mom was going to have a baby, she would have told me way before she would have told Rhonda or even Rhonda's mom. It was one of the longest days of my life, because I had to wait until Mom got home from work to prove that Rhonda was a liar. But then the surprise was on me!

"Mom, I have to ask you something," I asked the moment she walked in the door.

"Not now, Joanie," she said. "I need to change my clothes and get supper ready. Go outside for a while. I'll call you in when it's time to eat." Mom didn't seem to understand that I needed to talk to her right away. When I looked up at her with my eagerness, her straight lips and wrinkled forehead gave me the message to stop talking.

"Okay, Mom? Can I ask you something now?" I asked, later that night.

"Yes, what is it?" Mom said. She's settled on the couch, drinking a Hamm's. "Let's hear it. Did you get in trouble today or something?"

"No! I, well . . . "

"Oh, for goodness sake! Spit it out! What do you want?"

"Are you going to have a baby?" I asked quickly. My voice wobbled, and I became worried that I might cry. I wasn't planning on Mom being angry when I asked my question.

"What makes you ask me that?" Mom said in a loud voice—which sounds kind of like screaming and talking at the same time.

"Rhonda told me today when we were playing."

"Rhonda," Mom said, anger rising in her voice.

"But don't worry, Mom! I took care of it! I called her a liar; I told her you were NOT going to have a baby. And tomorrow when I see her I'll tell her she is mean for telling a lie like that!" But as I said these words to Mom, I noticed her face relax a little. Then, as she lifted a lit match to her cigarette, she looked at me with a little smile.

"Wait, Mom, is it true? You're going to have a baby?"

"Yep, I sure am," she answered. The anger scattered off into the air of the family room, and a huge smile spread across Mom's face. "Are you ready to be a big sister?"

"Yes! Yes!" I shouted, jumping and leaping for joy around the family room. When I calmed down a little, I climbed into her lap and gave her a big hug. "But how did Rhonda find out before me?"

"All I can say is people talk. I suppose someone told Rhonda's mom and then she told Rhonda. I was waiting to tell you so that it wouldn't be such a long wait for you. The baby isn't coming until around Christmas time. So you're going to have to be patient."

❧

Oh, man, it was so hard to be patient! I waited through the rest of the hot summer, and into fall while the leaves changed colors. I watched as Mom's tummy grew and grew—in October, when we made apple pies, she could hardly reach the table to peel the apples. When winter hit, her belly grew even bigger, and I could see, and feel, the baby kicking and squirming in anticipation of coming out. In the evenings, after supper, Mom had to put her legs up while she watched television, because her ankles were getting swollen. At first, I prayed every night for a sister. I told God it only made sense since I already have a brother. Mom told me all she wanted was a healthy baby—she didn't care if it was a boy or a girl.

❧

And now, here it is—the day the baby is coming. Dad took Mom to the hospital this afternoon, and Mark and I are waiting for him to call and tell us if it is a boy or a girl. Mom and Dad let us help pick out names for the baby. Mark's choice for the boy name is unbelievably weird: Judd. I think it's an awful name! Who names a baby Judd? But Mark says he thinks it's a cool name and that Judd would be the only boy in New Brighton with that name. After I found out about Mark's choice for a name, I told God in my nightly prayer that I thought it would be sad to have a baby named Judd, and I'm sure God agrees with me. Our dictionary has a list of boys' and girls' names in it, and I spent all summer and fall going through the list to help choose the girl name. I had it narrowed down to ten names, but Mom said that was too many—she wanted to know what my top three choices were. So if it is a girl baby she might be called Brenda, Gloria, or Chelsea—all much better names than Judd! Mom said she wasn't too crazy about Brenda, but she might consider Gloria or Chelsea.

"How long do you think it will take?" I ask Mark after we fix ourselves grilled cheese sandwiches for supper.

"I have no idea. I wish I could remember how long it took when you were born. We'll just have to be patient, I guess."

I decide to call Rhonda with the news, and she invites me to come over to her house. Before I go, I make Mark promise he will call me at Rhonda's as soon as he hears from Dad. And then, around 9:00 p.m., Rhonda's mom tells me that Mark is on the phone.

"You got your wish, Joanie. It's a girl!" Mark tells me. Oh, my gosh—I can't believe it! I'm a big sister, and it's a girl! I shout out the news to Rhonda, and the two of us dance around like crazy!

"What's her name?" I ask. But Mark says Dad didn't tell him what her name was, so we'll have to wait to find that out.

When I get home, Mark makes us popcorn and chocolate milk for our celebration. He is the best popcorn maker—I love to watch him pour melted butter over the top! I want to stay awake until Dad comes home, but once we finish our popcorn, I'm having a hard time keeping my eyes open. I decide to head to bed hoping to see Dad in the morning. As I lay my head down on my pillow, I thank my mom and dad, as well as God, for my new baby sister. I absolutely can't wait to meet her!

When I wake up the next morning, I hear Dad and Mark out in the kitchen. I run out to find out all the news from Dad.

"Well, she is beautiful, and she has dark hair like you and your mother. And we named her Gloria!" Dad announces proudly, as I jump up and down on the kitchen floor. I ask about a million more questions. Did she cry when she was born? Has she had a bottle of milk yet? What is she wearing? But most importantly . . .

"When can we meet her? I have to meet her, I HAVE to!" I scream.

"Your mother and the baby have to stay at the hospital for a few days, so you'll need to be patient a little bit longer." *Patient*—I'm starting to hate that word! What am I supposed to do for the next few days?

❧

The days passed by quickly, though, and today Mom, Dad, and Gloria are on their way home. When they come in, the entry is crowded with the three of them, and it takes a bit for Mark and me to get close enough—but when we do, Mom bends over so that we can peek into the layers of soft blankets surrounding our sister. And then I see her. She is sleeping, and guess what? She has her thumb in her mouth! She is absolutely the most beautiful baby I have ever seen.

"Okay, which one of you wants to hold her first?" Dad asks as he takes the preciously wrapped bundle from Mom. But Mark has already decided that I can be first, and I realize I have the best big brother in the whole wide world. Mom helps me get settled on the couch and tells me how to hold her, and then, ever so gently, Dad places Gloria in my arms.

"You can unwrap the blankets a little, just make sure you cradle her head," Mom says. Gloria is wrapped in layers of pink and white blankets made of the softest fabric I have ever felt, and I can feel her warmth penetrating through it. As I peel the velvety coverings away, I see my sister's tiny nose and her miniature mouth. There is just a hint of brown lashes at the bottom of her closed eyes and a smidgen of dark brown hair on her little head. Her hands look like little pads of flesh, and her fingers are curled in on themselves. Mom shows me her feet, and I giggle when I see her teeny-tiny toes! And now, there is no denying it: she is absolutely the most beautiful baby I have ever seen. As I cuddle her, I see her eyes open for a split second, and I see they are a light brown. I don't know why but tears begin to stream down my cheeks.

"I think her name is perfect, don't you, Mom? What else could you have named the most beautiful baby in the world?" I ask, looking up at her.

"Yes, Joanie, it's perfect—and so is she. She couldn't be more adorable," Mom says, and I see that she, too, is crying. "But now I think it's time for her brother to hold her." I lean over and kiss Gloria's warm cheek, and then, just before I hand her over, I whisper into what I am sure is the tiniest ear God has ever created.

"I will always love you, and I promise to always keep you safe."

LET'S BUILD

EARLIER THIS SUMMER, DAD started a project of epic proportions. The first I knew of it was when I saw Mark and one of his friends coming up the basement stairs, each carrying a bucket of dirt.

"Stay out of the way, Joanie!" Dad exclaimed as I tried to come through the back doorway. "Lots of dirt coming through!"

"What's going on?" I asked Mark, as he headed to the backyard. When he tips the bucket over, I saw the dirt was more like a goopy mixture of mud and rocks.

"I guess Dad's putting in a bathroom in the basement," Mark answered. "Kind of by the laundry room."

"That's right, Joanie! We'll be the first house on the block to have two bathrooms! What do you think of that!" Dad beamed.

I'm guessing Dad didn't run this project past Mom.

"Umm, well, I guess that's cool. Who's going to help you?" I asked.

"No one! My work crew is me, myself and I!" Dad exclaimed, proudly. "Well, and these two characters! I'm paying them one dollar for every bucket they haul out!" Dad continued, pointing at Mark and his friend. "I already tore out the cement wall, and as soon as the dirt is hauled out, I'll build the greatest bathroom you've ever laid eyes on!"

ᐧᐁᐧ

It took the whole summer, but I guess Dad did what he promised. He's been waiting and waiting for Mom to get home from the bank to show us his grand creation. "Lyla, Joanie—are you ready to see the bathroom?" Dad asks the minute Mom comes through the door. Mom's holding Gloria—she's already seven months old; they both look tired. "You better keep your shoes on, there could be some nails on the floor down here," Dad advises, already heading down the stairs. I can tell Dad is proud to show us what he created, eager for us to see the finished product. Over the past couple of weeks, he has hauled a whole bunch of stuff downstairs to help him build the bathroom. One thing he put in that I will like is a shower. It will be cool to take a shower instead of a bath.

At the bottom of the stairs, we take a right turn, and I see the bathroom door straight ahead. The door is surrounded on both sides by the huge white cement bricks that hold up our house, and is under what used to be a crawl space. I guess that's where all the dirt that Mark carried out must have come from. The door is shut, and I can see that it doesn't quite fit the opening. The light switch is on outside the door, and it looks exactly like the light switch in the garage.

"Are you ready?" Dad asks, opening the door. He flicks the switch, which turns on a light-bulb in the ceiling which is covered by a wobbling, square piece of white glass. An exhaust fan is roaring loudly above our heads. Maybe the whirring of the fan is what is making the light fixture shake? I peek in and start to examine the rest of the bathroom. I'm not sure what to say. Mom, still holding Gloria, is silent.

I'm no expert, but Dad's bathroom doesn't look so good. In

fact, I think it is going to fall apart while we're standing here. It looks like a wobbly cave with white, plastic walls. The floor looks like it could hurt somebody—apparently after Mark and his friend hauled out the dirt, Dad poured cement right over the top of the uneven surface. And then he painted the cement yellow. The pointy parts of the yellow cement—not a lemony color, more like the color of Heinz mustard—look like they could stab the bottom of your foot. The yellow paint must have been hard to put on the cement floor, because some areas have no paint at all and other areas are thick with what looks like yellow goo. There is a gross-looking drain in the floor which is closer to the sink than the shower. I'm pretty sure you'd have to stand on the drain to wash your hands.

The floor is gross, but it's the walls that make me nervous. They are made of some sort of flimsy whitish-silvery plastic and look as though they will fall into the room with the gentlest touch. They don't quite meet up with the ceiling or the floor in some spots. The shower apparatus is peeking through an uniquely shaped hand-cut hole. The sink and toilet are on the wall right across from the shower and look super wobbly.

The ceiling is creeping me out. It has the same white tiles that are in the rest of the basement, but I don't think Dad knew how to make the metal frames quite right. The openings for some of the tiles are way too big, and dirt from the roof of the cave is peeking through in a whole bunch of spots. As we stand there gazing at the bathroom, a spider jumps out of one of the openings and onto the toilet. Instantly, I make my decision: I will **never** use this bathroom. It is the ugliest and scariest room I have ever seen.

"Well, ladies? What do you think? Pretty good for an old man, ha?" Dad exclaims—and again, I see that he is so proud, literally beaming over his work. I almost feel guilty for hating it.

"John, it's, well . . . gosh, I don't even know what to say,"

Mom answers. I can see she's choosing her words carefully. She doesn't want to hurt Dad's feelings. The last thing she needs is to make him mad. But I can see that her lips are closed tightly together, forming the thin line that announces she is upset, angry. Tell-tale lines have formed on her forehead—she is not pleased. I take Gloria from her, so that she can go in a little farther for a closer inspection. "I guess it's okay. Does everything work?" she finally asks.

Dad demonstrates that the faucet on the sink shoots out water, that the toilet flushes (down goes the spider!)—verifying all is in working order. Mom asks him if the water is hooked up to the shower.

"Oh, certainly! You don't think I would put a shower in without hooking it up to water, now do you?" Dad replies. "But you'll have to stand back a bit if you don't want to get wet!"

Dad stands inside the lopsided doorway, reaches over to the shower faucet handles, and turns on first the hot, then the cold water. Water sprays everywhere, all over the toilet, sink, and floor and through the doorway. "Of course, you have to shut the door to take a shower—otherwise a ton of water will end up out in the laundry area!" Dad laughs a little as he explains the finer details of the shower. Mom does not.

"You didn't put in a shower curtain or anything to hold the water back? We have to clean the toilet and sink after every shower?" Mom asks. But even this question doesn't bring Dad out of his super happy, super satisfied mood. I can see that there would be no way to hang a shower curtain from the rickety metal frames the ceiling tiles are sitting in—the weight of the curtain would pull the frames right down.

"Always a clean bathroom that way, Lyla!" Dad exclaims. "Always a clean bathroom!" At that, Mom claims she needs to go upstairs to make supper. I follow her up the wooden steps and watch as she heads straight for the fridge. She pulls out a

Hamm's, and as she cracks it open, I hear her mutter something under her breath.

"Hey, Mom?" I ask.

"What do you want?" she replies, holding back her anger.

"I just wanted to say that I'm never going to take a shower in that bathroom," I proclaim.

"Yep, neither am I, Joanie," she answers, turning to the stove to fry up some hamburger. "Neither am I."

DYNAMITE, REVISITED

I WOULD SAY THAT TNT and I have become lifelong friends. He is such a good dog, and I tell him everything. The first thing I do when I get home from school is call his name—he'll come running from wherever he is and jump right up on me, nearly knocking me over. After he goes outside, we sit on the couch or lay on my bed, while I tell him all about my day. He is a good listener. He knows more about me than my teachers, or even my mom and dad. I take good care of him, feed him before and after school, make sure he has water, take him for walks, and tell him he is a good boy. When I change Gloria's diapers or help feed her, he is right there to help me. He is such a good boy.

Walking home from the bus stop today, I think of all the things I want to tell him. I didn't have the greatest day. My teacher, Mrs. Treleaven, told me I don't talk enough in school, that I don't answer her when she asks me questions. She also told me I need to work on raising my hand when I know the answer. I get too nervous to talk at school; my hands get all sweaty and shaky when she calls on me. I know that TNT will understand, he always does.

I can't find TNT. He wasn't in the window when I walked up the sidewalk, and he isn't coming when I call him. Maybe he's hiding somewhere? I call and call him, but he does not come. He's not in my room or any of the other rooms in the house. I check downstairs, too, but he is not in Mark's room or by the washing machine. Did someone let him outside and not go look for him? I think of what happened to Midnight and start to worry. Grabbing his leash and some treats, I head outside to look for him.

"TNT! TNT!" I call, over and over, all the way down to Hansen Park, and all the way back. I go around the block, then the next block over. I ask the neighbors if they have seen him, but no one has. Where could he be? My voice is getting weak as I continue to call his name as loudly as I can. I can't think of anywhere else he might be, so I decide to go back home. Where could you he be? I hope he hasn't been run over by a car.

When I get back home, I double check all the rooms in the house—still no TNT. I guess I have to wait until Mom or Dad gets home to figure out what to do next.

Dad is the first one home, and I can't get my words out fast enough to alert him to our missing dog.

"Dad!" I say. "You have to help me find TNT! I have looked everywhere; I can't find him! He isn't at the park or anywhere in the neighborhood. Can we go look for him in the car?" I ask.

"TNT is gone, Joanie," Dad tells me as he heads into the family room to lay down on the couch.

"I know, Dad. That's what I am trying to tell you. I can't find him. I need help!"

"You aren't listening to me, Joanie. TNT is gone. I just got home from Dr. Caldwell's office. TNT is with Midnight now."

"Dad, what? He was here this morning! He wasn't sick. Did he get hit by a car like Midnight?"

"No, he didn't. Your mother was sick and tired of that dog, she told me to get rid of him, so I did." What is Dad talking about? I am crying now, can't believe that TNT has been taken away. "Now stop asking questions, I need some sleep," Dad says as he rolls over onto a pillow.

I run to my room, fly onto my bed, sobbing. TNT can't be gone, can't be with Midnight at Dr. Caldwell's. But then I realize it is true: TNT is dead. I wish I could have said goodbye to him. I would have given him a big hug if I knew Dad was planning to kill him. I already miss him so much. He was the only one I could talk to, the only one who understood when I was sad, or happy, or worried. When I talked to him about something serious, I would hold the curls up from his eyes so that we could look right at each other. If I told him something sad, he always gave me a big kiss to cheer me up. Sometimes his curls would tickle my face, and we would giggle together. How could Mom be sick and tired of my sweet, sweet TNT?

When Mom gets home from the bank, I fly out to the kitchen to question her.

"Mom, did you tell Dad to have TNT killed at Dr. Caldwell's?" I yell at her.

"Oh, for God's sake, don't be so dramatic. I couldn't have him in this house anymore; he was peeing in my bedroom. He was too jealous of your sister."

"Jealous of Gloria?" I ask, staring at my sister, who is toddling around the kitchen without a care in the world. "What does that even mean?"

"It happens with dogs sometimes. A baby comes into the house, and they get jealous. This morning he peed in my bedroom for the hundredth time, and I told your dad I couldn't take it anymore."

"But he was MY dog! He was my best friend!" I cry out. "I didn't even get to say goodbye to him!" I'm stunned. I can't believe my mom and dad would do this to me. My best friend in the whole world, taken away without me knowing anything about it.

"Stop it now, you're nine years old and acting like a baby. This is my house, and I couldn't handle having that dog around here anymore. TNT was just a dog, Joanie, A DOG! Go to your room if you are going to keep crying about it."

I run into my room, crying and screaming the whole way. I hate my Mom and Dad. I pound my fists on my pillow. "I hate you! I hate you! I will never forgive you for this! Never!" I scream.

TNT was just a dog to Mom and Dad, but he was my best friend—the one I could talk to about anything.

My crying settles a little, and I pray. "Please, Jesus, help TNT find Midnight so they can be best friends in Heaven. Please."

THE NEW BANK

BIG NEWS IN NEW Brighton today! The First State Bank of New Brighton moved to a new location, and today is the open house. Mom told us that the bank outgrew its downtown location—they now have close to one hundred employees—so the owner built a brand-new building up by the Lund's shopping center. We've driven by it a few times to watch the progress, but today we get to go inside.

Along with the new location, Mom got another promotion. Last night she took us out to McGuire's, one of her favorite restaurants, to celebrate. As part of the celebration, Mark ordered a Coke, Gloria and I kiddie cocktails and Mom a Manhattan. Once the waitress brought our drinks, we toasted to Mom's success. She will be a loan officer now, helping people in New Brighton buy new houses, cars, cabins, or whatever they want, I guess. Though we'd heard the story many times before, Mom told us again how she started out as a teller, then worked her way up the ranks to get to where she's at today.

When we get to the bank for the open house, I am stunned at the number of windows. The time and temperature sign is on the edge of the parking lot, and Mom tells us they moved it there from the old location. As we walk through the enormous glass doors, there are customers and employees everywhere. Mom, dressed in her uniform, is talking to absolutely everyone—it's amazing how many people know her. I look up at her and see an unusual glow on her face. She is smiling from ear to ear, and I understand that this is the place that truly makes her happy. Without exception, each person addresses her as Mrs. Hicks. As she walks through the crowd, she holds her head up and looks straight at each person as she prepares to greet them.

Random people come up and congratulate Mom on her promotion. Others talk with her about how beautiful the new bank is. As we walk over to her desk, I see her nameplate, *Mrs. Lyla Hicks,* and I am filled with pride.

The windows—the ones inside the bank as well as the ones to the outside—are so clean, so shiny; I can see myself in them. I can almost smell the Pledge that probably gave all the desks their gleam. The teller stations are made of a kind of gold color, plastic I guess, but I guess they look nice. There is a downstairs and Mom gives us a brief tour of that as well. This is where the breakroom, the mailroom, and the bookkeeping department are. It's also nice, but I think the upstairs is better, because of the windows. As we go back upstairs, we are again greeted with another gathering of people.

A man comes up from behind us and shakes Mom's hand. "Hello, Mrs. Hicks! Who do you have with you today?"

"These are my daughters—Joanie and Gloria. Girls, this is Mr. Stahlmann, the bank president." He is amazingly tall and has the biggest smile I've ever seen. He shakes our hands, tells us how nice it is to meet us.

"It's nice to meet you, too," I say. "The bank is beautiful."

"Well, thank you. It's been a long time coming, for sure. I think it turned out great!"

At the end of the open house, Mr. Stahlmann and the owner

of the bank give a short presentation and thank everyone for coming.

On the way home, Mom can't stop talking about how many people were there and what a success it was. I try to think of a time when I've seen her this happy, this animated. She's trying to see if I remember meeting one of the customers.

"Do you remember him? He had a kind of frumpy look to him? A little short?" she asks me. But I met so many people I can't place him. "If you heard him speak, I know you'd remember," she says. "He has a speech problem—it's caused by a harelip."

We are home now, Mom has fixed herself a mixed drink, and she is still going on and on about the man, and I'm having a hard time understanding why it's so important for me to remember him. "Come on, Joanie, I'm sure you remember him—he talks funny—like this . . . "

Sitting across the table from my mom, I watch as she carries on a pretend conversation with the funny-talking man. I listen as she cleverly trades her normal voice for his lisping one. A few times she's laughing so hard, she has to take a break.

"Oh, my God," she says once the pretend conversation between her and the man comes to an end. "It's hilarious to listen to him talk!" She is primarily taken with how the man pronounces "Mrs. Hicks"—apparently, the lisp causes some spit to come out when makes the "s" sound, which makes her laugh. Mom is telling me something that she thinks is hilariously funny, but unfortunately, I don't. I'm worried that if I don't laugh, she will get mad, so I chuckle a little here and there.

While she's finishing up her skit, I think about the boy in our class that has a stutter in his voice. Our teacher told the whole class about it on the first day of school and said there is no reason to make fun of him—we are all born with something, and this is just what he has. I don't know him very well—he doesn't live in our neighborhood—but I have tried as hard as I can to be nice to him. Last week we made dioramas of the ocean floor, and each of us had to have at least one interesting fact to share with the class. When it was his turn, I could tell he was nervous, and I tried to send him a mind message that it was going to be okay. The whole class sat patiently while he told us about the kelp forest he had created, and everyone, even the teacher, clapped for him when he was done.

And so, as I think about this man coming in to cash a check, to take out a loan to buy a new car or whatever he has to do at the bank, I decide I'm going to stick with what my teacher told me. We are all born with something, and there is no reason to make fun of anyone.

SKUNKED

A FEW WEEKS AGO, Mom told me that Dad was not going to live in our house any longer. A dad not living with their family? How does that work?

"Where's he going to live?" I asked, but she didn't know.

"All I can tell you is, not here. Anywhere but here. At least not for a little while. We are trying to sort some things out," Mom explained.

I'm not sure Dad agrees with this plan, though, because it seems like I see him more now than before he moved out. One night, he walked right in while we were watching television. Another time, he woke us all up by trying to break through the side door in the middle of the night. Mom yelled at him to leave, and he finally did. But last week, it happened again, and Mom had to call the police. They got here just when he was starting to beat her up. The next day, when Gloria and I came in from sledding, there he was, at the table having coffee with Mom, drinking out of his brown-striped mug as if he still lived here! He also brought Mom a gift, not something I would want for a gift, but she seems to like it: gold drapes for the family room.

The new drapes don't fit the windows quite right, but they do make the red carpet stand out!

I'm glad my dad is gone. I suppose I should miss him, but I don't. When he's gone, I don't have to worry about Mom getting hurt. What would happen to us if she had to go to the hospital or something?

But here's who I do miss: Mom. It feels like she is gone—not like Dad. I mean, I know she lives here, but I can't find her. Even when Mom is sitting right next to me, it feels like she's a million miles away. I miss her smile; I miss her piano nights. When I try to talk to her about anything—even something good—she gets angry and yells at me to leave her alone. I try to keep Gloria as quiet as I can, but that isn't always as easy as it sounds. I don't want Mom to yell at Gloria, so the two of us spend a lot of time in my room. I suppose Mom might be sad because I'm not helping her enough. But even when I tried making supper a couple of times and cleaned practically the whole house, she didn't smile. The only thing she likes to do is sit on the couch and watch television while she drinks her beer. Well, that and play cribbage with Bernice. I think if I could get her to smile one time, then maybe she will like it and start smiling more and more.

A few days ago, I told Bernice I had the perfect idea to cheer Mom up. Bernice offered to help me, and we cooked up something special: a surprise birthday party! Today, February 28, 1972, is not only the day of Mom's forty-third birthday but also the day of the party! It's called a cake and coffee party, and we invited Nancy's mom, Mrs. Kewatt, plus three of Mom's friends from the bank.

When Mom got home from work tonight, I wished her a happy birthday right away so she wouldn't get suspicious. It was hard to keep the secret throughout dinner, but I did it! and then, right after supper, Bernice called our house to invite Mom over for cribbage and beer, and off she went!

I hadn't told Gloria about the party, because I was afraid she might get too excited. It's a good thing I didn't, because now she's running around the house yelling "party!" over and over.

The guests are supposed to arrive any minute—the official start time is 7:00 p.m. Once everyone is here, the plan is for me to call Mom at Bernice's and tell her Gloria and I are scared and I need her to come back home. Then, Bernice is going to suggest they move the cribbage game to our house.

All the ladies are here now, and it isn't even 7:00! The gifts are stacked by Mom's spot at the table, right in front of Bernice's beautiful homemade cake. The party is off to a good start! The ladies are all talking and laughing—I ask them to quiet down a bit, so I can explain about the phone call. The phone is on the wall inside the family room, right above Mom's television watching spot on the couch.

"Hi, Bernice, is my mom there?" I ask, trying not to giggle.

"Yep, hang on a sec. Lyla, it's Joanie for you," I hear Bernice say.

"Hi, Mom. Can you come home? Gloria and I are scared!" I'm standing on the couch while I talk, because the phone is easier for me to reach from there.

"Scared? I just got here, for God's sake!" Mom shouts through the phone.

"Um, well, I keep hearing a loud noise," I try. Mom doesn't believe me? I wasn't expecting that to happen. I turn my face towards the wall, so the ladies can't see me.

"I'm sure it's nothing. Stop being such a worry-wart," Mom concludes.

After she hangs up, I know the ladies are waiting to find out how the call went. I don't want them to know that Mom doesn't believe me.

"Bernice and my mom should be here any minute!" I announce to the partiers.

The ladies go back to chatting, and while we're waiting I get a few more things ready. I set a First State Bank of New Brighton matchbook by the cake to light the candles with and put the plates and napkins that Bernice bought next to the matches. I wish I knew how to make coffee. Then at least I would have something to serve my guests. The ladies check out the cake, all are certain Mom is going to love it. Gloria is sitting on Mrs. Kewatt's lap, and they are practicing saying "SURPRISE!" Gloria raises her hands up in the air as she yells the word, and the little audience giggles at her.

But now it seems like it's taking too long for Mom and Bernice to get here. I check out the window for about the hundredth time, still no sign of them. Bernice's back light isn't even on. I check the clock: ten minutes after seven.

"How far away does Bernice live?" someone asks.

"Right across the alley. The plan was for them to hurry right over once I made the phone call," I say, trying to sound confident. And yet, where are they?

The ladies seem to have run out of things to talk about. Gloria is now a master at the "surprise" thing and is repeating it over and over. Adorable, yes, but I admit it's starting to annoy me.

I'm getting a bad feeling in my stomach. Something is wrong, but what? Is Bernice having a hard time convincing Mom to come home? Did Bernice decide the party was dumb? Maybe she thought the whole thing was a stupid idea right from the beginning? But she delivered the invitations for me and made the birthday cake, so she must have thought it was a good idea at some point. The ladies, quiet now, are looking at me, but I don't know what to do. I look at the clock: twenty minutes after seven.

"Guess I'll call Bernice's house again. Maybe Bernice didn't remember the party started at 7:00," I say. I hope they don't notice that my voice is trembling a little.

"Hi, Bernice. Is my mom on her way home?" I say, trying to

sound older, not like the eleven-year-old kid that I am. It's kind of like being a kid actress—I'm nervous inside myself, but on the outside, I'm trying to be as cool as a cucumber.

"Nope, she's sitting here shooting the breeze and playing cribbage with me," Bernice says, with a giggle. What is going on? How am I going to get Bernice back on track?

"Oh, um, well the ladies are all here waiting, for her, for the party? Are you going to bring her over like we planned? It was supposed to start a while ago—at 7:00."

"Pretty soon, sunshine. Pretty soon," Bernice replies. I don't think she's understanding how important this is.

"Okay, well. Could you put my mom on the phone again?"

"Hi, Mom. Sorry to call again, but, honest Mom, we're scared," I say, trying to make my voice sound wobbly and frightened, which actually isn't that hard. "Gloria's crying and I can't settle her down! Plus, I heard a loud noise outside! Can you come home? Maybe you and Bernice could play cribbage here?" The lies are multiplying way beyond what I thought would be needed, spreading like the dandelion weeds in our front yard in the summer.

"Why are you scared tonight, of all nights? I'm over here celebrating my birthday with Bernice. Why don't you and Gloria hop into bed and try to fall asleep? I'll check on you later," Mom sighs loudly into my ear. It's crystal clear that Mom does not feel it's necessary to react. On top of that, she's angry at me for trying to put an end to her fun. I suppose a Mom should be able to do what she wants on her birthday and not be bothered by her kids. But what am I supposed to do? It's way too late to change the plan. I'm so confused.

"Okay, Mom. I'm sorry I bothered you. Can I talk to Bernice one more time?"

"Hi, Bernice," I can feel tears sitting on the bottom of my eyelids now. I blink fast to try to push them back into my eyes and prevent the salty liquid from leaking down my cheeks. I will NOT let my mom's friends see me cry. "Should I tell everyone to go home?"

"Don't worry, honey. We'll be there soon." Somehow, I don't feel reassured by Bernice's words. After I hang up the phone, I stay facing the wall. What should I say to these ladies, all sitting here in our family room? They are sitting right behind me, so I know they heard my side of the phone conversation. These ladies have never been in our house before, never seen any other side of Mom than the Mrs. Hicks I watched stroll through the new bank last summer. Even Mrs. Kewatt, who lives right across the street, calls my mom Mrs. Hicks, and she doesn't even work at the bank. I don't think I should say Mom got carried away with her beer—these women probably don't even drink beer. It also doesn't feel right to let on that Mom doesn't believe me when I say I'm scared. I try to think of some sort of excuse for all this, something to say that won't make it look like Mom is letting me down. I hear the ladies start to murmur; it's time to turn around and face them.

"I guess Bernice and Mom completely lost track of the time! It may be a few more minutes before they get here. Sorry! I thought we had worked out the perfect plan!" I'm trying to use a cheerful voice, but it's coming out weird—I can't fake everything, I guess. I watch as the ladies all look at each other with confused looks on their faces. They don't know what to do either.

I check the clock: twenty minutes to eight. The phrase *Be Brave* repeats over and over in my head, like when the needle gets stuck on one of my scratched records. If only I had special powers like Samantha on *Bewitched*. With a simple twinkle of my nose, Mom and Bernice would magically appear right here, right now.

"Where is your dad tonight, Joanie?" Mrs. Kewatt asks. And now, the bundle of nerves that's been waiting to spring has sprung. I hadn't thought of Dad popping in tonight. Do these ladies even know anything about my dad? Now, I am scared—for real. Dad arriving on the scene would surely ruin everything. My stomach starts whirling, like the clothes in the washer during the spin cycle. What if he comes flying in here and sees all the guests? He'll probably start yelling—or worse. I should send everyone home right this minute and lock the door. This party is quite possibly the dumbest idea I've ever had.

"I think he's at work," I say, though Dad hasn't had a job in I don't know how long. Another lie. I guess I'll be assigned a lot of prayers for penance at my next confession.

"You know what, Joanie? I think it might be best if we all went home. It's almost 8:00 and I bet you girls need to go to bed soon," Mrs. Kewatt says. She's right, of course, but I don't want to admit it. And then I feel a wetness collecting in my eyes. I can't stop them; the tears stream down my cheeks. I had my eleventh birthday a few weeks ago, and here I am crying like a little kid in front of Mom's friends. Why couldn't Mom have believed that I needed her to come home? All I wanted was to see her smile.

The ladies are putting on their coats, and I suppose I should use my manners and thank them for coming, but my voice simply won't work.

Wait—what? Mom and Bernice are bursting through the door—laughing? I watch Mom bend over to take her boots off and hear the ladies shout "Surprise! Happy Birthday, Lyla!" Gloria puts her new word to good use, shouts "Surprise!" over and over. And now the cheery group is singing the "Happy Birthday" song. But not me. I don't want to have this party anymore. I back myself into the family room, sit on the couch, tears spilling.

As the little group drifts its way back to the Duncan Phyfe, I try to wipe the tears from my eyes, try to put a smile back on my face. Bernice brews up the Folgers, pours a cup for each guest. She asks me to help serve the cake and ice cream, but I tell her I have a stomachache and cannot help. Gloria hops up on Mom's lap while she opens her presents. Everyone is giggling, chatting, laughing.

And now the ladies are putting on their coats to go home—for real this time. Bernice is going to stay so her and Mom can finish their cribbage game and have "one more beer." I pull myself up off the couch, slowly walk over to give Mom a goodnight kiss. I kind of want her to say thank you to me for planning the party, but she doesn't. I say goodnight to Bernice. I kind of want her to say she's sorry for getting Mom here so late, but she doesn't. What did I do wrong, anyway? If I wasn't such a dumb kid, I could probably figure it out.

I pick Gloria up and carry her into her room for bedtime. Tucking my sister into bed, I try to sing her favorite goodnight song, the one from *The Lawrence Welk Show*.

Goodnight, sleep tight, and pleasant dreams to you
Here's a wish and a prayer that every dream comes true
And now 'til we meet again
Adios, au revoir, auf wiedersehen

A few more tears leak out and trail down my cheeks. I don't even try to stop them. Gloria pulls her thumb out. "Sad?"

"Yes, Joanie is sad," I answer.

Putting on my pajamas and climbing into bed, I hear Mom and Bernice carrying on their cribbage game. "Fifteen for two!" Mom howls. She's smiling now, that's for sure. I lay my head down on my pink pillowcase, stained with tears, and pull the covers up over my ears. I don't need to hear who gets skunked tonight.

BURNED

Today started out about the same as every other one from this summer. I woke up to Rhonda knocking on the door, trying to roust me from my slumber. She gets up way earlier than I do, and we always joke that she is my summer alarm clock. This summer we have been spending most of our time at Long Lake Beach.

"What should we do today, Joanie? Want to go to Long Lake? It's a great day for swimming!" Rhonda suggests as I wipe the sleep out of my eyes.

"Yeah, sure," I say. "Wow, it's 10:00 already? I slept in today!"

"Okay, well get your stuff together and then we'll stop by my house, so I can change into my swimsuit!"

The only part about going to the beach that I don't like is that I don't have a swimsuit. I usually wear a pair of short-shorts and a tank-top, but it isn't the same as having a swimsuit. Rhonda and Connie both have cute swimsuits, and when they do handstands in the water, they don't have to worry about their shirt coming up. Mom said she would work on getting me a suit, but since the summer is almost over, I don't think I'll get one this year. Once I'm dressed, Rhonda and I head over to her house.

"Ready?" Rhonda asks as she comes out of her bedroom.

"Yep, let's get this show on the road!" I say, happily. "Wanna race?"

We used to ride two-on-a-bike—it's called giving someone a buck. If we took her ten-speed, I would sit on her front handlebars, and she would pedal us to the beach. If we took my banana seat bike, she rode on the back while I did the pedaling. But one day we crashed on the bridge that crosses over the freeway, and both of us got pretty banged up. After that, we decided we were too big for bucking, so now we ride our own bikes.

As we fly down the hill to get to the beach, I raise my hands and wave my towel in the air. I love riding my bike no-hands! As we approach the bike rack, we see that everybody in New Brighton must be here! After we park our bikes, we try to find a place to play our towels out. My bare feet are burning up walking through the hot sand, and I can't wait to get them into the cool water. As soon as we drop our towels—whoosh!—into the water! I dunk my head under the clear surface and let the coolness rush all over my warm body. Rhonda and I practice and practice our handstands—we've been trying to master them all summer. Then, we swim out to the first drop-off, where we can't touch the bottom, and practice dog-paddling.

After swimming for a long time, we decide to get a suntan and head up to our towels. Along the beach, some of the little kids are building sand castles and moats, a group of boys are playing Frisbee, and, at the back edge of the beach, I think I see my brother, Mark, and his friends. It's amazing how much fun everyone is having today.

After we suntan, we go for one more swim and then decide to head home. Pedaling up the steep hill to get to Long Lake Road makes my thighs and calves burn and tingle like they've been attacked by fire ants. Rhonda can make it all the way to the top because she has a ten-speed, but I hop off my bike and walk the

last part. Once we're at the top of the hill though, it is smooth
sailing. We fly over the freeway bridge, cross over it at just the
right moment and there we are—at the start, or end depending
on how you look at it, of Eleventh Avenue. This part is a dirt
road, and it's easy to wipe out if you aren't careful. Rhonda and
I know where all the bad spots are, so we don't crash too often.
Once we get to the cemetery, the road is paved, and two blocks
later, we're at my house.

"I'm starving!" I say as we head into the house. "Want some
lunch?"

After lunch, we decide we want a little more fun in the sun
and try to come up with an idea. We finally decide on a water
balloon fight in the backyard. We search around and finally find
Mom's stash of First State Bank of New Brighton balloons (these
are what the kids get if they go to the bank with their parents) and
head outside to get started. It's a little tricky getting the balloons
filled, but once we do, we pelt each other like crazy. So much
fun! After we've used them all, we pick up all the little balloon
pieces and head back in the house to play *The Dating Game*.
This is our favorite board game—we both want a real date with
the blonde-haired guy!

"Let's put our wet clothes in the dryer. I'll wear my nightgown,
and you can wear my robe. They should be dry by the time we
finish the game," I suggest to Rhonda. We run downstairs, take
off our wet clothes and throw them in the dryer. As we start to
run back up the stairs, I hear the back door open. Is it possible
Mom is home from work already? Apparently, Rhonda and I were
having so much fun that we lost track of time. I look up the stairs
and am about to welcome Mom home, but she beats me to it.

"My God in Heaven! What the hell is going on here?" Mom
yells, glaring down at us. Rhonda, on the step behind me, does
not move.

"Mom? What?" I ask, but she is in no mood to listen to me.

"I said, what the hell is going on here? And what are you doing wearing Joanie's robe?" she asks Rhonda.

"Mrs. Hicks, our clothes were wet . . . " Rhonda starts, stuttering a little.

"Your clothes were wet? Well, don't you have a dryer at your house? What the hell do you think this is, a laundry service or something?"

"But Mom, I told her she could dry her clothes here while we played a game," I try to explain.

"DO NOT argue with me!" Mom roars, the sound filling the stairwell. I swear the walls are moving in response.

Rhonda and I do not move. I have never seen my mother this way. From my vantage point on the stairs, I can see that every fiber of her being is wrapped up in her anger. I can't imagine why she is so furious. I know how to use the washer and dryer, I do laundry all the time. And isn't that what a dryer is for—getting wet clothes dry?

"Now get back down there and get your clothes on! Both of you!" Mom continues. And then she raises one of her arms and points her long index finger—it is topped off with the longest, pointiest fingernail anyone has ever seen—right at Rhonda. "I'm going over to Bernice's to get Gloria, and SHE better be gone when I get back! DO I MAKE MYSELF CLEAR?" I can't describe her yelling as roaring anymore—it's like a different person has taken over her voice.

"You want Rhonda gone?" I ask. "We were going to play a game." But this is not what Mom wanted to hear. Her anger surges, I think her head might blow right off, she's so outraged. She moves so that she is standing on the top step, leans down towards us. She grabs onto the railing, and I see her arm is shaking so hard the wood railing is wiggling.

"Are you still arguing with me, young lady?" Mom is staring at me with a look of hatred and disgust. "I can't believe you have the nerve to argue with me! I suppose Rhonda taught you how to do that too, ha? How to talk back to your own mother?"

"No, Mom, you know Rhonda's my friend. We were having some fun today like we always do," I reply, trying not to cry. I can't imagine why Mom hates Rhonda so badly all of a sudden. We have been friends for a long time now, and, though Mom has never been nice to any of my friends, she has never been this cruel, has never scared anyone away.

"Out! I want her OUT!" Mom screams, then turns and slams out the door to go over to Bernice's.

Rhonda and I stay on the steps for a split second before turning and running to the dryer. I am so upset, crying hard, and for some odd reason, I feel like I'm on fire. My skin is tingling, and I can't seem to concentrate. Rhonda gets to the dryer first, and I stand next to her as she quickly opens it to take out her swimsuit.

"Rhonda, I don't know what to say. I'm sorry my mom yelled like that," I say, barely able to get my nightgown off to put my shorts and top back on.

"Yeah, well, that was something," she says. "I'm leaving as fast as I can, that's for sure."

"My mom gets mad over the dumbest things. Does yours?" I ask.

"Well, yeah. Sometimes my mom gets mad at my little brothers, but I have never seen her like that. Your mom scared the crap out of me; I'm shaking right now. Okay, I've got my suit back on—I'm out of here. Maybe I'll see you tomorrow," Rhonda says, flying up the stairs and out the door.

As I finish putting my clothes back on, become furious. I am so mad at Mom for treating us like that. I know she thinks I am a stupid idiot, but she has no right to treat any of my friends like that.

I'm at the kitchen sink washing dishes when Mom walks in the door with Gloria. I do not turn around, do not acknowledge her presence. I can feel her authority behind me, feel her fierce glare on my back—the burning sensation feels like a lit flame is touching my back. Apparently, she has not calmed down.

"I'm telling you right now. That girl is never to be in this house again. Are you listening to me? Never! This is my house, and I decide who is or isn't going to be in it! Did you hear me? Turn around and look at me, I'm talking to you!" Mom's voice hisses behind me.

I stop washing but leave my hands in the dishwater while I try to think of what to do or say. Tears are streaming down my face, and I know that if I let Mom see my tears, it will give her a satisfaction that I don't want her to have. At the same time, I know I can't stand at the sink all night.

"Turn around!" Mom thunders. And finally, I do.

Her brown eyes glare at me, try to bore through my heart. The look on the rest of her face is one of disdain, and I know that I am scum to her. I search her eyes to see if there is any part of her that understands me, that can sense what she is doing or how she is making me feel. There is nothing but pure disgust mirroring back to me. By allowing Rhonda to use our dryer, I have been deemed even more senseless than I was before.

"Here, take your sister. I need to make supper," Mom barks at me, trying to hand Gloria over. But in the few minutes I had to think, I made some decisions of my own.

"You're on your own with supper and Gloria tonight, Mom. I'm not hungry. I'll be in my room for the night," I reply, holding back on what I really want to say. Mom's rage in response to my words ratchets up, and I sense that she is on the border of being unable to control herself. Mom sets Gloria down, continues staring at me, drilling me with her wicked look. As her right hand with its long fingers extended, raises up and comes towards me, I grab her wrist with a strength I didn't know I possessed, and raise her arm to the ceiling.

"You want to slap me, Mom? You think that will teach me some sort of lesson? Teach me not to use the dryer, which I have used some hundred million times? Will keep me from having my best friend over to play? Do you think Rhonda would even want to come here again after the vicious way you treated her? I doubt it. Well, guess again, Mom, because you are NOT going to hit me. I think I've had about all I can handle for one day." I hold on to her wrist for just a minute longer as dishwater streams down our arms, then let go and watch as her arm drops to her side. I take a few steps to move around her, and head for my room.

"Just so you know, Bernice is coming over after supper to play cribbage," Mom says as I move through the side entry. Is she mocking me? I can't have my friend over, but she can? I have no idea. Well, good for Bernice—she can have a grand old time with Mom if she wants to.

Standing in front of my mirror, I watch as beads of tears flow down my cheeks, land on the top of my dresser. The salty mixture is coming from deep within my heart and my soul. White streaks form on my puffy, red cheeks. Soon, the beads turn to goblets. I've cried myself to sleep plenty of times, but this time I'm so sad, so devastated that I'll probably cry until I die. Turning away from the mirror, I take off my damp clothes and move to put my nightgown back on.

Out of the corner of my eye, I catch a glimpse of my back in the mirror. What in the world? My back and shoulders are the brightest red that I have ever seen—brighter than the ripest apple on our apple tree, brighter than any lipstick Mom has ever worn. I turn a bit more, and then I see the white stripes marking where my tank top had been. No wonder my skin felt like it was on fire! I thought it was from being so upset, but no—I am sunburned and, though I have been sunburned plenty of times before, I can see that it is worse than ever.

I put my nightgown on but instantly take it back off. The

pressure of the lacy fabric is more than I can bear. Climbing into bed, I grab a book; maybe if I read, I will stop crying and it'll take my mind off the pain of what has turned into a dreadful day. The instant my back touches the pillows, I flinch and bolt out of bed. I don't think I've ever been in so much pain. I re-examine the sunburn in the mirror—is it possible it is redder than it was a few minutes ago? It sure looks like it. I wonder if a person can die from sunburn? Finally, I decide to lay on my stomach. I pull the sheet up to my waist, leaving my back exposed to the air. Since I can't read in this position, I decide to go to sleep.

I wake up to the sounds of Mom and Bernice playing cribbage. I can tell that Mom's beer and Bernice's brandy have amped them up. While I'm listening to their banter, Gloria comes toddling in and stands by my bed, thumb in her mouth. She's looking at me, with her big, brown eyes. I suppose she's trying to figure out why I'm in bed. I stare back into her eyes.

My God, she's beautiful. Everyone who meets Gloria falls in love with her eyes, but no one loves them as much as I do. Tonight, I see pureness and innocence in them, and it takes my breath away. I watch her soft lashes open and close like butterfly wings and realize that I could stare into her eyes and absorb the love for hours. But alas, I know there is an actual reason she came to me, and it doesn't have anything to do with staring into each other's eyes.

"You stink," I say, reaching out to tickle her belly. She nods her head in agreement, smiling around her thumb that is firmly planted in her mouth. "Remember, you're only going to use your thumb at night from now on." I reach up and gently tug her thumb out. "Save it for bedtime, okay?"

"Okay," she says, her lower lip pushing out a bit. One thing about Gloria is that she hardly ever cries. If she does, it's most likely because she got hurt, or got into trouble. But she can pout!

"Alright, let's get that stinky diaper changed!" I hop out of bed, put on my nightgown and then remember the sunburn. "Ouch!" At this Gloria jumps a little. "Don't worry," I reassure her, "I just have a big owie on my back."

Once I get her diaper changed, I help her into her pajamas, and we head to the kitchen. Mom and Bernice are having a grand old time playing cribbage at the Duncan Phyfe and hardly notice we've entered the room.

"Hi, Bernice," I say, pouring some milk into a cup for Gloria's bedtime snack. "Who's winning tonight?"

"Well, hello there, doodlebug!" she bellows, and I realize that even though I'm a little old for it, Bernice will never stop calling me weird names. "Oh, your mom is the winner, of course. She's skunked me twice already!" Mom says nothing to me, and I don't speak to her either. As I turn to help Gloria with her cup, Bernice gasps, "Joanie, what's wrong with your back? What happened?"

"Oh, yeah. I guess I got a little too much sun today," I answer. Bernice walks over and examines my back.

"Wow! Holy smokes, that looks like it hurts! Do you have anything to put on it? Any lotion or spray or anything? Did you put a cool cloth on it?" Bernice asks. As she looks me over, I try to figure out why this woman cares so much about me. She's Mom's best friend, and even though my mom could care less about me or my sunburn, here is Bernice looking like she could cry—like she's the one with the sunburn. Bernice reaches out and ever-so-gently touches my shoulder with a fingertip. When she removes her finger, the small area stays white for a split-second before the fiery red color reappears.

"Yeah, it hurts like the dickens," I say. "Even my nightgown makes it hurt. I don't have anything for it."

Bernice is talking to Mom now, who doesn't turn and look at me, so I guess she still hates me. I have no idea how long she'll be mad. I guess I don't care.

"Okay, well, I'm going to put Gloria to bed," I say, as Bernice sits back down at the table. Gloria gives them both a kiss goodnight, and we head through the living room to her bedroom. Once she's settled, I go back to my room to re-examine the burn. The areas on my upper back and shoulders are now a bright raspberry color. The skin is so hot I wonder if it would burn my fingertips if I touched it. There are also some raised areas on my shoulders where I assume blisters are forming. I take off my nightgown and position myself stomach-down on my bed with my arms spread out.

A bit later, I hear a knock on my door. "Can I come in for a minute?" Bernice asks.

"Sure. Did Gloria wake up or something?" I ask, trying to figure out why Bernice would be in my room.

"No, everything's okay, sweet pea. I went home to get some lotion for your sunburn. I use it when I get sunburned up at Lake Mille Lacs," she says, quietly. I notice that her usual jovial personality is dulled a bit. She is quiet, peaceful even. "Do you mind if I put some on your back?"

As I lay on my stomach, Bernice gently massages the cool lotion onto my skin, and I feel kindness and love in each delicate stroke of her hands. Instantly, I feel the pain decreasing, the burn easing. "I've never seen a burn quite this bad, Joanie. Unfortunately, the lotion only helps for a little while. It should be put on every couple of hours," she says. "Do you think you can reach around and do it yourself?" Apparently, Bernice has picked up on the fact that Mom will be of no help to me, at least not tonight.

"I'll try," I say. Bernice puts the cap back on the lotion, sets it on my nightstand and turns to leave.

"Okay, and then tomorrow, try to put a cool cloth on it a few times during the day. And—no sun tomorrow, okay? I'm ordering R & R for you, little lady!"

"Bernice?"

"Yes, honey?"

"Thank you. Thank you so much."

"You're welcome, sweetie pie. I wish I had something to take the pain away altogether," she says as she walks out my door.

I wonder if anyone else has ever had a day like this? One where it starts out as a normal, super fun day, then turns into one of the worst, most embarrassing and horrible days of all time? It's hard to imagine that this morning when I woke up I was the same eleven-year-old kid I was yesterday—and that the day was just like every other hot day this summer—and that now, as I try to fall asleep for the night, I feel like a whole different person in a whole different world. I'm in pain, yes, but I also feel alone, profoundly sad, almost as miserable as when Midnight and TNT died.

But then I think of the end of the day. Bernice's gentle touch on my shoulders and her kind words—how that despite her being Mom's best friend, she showed compassion towards me. And as my eyes close and the tears stop trailing down my cheeks, I wonder if it's possible that she loves me.

LISTEN TO ME

I TRY TO HELP Mom with Gloria as much as I can. Bernice babysits Gloria during the day, and I pick her up after school. If we're lucky, Bernice has homemade chocolate-chip cookies ready for a snack, and, if we're extremely lucky, she invites us to stay for one of her famous fish fry dinners. But if not, Gloria and I head home, have a little snack and watch *Sesame Street* and *Electric Company*.

In addition to being smart, three-year-old Gloria is on the move! She can walk, run, climb on countertops, throw things in the toilet, hide in closets, and open cupboards. I try to keep my eyes on her all the time so that she doesn't get hurt or into trouble. Her cute little voice puts a silly grin on my face, and I beam with delight whenever she learns a new word. She can already say a lot of words, including my name, her name, and Mom. Sometimes she asks me "Why, Joanie?" over and over, and, as cute as my little sister is, it's a little annoying. I read to her just about every day, but her absolute favorite thing to do is listen to music. Most of the records I have are little kid songs, which she loves, but "These Boots Are Made for Walking" by Nancy Sinatra, seems to be her favorite. As soon as Nancy starts to sing "One of these days these boots are gonna walk all over you!" I start to tickle Gloria's feet and then her legs—I keep tickling all the way up to her belly until we are both laughing and tumbling on my soft bed.

After supper, when Mom is trying to watch television, I usually take Gloria for a walk in the stroller. She loves our stroller walks! Usually, we go around the neighborhood, but sometimes I take her to the park or the school playground. Once we get home, I help Mom put her to bed. If Mom's in a good mood, she will come into Gloria's room to say goodnight, but most of the time they say goodnight in the family room while Mom finishes her television show. Once Gloria is tucked into her bed, she usually pops in her thumb and goes straight to sleep. The only time she has trouble falling asleep is when Mark's band is practicing at our house.

Mark plays the electric guitar in a cool band that also has a drummer, bass player, and singer. The instruments are hooked up to enormous amplifiers and speakers so that even though they practice in the basement, the music is overwhelmingly loud. With each rock-and-roll song they play, the floor shakes and vibrates under our feet. During band practice, Mom turns the television volume way up so that she can watch her shows despite the loud musicians below her. I don't know what the name of their band is, but they play songs that are on the radio, and I guess they're going to perform on a stage somewhere once they do enough practicing. My favorite song they play is "Sunshine of Your Love." I can't imagine how Mark learned to play the guitar like a true rock star, but I guess if you know how to play the piano, you also know how to play the guitar. Maybe someday I will hear his band playing on my favorite radio station, WDGY, but for now, I listen to them right here in my own house. When Mom goes to bed, she signals the musicians to stop practicing by flicking the basement light on and off a bunch of times. It's amazing how quickly the house goes quiet when they stop; sometimes it causes a ringing noise in my ears.

On Friday nights, the bank is open late, so I babysit Gloria until 8:30 or 9:00 p.m. Usually, I make macaroni and cheese for supper, then we play outside for a while. After we come in for the night, we put on our pajamas and snuggle on the couch to watch the *Partridge Family* and the *Sonny and Cher Comedy Hour*. Occasionally, the Kewatt family will call and invite us to go out for dinner with them. We always go to the same place: Ponderosa Steakhouse. It's a lot of fun, because Mr. and Mrs. Kewatt think Gloria and I are the greatest girls they have ever known (well, except for their own two girls) and we love to be around them.

I go to school at New Brighton Elementary now instead of St. John's. It's kind of a long story, but basically, Mom and my teacher from last year, Mrs. Treleaven, had a big fight. What happened was that Mrs. Treleaven talked to me about my grades and asked me who was helping me with my homework. She was mainly worried about my science and spelling grades. I told her that my mom and dad were busy with a ton of stuff, so it was hard for them to help me. I also told her I was kind of busy, too, helping to take care of my little sister. I promised to try to find more time to study. But when Mom got home from work that night, she announced that I wouldn't be going back to St. John's—she said she couldn't believe that Mrs. Treleaven had "the nerve to call me at the bank to talk about spelling, of all things!" I guess my teacher didn't know the rule about not disturbing Mom at work. I studied like crazy for the rest of fourth grade, hoping that Mom would change her mind, but, I guess it didn't work. I was a little nervous to start a new school in fifth grade, but there are three good things about it: 1) I get to walk to school, 2) I don't have to wear a uniform, and 3) my friend, Nancy, also goes there.

I guess the whole finding-another-place-to-live plan didn't work out for Dad, because he's living with us again. When he moved back in, he brought a very interesting gift for us—a dishwasher. The problem is, there is no place to put it, so it sits right smack in the middle of the kitchen floor. At night, after we load the dishes, we stretch a hose from the back of the machine and attach it to the faucet on the sink, so the dishwasher can do its job. Another hose stretches into the bowl of the sink, allowing the water to drain out. It would be easier to wash the dishes in the sink, but I'm not about to tell Dad that.

Also, since he moved back in, Dad is acting downright weird. Sometimes I can't make any sense out of what he is saying, and if I ask him what he's talking about, his anger flares up like Bernice's Zippo cigarette lighter. "Meanwhile, down on the ranch" is one of the phrases he repeats over and over. Occasionally, I try to change the subject, but then he doesn't seem to understand what I'm talking about. Another super weird thing he does is whistle—a lot. And then, the other day, he took apart his stereo and set it up under the workbench in the garage. He keeps beer out there, too, so sometimes instead of coming in for supper, he stays out in the garage and drinks beer while he listens to his music. It's kind of embarrassing because none of my friends' dads do that!

Mom and Dad argue a lot. Sometimes I want to scream at them to stop. During supper last night, I was trying to tell my parents about something that happened at school, but they were fighting and didn't even hear me. I finally got so mad that I started yelling myself to see if one of them would notice me.

"Why isn't anyone listening to me?" I screamed, slamming my hands down on the table.

"Shut your mouth, young lady!" Mom shouted. "Who do you think you are talking to your parents like that!" I don't know why, but I got even more furious because of what Mom said. I guess I was trying to figure out why it's okay for them to yell at each other all the time, but when I do it, I get into trouble.

But I have no explanation for what I did next—it was like a rage was overtaking my body—my hand went into action without me even realizing what I was doing. I stood up, reached across the table and slapped Mom right across the face. Instantly, it felt like my own face had been slapped—my cheeks felt on fire, like they were being torched with a pack of lit matches.

Then I started to cry. I couldn't believe I had hit my mom! I was shocked, and I think she was, too, because she didn't say a word. As I looked at Mom, our eyes met, and I understood that, not only was she furious with me, but that I had hurt her deeply. Her lips were straight, eyebrows curved in towards her nose— letting me know that she was angry. But her eyes. Her eyes showed me how much I had hurt her. Her upper eyelids looked droopy, like she could hardly hold them up, and her pupils seemed larger than normal, circled only with a thin, dull sliver of brown. When I looked into them, it felt like I was looking into a deep, dark tunnel. A wet film started to coat her eyes, and, as she looked at me, I thought she might cry. I was so ashamed of myself I didn't know what to do. I wondered what Father Paul would say when I confessed this shocking, awful sin. My chances of ever getting into Heaven were now very slim, I realized. How could I have done such a thing?

"Joanie, how dare you hit your mother like that!" Dad yelled, breaking the brief trance that Mom and I were locked in. "Your mother does so much for you, and you treat her like that? You need to have some respect for her! Now say you're sorry, right now!" They both stared at me, waiting for my response. And even though I was, and still am, sorry, I couldn't make the words come out, because I was crying too hard—not even one word would form. Then, Gloria, sitting in her high chair, sensed something had shifted in her little world, and started to cry.

"Now see what you've done!" Mom yelled, taking Gloria out of her high chair. And I knew she was right: I'd ruined everything. My idea to have my parents talk to me, to listen to me instead of fighting with each other, was quite possibly the worst idea I have ever had.

"I'm sorry for slapping you on your face, Mom," I finally blurted out. "I was trying to get someone to listen to me!" And then, because there was basically nowhere else to go, I ran to my room.

TRAVEL

YESTERDAY WE MET GRANDMA Tighe at the Dairy Queen in Belle Plaine. After we all had a treat, Mom and Gloria headed back to New Brighton, and Grandma and I drove to Madelia. Usually, I spend a week every summer at Grandma's house, but this year, we are going on a road trip. Tomorrow, we will drive to Milwaukee, Wisconsin to visit Aunt Sharon—my mom's youngest sister—Uncle Lee, and their kids.

It's a little different driving to Madelia now, because Grandma doesn't live on the farm anymore. My Grandpa Tighe died right before Gloria was born, and Grandma decided it would be too much for her to be a farmer, so she moved into a cute little house on Second Street. The route to her new house bypasses most of my favorite landmarks, like the chestnut-colored horses and the corn silo that has the 7-Up logo painted from top to bottom.

Last night, Grandma and I had hamburgers for supper, and this morning, we packed the leftover burgers in a cooler, along with some lemonade and chips, so we can have a picnic on the way to Milwaukee. I've never been on a trip with Grandma, and I'm a little surprised she chose me to go with her. She has a cool car—a brand-new Oldsmobile—and I helped her get it all packed this morning. Mom told me to be on my best behavior and be sure to thank Grandma for everything she does for me. But after about the fourth time I said thank you, she told me I was overdoing it.

"Let's just be glad we have this time together, okay?" Grandma Tighe suggested.

About the time my stomach starts to rumble with hunger, Grandma suggests stopping off for lunch. I thought it would be gross to eat cold hamburgers out of the cooler, but they taste okay. After I help Grandma clean up, we hop back in the car. Grandma suggests I get one of my books out, because we still have another three hours or so to go.

"What are you reading?" she asks, maneuvering the car back onto the highway. Grandma reads a lot of books, and I know she is proud of me for being a good reader.

"I'm reading *Charlotte's Web*. It's so good! Do you know what it's about?" Grandma says she does. We talk about how fun it is that Charlotte, who is a spider, has a pig as her best friend. "It reminds me of some of Mom's pig stories from growing up on the farm!"

"Oh, yes. There are lots of pig stories, that's for sure!" Grandma says, with a little chuckle.

I haven't quite finished the book when we pull into Aunt Sharon and Uncle Lee's neighborhood. I'm amazed as to the size of the homes on their block—they're enormous! As Grandma pulls her car into the driveway, I'm stunned into silence. I can't be sure because I've never seen one before, but I think Aunt Sharon's house is a mansion. As we get out of the car, Aunt Sharon comes out to greet us.

"Hello, Mother. How was the drive? Are you tired? Did you eat lunch?" Aunt Sharon is full of questions for Grandma. "And how about you, Joanie? What did you think of that long ride?"

"It was great! We stopped for a picnic, and I almost finished a book," I answer.

"Well, okay then! Let's get the two of you in the house, get you settled in your rooms."

Aunt Sharon and Uncle Lee have three kids—Kelly, Katie, and Steve—and they are all a little younger than me. I'm twelve, Kelly is ten, Katie eight, and Steve six. As my aunt takes us up the stairs, she explains that Grandma will sleep in Kelly's room. Kelly will move in with Katie while we are here, and I will sleep in that room as well. After we put our suitcases in our rooms, Sharon takes us on a tour of the house, and it is truly amazing. On the main level, there are rooms that are only for special occasions. One is the living room, which has white carpet and extremely fancy furniture. I can see that no one has walked on the carpet—all that shows are vacuum markings. The other is the dining room—their beautiful table is nothing like our Duncan Phyfe at home! We finish the tour in the kitchen, which has a large eating area next to it. Aunt Sharon explains that the wood used to make the table in this room was hand-selected by Uncle Lee—it's very long and remarkably heavy-looking. Right behind the table, there is a door that opens to the backyard, and when Aunt Sharon opens it, an enormous dog comes trouncing in.

"This is Morgan! Get ready for some kisses!" Aunt Sharon steps aside, and Morgan gallops straight over to introduce himself to me.

"My goodness! He's huge!" I say. "What kind of dog is he?" I sit down at the table, and Morgan looks me right in the eye, then gives me a big lick on my cheek. He nudges his head next to mine as though he wants a hug—I've never seen a dog this tall!

"He's an Airedale. I think he's about two feet tall. Three years old and crazy wild! I don't think this dog is ever going to settle down!" Aunt Sharon informs us. "How would you like some lemonade?" As Morgan licks me all over my face, I designate him the third-cutest dog I've ever seen.

About the time she gets our lemonade poured, the back door opens, and Kelly and Katie come in. They have been swimming with friends, and after saying hello, they head upstairs to change. Soon enough, Steve comes home—he's been out playing basketball. And finally, Uncle Lee comes home from work.

"Well, who do we have here! Grandma Tighe and Joanie! Wonderful! Just wonderful! Joanie, did you see my spiral staircase yet?" Uncle Lee is talking and walking so fast I'm afraid I won't be able to keep up. I think he has more energy than Morgan!

Uncle Lee leads me to the spiral staircase, and I follow him up. At the top of the black metal staircase is his office. There are a lot of papers on his desk, and family photos cover the walls. While the rest of the house is nearly spotless, Uncle Lee's office looks slightly messy—I'm guessing Aunt Sharon doesn't clean up here as often as she does the rest of the house. Once he's done showing me his office, he leads me back downstairs, and Aunt Sharon asks him to start the grill.

It's positively noisy during dinner—everyone in this family has something to say, and they are all talking at the same time. The girls tell everyone about their day of swimming and start a conversation about going over to a friend's house later tonight. Steve wants to know if he can go to a movie with his buddies. In between the hubbub, Uncle Lee tells about a hundred jokes— sometimes we laugh, but sometimes we don't.

"For goodness sake, Lee! That isn't even funny! Where do you learn these jokes anyway?" Aunt Sharon teases. And at that, everyone, including Grandma, laughs.

The amount of food reminds me of Thanksgiving. How Aunt Sharon cooked all this in one day is beyond me. Besides the hamburgers, there are hot dogs, potato salad AND potato chips, corn on the cob, and baked beans. And for dessert—chocolate brownies!

Once dinner is done, the kids scatter, and Uncle Lee goes out to the garage to work on his car. It is quieter now, but not silent like my house is.

"Thank you for that wonderful dinner, Aunt Sharon," I say after we get all the leftovers put away.

"You're welcome. Now, don't forget, tomorrow we're going to the Brookfield Zoo. I think you're going to like it!" Grandma and Aunt Sharon pour themselves a cup of coffee and settle in at the table to catch up on the latest family news—I sit near them and try to finish *Charlotte's Web*. This is such a different house and family than what I'm used to—so bright, so full of energy. It astounds me that after all the hard work they did today, neither Aunt Sharon or Uncle Lee spend the night relaxing in front of the television.

ি

It's been a great few days in Milwaukee, and I'm glad to have gotten to know my cousins a little bit better. But today, after breakfast, Grandma and I are headed back to Madelia. While Grandma packs up her stuff, I head to the kitchen for breakfast.

"So, Joanie, how's your dad?" Aunt Sharon asks me, as I'm eating a blueberry muffin. I'm shocked at this question, temporarily stunned. No one has ever asked me about my dad— not my mom, Grandma Tighe, Bernice—no one. I don't know what to say—what does she already know? Does she know about the beatings? That Mom has asked him to go live somewhere else, but he keeps coming back? That he talks in nonsense? That his very presence in our house makes all of us jittery? That sometimes he looks like he is on the verge of crawling right out of his skin?

"What's the matter? It's just a question, my goodness, what happened to you—I remember when you were a wild child, and now, you hardly talk or move at all!" Aunt Sharon says, pointing her finger at me. It's the same finger that Grandma and my mom have—and when she points it at me, I shut down even more.

"Well, I . . . he doesn't always live with us, so I don't exactly know how he is," I say, trying not to cry.

"I want you to know something," Aunt Sharon continues, still pointing at me. Honestly, I wish she'd stop pointing that damn finger at me. "Your dad is a nice man. I want you to remember that," she finishes.

I say nothing. I mean, what can I say? I have little evidence of this nice man she's talking about, but I don't see the point in arguing. I wait to see if she offers something more—something about my dad I don't know—something that would convince me of her characterization of him, but she offers nothing. The only happy memory I can think of is the time he made homemade ice cream with us. Mark has tried to tell me about happy times—a trip to South Dakota to see Mount Rushmore, a vacation to Bemidji, Minnesota to see the Paul Bunyan and Babe the Blue Ox statues. I've seen the Polaroid photos that Dad took that proves I was there, but I have absolutely no memory of being there, of being a part of a normal, happy family.

"I don't understand why you're so quiet. I remember visiting your mom in the hospital when she had one of her babies. You were about three, I think. You and Mark were in the waiting room, and you were screaming and jumping around like a wild monkey. Your behavior embarrassed me! And now, nothing. You hardly say a word!"

It feels like there is a tornado in my brain. Aunt Sharon's statements are swirling around and around, repeating themselves over and over. I can't make them stop, and I can't slow them down.

> *Dad is a nice man? I was a wild child? Mark and I were at the hospital by ourselves? Mom had a baby when I was three? Dad is a nice man? I was a wild child? Mark and I were at the hospital by ourselves? Mom had a baby when I was three?*

"I wonder if you're thinking of a different wild child. I don't remember ever acting like a monkey," I finally say, holding back what feels like a torrent of tears behind my eyes. "Plus, Mom didn't have a baby when I was three. I was eight when Gloria was born. I know about Steven and Cecelia, but they would both be older than me."

"No, it was you, for sure. This wasn't a stillborn baby—it was after one of her miscarriages. She got incredibly sick afterwards— had her gallbladder removed or something like that—and you and Mark were in the waiting room when I came to visit."

Aunt Sharon is staring at me. The energy cloud around her is demanding a response from me. But I can't say anything at all now. I have no idea what Aunt Sharon is talking about, and if I try to say anything, I will cry. Mom had a miscarriage when I was three? And it wasn't her only one? How is a miscarriage different from a stillborn baby? And I can't help but think, if this truly did happen, why were me and Mark in the waiting room all by ourselves, with no one watching us? Who could blame me for acting like a wild monkey?

"Aunt Sharon, I . . . I didn't know anything about this," I stammer.

Just then, Grandma Tighe comes in the kitchen and announces it's time to go. She wants to get home before dark.

I want to tell Grandma that despite it being 8:00 a.m., darkness has already set in.

MIRROR, MIRROR

MOM IS OBSESSED WITH the size of my thighs. She will not stop talking about the fact that a twelve-year-old should not have thighs as fat as mine.

"Joanie, my God. Look at your thighs, just look at them. Are they getting bigger for some reason? Stand up," Mom starts in, from her spot on the couch. I'd rather do anything—clean my room, do the laundry, anything—than show her my enormous thighs again. But she insists, so finally, I stand up off the couch and pull my navy-blue shorts up to my crotch so that she can inspect them—again.

"I just don't get it. Who did you get those thighs from? I think they are bigger than mine, and I am a grown woman!" I have nothing to say: I quit responding to this thigh routine a long time ago. I keep standing there, waiting for her next verbal assault. She takes another swig from her Hamm's and loudly proclaims, "I think we should measure them! Go get the tape measure out of the drawer in the kitchen. I have to know if your thighs are larger than mine."

"Mom, what? No, I—" but she has already decided. She is smiling now, excited even, hopeful the outcome will be in her favor.

"There you see! I knew it! Yours are a half an inch bigger!" Mom exclaims once both our thighs have been measured, the inches written down in pencil on her First State Bank of New Brighton notepad.

I will not cry. I have given that up: it does no good.

"How can I make them smaller, Mom?" I ask, thinking maybe a piece of advice will come my way.

"I don't know, I guess you are stuck with them. Too bad," Mom laments, finishing the conversation. "Looks like *Mannix* is coming on. Do you want to watch it with me?"

In my room, trying to fall asleep, I still don't cry—what good would that do? I pull my nightgown up and stare at the offenders, these huge thighs of mine—they are so fat that when I am laying down, they touch each other. There must be a way to reduce the outrageous size of my upper legs; there must be. Could some of it be cut off? Could I wrap something around them to squeeze the fat out? Should I stop eating for a while? Tomorrow I'm going to request that Mom make a doctor's appointment—maybe the doctor will have some treatment for this blight on my body.

At school today, all I could think about was how fat my thighs are. I'm sure everyone at school is aware of them and now I just want them removed for good. I hope Mom will agree to make a doctor's appointment for me.

Once we are seated at the table for supper, I try to ask Mom about the appointment. But before I speak even one word, Mom turns her attention to something new. It seems my face is not meeting Mom's expectations, has taken my thighs out of her limelight.

"What is that on your face?" Mom exclaims during dinner.

"What, Mom? What do you see on it?" I wipe my face with a paper towel. Maybe it's some ketchup on my upper lip?

"It's a pimple! How could you not know you have a pimple on your face? It's huge, just disgusting looking."

A pimple, not something I have had before. Usually, her criticism about my face has to do with my freckles, or my constantly sunburned nose—or the fact that my pale, white face turns fire-engine red when I am upset or embarrassed. These have all been discussed, but not a pimple.

"I don't know how I got it, Mom. What should I do about it?"

"Well, pick it open—you have to pick it until it is gone. It's too gross to look at," she advises. "Oh, my God, not now!" Mom yells as I trace my cheeks with my fingertips, trying to find the offensive boil. "We are trying to eat here. Go in the bathroom after supper and pick away until it's gone."

In the bathroom, I feel my face to find this newly revealed infraction. I don't look in the mirror; there is no need to see what it looks like. In fact, I have quit looking into mirrors altogether. The beautiful, oval-shaped mirror that stands up from my white dresser in my bedroom could be removed and thrown out for all I care. I don't need a glass reflection to confirm what I look like; Mom has become my mirror. So, no, I don't spend any time in front of mirrors, I don't even glance up to look in the mirror while I'm washing my hands or brushing my teeth.

My fingertips find the lump, high on my cheekbone. Placing a piece of toilet paper over it, I try to pinch it with my fingers. I squeeze so hard it hurts, but it works—yellowish-white fluid seeps out, and I think I have solved the problem.

"Is that better, Mom?" I ask, hopefully. She has moved from the Duncan Phyfe table to her spot on the couch and is watching television. Her usual can of Hamm's is sitting next to a pack of Winstons on her side table. I stand in front of her, bend over so that she can study my face.

"Well, a little. At least it doesn't look like it'll explode anymore," she replies, frowning while re-inspecting my face. "It's super red now." But now she is not looking at my face. Her gaze is cast downward, and I realize I have stood in front of her too long, given her time to find something else to worry about.

"Your stomach, Joanie. How long has it been that big? It looks like you have a pouch there. You're not hiding a baby kangaroo in there, are you?" Mom says with a little laugh.

"My stomach? My stomach is sticking out?" I feel myself starting to panic. My God, what is happening to me—a pimple, my belly sticking out? I don't want all of this on top of my super-sized thighs.

"Yep, sticking out is putting it mildly," she says, poking her long index finger into my belly, her sharp, yellowish fingernail piercing the newly discovered roll of fat. "You're starting to look like—oh, what's her name, the wife on *All in the Family*?"

"Edith, Mom?" Oh God, I can't believe I resemble the old lady on the show. "I look like Edith Bunker?"

"Well, not your whole body, but your stomach does," Mom clarifies.

I stare at my mom and see something in this mother mirror that I have not noticed during previous critical reviews. Her smile is different. It's more like a sneer, and now I see that her eyes have just a bit of a gleam to them. And suddenly, I realize she is enjoying this—my mom is getting a kick out of watching for my reaction to her harsh words. And as the realization hits harder—connects to my heart, to my soul—my telltale face flares fast into its emergency shade of red. And now, she has her satisfaction; she knows she has hurt my feelings.

"Oh, Joanie, you take things so seriously. You need to learn to lighten up, learn to laugh a little," she says, her dried-out lips now in a full smile.

And I wonder. Should I try to run away again? But I know that is not a good idea—now that I'm older, I can see that I'm a misfit, that no one would want me as a part of their family. So I'm stuck with a mom that doesn't like me, and truthfully, I don't like her either. She makes me so mad I could scream for thirty days and thirty nights. What would happen if I let the rage that is boiling inside of me out? Unleashed the building fury at this woman, this mother mirror, this woman I have watched almost die at the hands of my father? What if I let not only my face but my whole body turn fire-engine red while I yell at her, vomit it all up, tell her what a mean person she is?

I've already confessed that I slapped her across the face, but this is different. When I did that, I was sorry for what I had done. But right now—I don't regret what I'm thinking. So then what? What does a priest say to someone who isn't sorry for what they have done? Would I be forgiven at confession anyway? I can just picture it, sitting in the dark confessional, anonymous to the priest on the other side, telling the old man in his flowing white robe my sin: "I have broken the commandment that requires me to honor my parents at all times." And after saying my Act of Contrition, await his penance. And finally, waiting for the words that tell me the session is concluding: "All is forgiven, my child. Now go. Go in peace to love and serve the Lord."

Forgiven by this human representation of God maybe, but how will I ever be able to forgive myself?

John Hicks; circa 1947

Lyla Tighe, High school graduation; 1947

Hicks family photo. John Hicks front row, far right; circa 1939

Mr. and Mrs. John Hicks; 1949

First apartment
as a married
woman; 1949

Tighe Siblings:
Sharon,
Sharlene,
Charlotte, Lyla,
& Earle

Lyla on the phone. Kitchen/Family room of 509

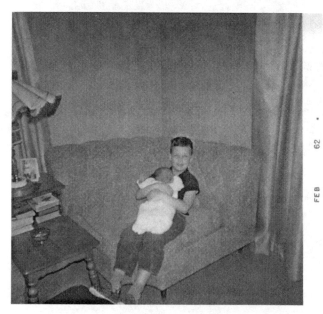

FEB 62

Joan and Mark; 1962

Joan and Her Parents. Living room of 509; 1963

Joan and her Mom. Front of 509; 1963

Joan with stuffed puppy; 1964

Joan and Lyla on the steps of 509; 1965

The Gardner Hotel in Duluth, MN

Joan and Mark; 1966

Brenda (white swimsuit) and Joan (pajamas); 1966

Joan with her dad; 1967

John Hick; 1968

Joan and Midnight (Mark with his guitar); 1968

Lyla and Joan, piano night; 1970

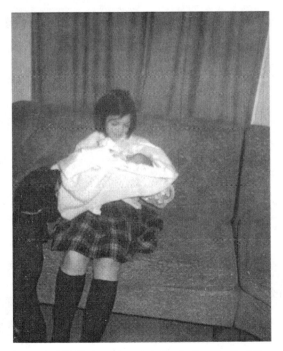

Joan and TNT checking out Gloria for the first time

Joan and Gloria; 1972

Joan and best friend, Sharon; 1973

Mark, High school graduation photo; 1974

Gloria; 1975

Mark, Joan, and Gloria. Spearman, TX; 1976

Joan and Gloria in their matching outfits

Joan and Gloria; Christmas 1979

Joan and Gloria with Bernice

AUTHOR'S REFLECTION

ONLY ON THE RAREST of occasions did Mom speak of the violence that pervaded our home. In fact, as she entered her sixties, it seemed like everything had been wiped away, erased from her brain. Talking with her on the phone, she would read articles to me about domestic violence, child neglect, and so on. Her responses to the news articles astounded me—"I can't imagine how anyone could live through such a thing!" and "How could anyone be so mean, to treat their wife/husband/child like that!" or "Those poor children!" Though I never did, there were times when I wanted to scream "WE LIVED THAT!" There was one time, however, when the two of us were out for lunch, that she broached the subject.

"Do you remember the time when we went to Annie Sawchuck's house?" she asked, catching me by surprise.

"I do. That was a bad one," I answered. As we looked at each other, a tear or two trickled down her cheek. Since it was also rare for Mom to show any emotion, I was temporarily taken aback. Was there something about Mrs. Sawchuck, or the day, that I didn't remember?

"Did you ever wonder why we went there—instead of to Mrs. Stedman's?"

"Yes, I remember thinking that right away. Why did we?"

"Well, while we were running down the street, I felt a tugging on my shoulder and heard a clear message. Something like: *Turn here, Annie is waiting for you.* And when we walked in, didn't it feel like she and Jeannie were waiting for us?"

"Yes," I whispered.

"I found out later that Stedman's house was the first place your dad went looking for us. If we had gone there, he would have found us for sure. It was an angel, Joan. A guardian angel spoke to me that day."

"Oh, Mom," I said, thinking about my four-year-old self running down the street—wondering why there had been a last-minute change in our escape plan.

"I called Annie yesterday and told her I wanted to take her out to lunch. She seemed surprised to hear from me. We've never been close, you know. Well, anyway, I'm going to thank her for what she and Jeannie did for us that day. I need to do that. I want to."

"She will like that, Mom. I'm sure she has never forgotten that day. Please tell her thank you from me, too."

Later, after I had dropped Mom off at 509, my mind drifted back to the events of the day, and what struck me was how I had never considered the risk that Mrs. Sawchuck had taken on for us. Even though Dad did not come there to look for us, I suppose he could have, and I wonder now if Annie considered this when Mom, bleeding and broken, arrived on her back steps with little Joanie in tow. The way she instantly opened her home to us and summoned her daughter to care for me while she cared for Mom leads me to believe she didn't think twice about it.

The manifestation of the angel did not surprise me. I have felt the aura of a spirit guiding me at many times throughout my entire life. I wish that I had asked Mom more about what it felt like for her, what she thought the angel looked like. As for me, I picture a female angel, dressed all in white, with wings. I imagine her floating above us as we run down Eleventh Avenue, imagine her tugging at Mom's shoulder at precisely the right moment to alter our course. I imagine one of her wings cushioning my bare feet, making sure I don't trip and fall while I run like the wind. In my mind's eye, I watch as she follows us all the way to the back door. And I watch her glide in, place her face right next to Mrs. Sawchuck's ear, and whisper: "Annie: Lyla and Joanie need you. I have faith in you."

Persons who have experienced traumatic events often have flashbacks to them, and this is what happened to me regarding our reckless journey to Duluth. I was old enough at the time to realize something was dreadfully wrong, but it wasn't until well into adulthood, when I started having flashbacks, that I sought out help. When I told my health care practitioner what I could remember about the incident, she referred me to a therapist trained in Eye Movement Desensitization and Reprocessing (EMDR). At my first appointment, all I could tell the counselor was that Dad had whisked us off to Duluth in the middle of the night, and then left us there with no way to get home. I could not bring forth what Mom and I did after that moment or how we got back to New Brighton. The counselor educated me on the EMDR process, which involves looking at a blinking light as it moves across a bar. Research had shown that as a person's eyes track the light, their mind is able to find the memory and relate it orally to the counselor. I agreed to try it.

Processing this memory took three one-hour EMDR sessions. During the first, as I followed the light back and forth with my eyes, I got as far as walking on the sidewalk with Mom and could identify how scared I was and how I had decided to be brave so that I wouldn't become a worry to her. By the end of the second session, I identified how badly I had to go to the bathroom, how worried I was about my brother, and an image of the hotel. And during the third, I pictured Uncle Lee picking us up, driving us home and my happiness upon seeing my brother the next day. Once I had the full memory, the counselor worked with me on identifying feelings of abandonment, fear, worry. We talked at length about how I had learned at such a young age not to cry or make a scene when I was scared.

Though I was never successful, running away from home became one of my top coping skills. As soon as something bad happened, I reverted to the underlying feelings of being unloved, unwanted, and a burden to my mom. All the pain and suffering that I took in translated into the thought that all would be better if I was gone. In the early years, such as after the stealing incident, I would pack up a few items in my Barbie case and basically go around the block. As I got older, loneliness took over, became an almost a constant companion, and so I tried running away again. I had one mission—to find a place where I belonged. I was devastated when Mrs. Somebody found me, foiling my plans. But my devastation paled in comparison to the heartache I saw in Mrs. Somebody's eyes when the conversation at the bank didn't go quite the way she expected it to.

As my dad's behavior became more erratic and unpredictable, I had a hard time figuring out what was going on. Everything he did scared me. The finished bathroom freaked me out. I couldn't keep up with whether he was living with us or not. Ours was a household running on fear and confusion, and yet, most of the time, it didn't seem to be of concern.

Mom was so angry and sad that she had very little energy for child raising. I couldn't stand to see her so sad, and made it my number one goal to cheer her up, as shown by the birthday party Bernice and I planned for her.

Bernice and her husband Lawrence built their home around the same time as my parents did and the two couples became friends almost immediately. As their friendship blossomed and our family life plummeted into dysfunction, Bernice was the only person from the outside who had a ringside seat, the only person who *knew* what was going on. I imagine there were many moments, such as the night of the birthday party, where Bernice was conflicted—wanting to honor Lyla's friendship, but at the same time wanting to do the right thing. Because Bernice was who she was—a kind, loving person who pursued goodness in everything and everyone—I choose not to think of her as having let me down that night. Instead, I choose to believe that Bernice tried as hard as she possibly could to convince her best friend to go home, to attend to her children. I think it's safe to assume that Bernice ended up telling Mom about the party, finally convincing her to come home.

I was a member of a writing group for a short time, and at one of our meetings, I read the first draft of the birthday party chapter to the group. One of the members thought I had portrayed my mother too harshly: she wanted to know why I couldn't "give my mom a break." The truth is that I did. I did, and still do, give Mom the benefit of the doubt. The burdens she carried were many—to be the breadwinner, to maintain her image at the bank, to keep up with the bills, to raise three children on her own, to wonder about her marriage, to worry about her safety—she carried all this on her shoulders. Dad's threats and behavior cut her off to some degree from her extended family, severely limiting her support system.

I know this now, as an adult. But, my message here is about the children who are growing up in the home. Unless significant interventions are put in place, they do not, and cannot, know and understand the whole picture. Children process what is before them: that Mom is going to die. Add other dysfunctions —alcoholism, neglect, verbal abuse—and the child is left without a clue as to what is normal and how to move on in life.

ADOLESCENCE

SIXTH TO SEVENTH

SUMMER BREAK WENT BY too fast! It was such a fun summer—I hung out with Sharon mostly. Sharon and I have become super good friends—it reminds me of when I had Brenda for a friend. We even came up with secret nicknames for each other! Sharon also likes Gloria and doesn't mind helping me babysit or going for stroller walks. She has two older sisters and two younger brothers—we're both middle children, which is cool. Sharon also plays the clarinet, is crazy smart in math and plays lots of sports. She even got the Presidential Fitness Award at the end of sixth grade last year. I worry that Sharon will stop being my friend since I'm not too smart and don't know how to play any sports. But so far, so good. We are both hoping we have some classes together at Johanna.

Though everyone else seems excited to start junior high, I'm a little worried about seventh grade. The school district boundaries changed, so now my neighborhood has to go to Johanna Junior High instead of Highview. Johanna is about three miles away from our house while Highview is only a mile away—I could walk there if I had to. It makes no sense to me why the school board thinks this change is a good idea. Luckily, Sharon will also be going to Johanna.

Today is the first day of junior high, and for some reason, the thought of a bus ride is making me sick to my stomach. Maybe it's because we have to be out here by 7:00 a.m., way too early in my opinion. Sharon and I don't have too much to talk about this morning. Maybe she's a little anxious, too. It seems like it's taking forever, but finally, the bus comes chugging up the hill towards us.

As Sharon and I step on, it's immediately clear there is no way we are going to be able to sit together. The bus is jammed with kids—there are no empty spots—every seat already has two people in them. I walk down the aisle, looking for a familiar face. Ahead of me, Sharon finds a seat with two girls in it and asks if she can sit with them. It's taking me longer to work up the courage to ask someone if I can sit with them. Suddenly, the bus jerks forward, causing me to lose my balance. It feels like everyone is watching me and my face is burning, so I'm guessing it's turning red. Finally, two girls skootch over and I wedge myself onto the end of their seat. We pick up a few more kids, then the bus driver makes one final stop on Ninth Avenue, where Elise, another one of my friends, hops on board. And now, we are on the way to Johanna.

After a long ride with my butt sitting on less than an inch of the plastic seat, we finally arrive at the school. There are about fifty other buses lined up in front of the school, and the driver tells us to remember our bus number, as we will have to find it amongst all the other buses after school. Getting off the bus, it feels like I'm at a carnival or something. Where did all these kids come from?

The first thing we are supposed to do is try out our locker combinations, which isn't as easy as I thought it would be. There is a swarm of kids in front of the block of lockers, and as I try to squeeze through a small opening, my shoulder accidentally bumps into a girl with long brown hair. Apparently, bumping into someone is not allowed.

"Watch it, you idiot!" she yells. "Who do you think you are, anyway?"

"Sorry. I'm trying to get to my locker—it's behind you." As I finish my explanation, I see she has two blonde-haired friends with her. All of them are dressed in tee-shirts and shorts and have cute tennis shoes. These girls are skinny, they do not have thighs that touch each other, and I understand instantly that they are part of a group that I am not: cool and beautiful. The one doing the talking is swishing her long hair around like the disco dancers on television. They make no motion to move out of my way.

"Hey girls! Check this out! This ugly loser wants to get to her locker," the brown-haired beauty announces to her friends, at which point the three of them join more closely together, forming a line of icy coolness right in front of my locker. "Just how do you think you're going to get there?" she asks me. I attempt to go around them, but they change from disco to line dancers and side-step to block me. Is it possible they hate me already? Their six eyes look right at me, through me, around me—waiting for me to make my next move. I look at the floor, unsure of what to do. Nothing like this ever happened to me at New Brighton Elementary. Suddenly, the bell rings; an announcement follows alerting us that we have five minutes to get to homeroom. The girls decide to head off to class, but I don't make a move until I can't see them anymore. With only a few minutes left to get to homeroom, I decide to skip exploring my locker for now.

In between classes, I check the hallway carefully—trying to make sure the trio of girls that greeted me this morning are not around. Math and science go okay, and, surprisingly, I haven't gotten lost trying to find any of my classes. Arriving at gym class, I find out it is way different than in elementary school. Our teacher, Miss Wiig, has a full head of gray hair; it's possible she's older than my mom! Miss Wiig's gray hair is offset by her all-white outfit—her shorts, shirt, socks, and shoes are all bleached to perfection. She blows on the whistle around her neck and, in a whispery voice, orders us to quietly find our gym locker.

"Time to review the rules," Miss Wiig starts, as we find places to sit on the narrow wooden benches. "You must wear your uniform every day, and, starting tomorrow, you are to have it on and be in the gym by the start of class or you'll be marked tardy." A bunch of girls on the bench next to me are talking, making it hard to hear Miss Wiig's soft voice. Until today, I thought gym teachers were required to have loud voices. "Before you leave class today, each of you will be given a uniform. It should be locked in your locker for tomorrow."

The square lockers are stacked and mine is in the middle of the bottom row. Sitting on a bench, I bend over and try to stuff my uniform inside.

"You again, ha? Hey guys, look who just happens to be in our gym class. It's the girl that knocked into me this morning. What size uniform did you have to get? Do they even make one for a giant like you?" I look up, and sure enough, it's the brown-haired girl from earlier today. "I dare you to try pushing me around again!" she continues.

She's still mad at me for bumping into her? I already tried to apologize, so don't have a clue what to say now. One thing is for sure—I don't want her to know my uniform is a size large, because I'm positive she wears a small. Luckily, Miss Wiig comes by and tells us to line up and wait for the bell—gym class is over for today.

After gym, I head upstairs for home economics, which is basically a fancy way of saying cooking class, and then on to the cafeteria for lunch. Entering the cafeteria, my hearing is instantly bombarded. It is an enormous room, the size of a large gym; some kids are eating, some are in line—but all of them are talking, yelling, screaming. I finally make it through the outrageously long line only to find out there is no place to sit. Whose bright idea was it to have more kids than seats? I eat as much as I can leaning against a wall, then dump the rest into the trash and head off to English class.

My last two classes are social studies, which I can tell is going to be the worst class ever, and concert choir. I'm certain I'm not a good singer (Mom doesn't even want me to sing in church), but Mrs. Peterson seems to think we all have good voices, so we'll see. At the end of the day, I finally stop and try my locker combination—it opens easily, and I place my books on the top shelf.

Outside, once I find the correct bus on the long circle drive, I climb aboard and grab a seat. It's hard to believe Sharon and Elise aren't in any of my classes. It's such a drag! The boys from my neighborhood climb the steps and move to the back of the bus. I didn't even notice them this morning. Nancy hops on and walks past me to sit in the back with the guys. She has been extremely interested in boys lately, and I'm not, so we haven't been the best friends we used to be. Finally, Sharon and then Elise get on the bus. Unfortunately, my seat is full, so we can't sit together, but somehow seeing their faces makes me feel better.

One thing about junior high is that you get home at 2:30 in the afternoon. I don't have to pick up Gloria yet, because it's still her naptime. I have a quick snack, watch a little television, and then head over to pick up my sister. Bernice wants to know all about my day, but it's kind of hard to describe.

"Lots of kids," I say. "It's hard to move around in the hallways, and I didn't have enough time to eat lunch."

"Oh, I'm sure it will all work out," she says. "Just give it some time."

∽

At supper, I can't believe how hungry I am. As we sit down to eat, Gloria spills her milk, which sends Mom into a huge tantrum. We still have the same stupid dining room table—the Duncan Phyfe. It only has one support leg, right in the middle. So when you sit at either end of the table and lean a little too much, the whole table tips, leading most often to spilled milk.

"My God, every night, one or the other of you spills their milk! Help me clean this up, Joanie!" Mom barks. "Get some paper towels. NOW!" she yells, causing Gloria to whimper a little. "When will you girls learn not to lean on the table?"

Mom and I get the offending spill cleaned up, refill Gloria's milk glass and try to resume dinner. I want to tell her about the trio of girls at school, the stupid lunchroom, the cool kitchens in the home ec room, and how unfair it is that Sharon and Elise aren't in any of my classes. But even after the milk is cleaned up, Mom keeps a scowl on her face, so I'm guessing she wouldn't want to hear about any of it.

After I wash the dishes, I take Gloria for a stroller walk, and by the time we get back, it's her bedtime. Once I sing her the Lawrence Welk song and get Gloria all tucked in, I go out to the family room and tell Mom I'm heading to bed, too. It's been a long day, and I'm exhausted. She's all settled in her spot on the couch, watching *Mannix* or *Barnaby Jones* or some other dumb show, drinking her beer.

"Sleep tight! And don't let the bedbugs bite!" Mom says.

NOTHING FITS

SEVENTH GRADE SUCKS. I'VE never hated school before, but I do now.

Gym class is the worst. We started out playing softball, a game I didn't even know existed. Yesterday was the last day of the softball rotation, and I still had not hit the ball, caught the ball, or tagged anyone out. And now, today, we're gearing up to play basketball—another game I know nothing about. It's not like playing a board game like Monopoly, where you get a set of written instructions telling you how to play the game— somehow, we're supposed to magically know how to play.

Sitting on the gleaming wood floor of the gym, we go through the process of choosing teams. Just like in softball, I'm the last one chosen—but there is one thing in my favor: the Trio is on the opposing team. They have become my own personal tormentors, and, if I've learned anything in gym, it's that we should never be on the same side. Miss Wiig comes over and tells us to stand up.

"Hicks, you're tall, so you're going to be center," she says in her raspy, whisper-like voice. Miss Wiig calls off the other positions, and we run out to the middle of the gym to start the game. I'm five feet, six inches tall, about an inch or so taller than the girl facing me, but I don't know what a center does. As Miss Wiig blows her whistle and tosses the basketball up, I don't move. The girl from the other team does a little jump and taps the ball, and I watch it soar off to the side. Girls are now running in every direction—shouting, jumping, running for the ball. I try to join in, but can't keep track of who my teammates are. The ball comes flying towards me, and I'm positive it's going to hit my leg and break it into a billion pieces. To avoid the impending injury, I jump away from it causing Miss Wiig to blow her whistle. In a flash, the Trio surrounds me.

"How's it going, Hicks?" the brown-haired girl sneers. "Look at those gross shoes! Where'd you get 'em, a garage sale? They don't sell anything like that at Kinney Shoes! What are you, some kind of scaredy-cat giant? Sooo tall, but scared of everything?" The sound of her voice sounds like a hungry mosquito buzzing around my ears, which makes sense, because whatever she says always ends with a sting. "Guess what? I'm guarding you, so don't make any fast moves or you WILL be sorry!"

When the game resumes, the two blondes come up behind me and, as I try to run toward the ball, one of them gives me a little push so that my stupid tennis shoe catches on the floor, causing me to fall onto my hands and knees.

I quickly decide I don't like basketball any more than softball and make a plan to stay down on the floor as long as possible. Maybe Miss Wiig will deem me injured, permanently, and I will be able to sit out the rest of the game. How in the world does everyone else seem to know how to play these absurd games—games that involve balls that could hurt, possibly even kill a person? Whatever happened to four-square, dodgeball, or kickball?

"Wow, Hicksy, you're such a Dicksy! So uncoordinated! What a disgusting basketball player you are! Worse than softball, even!" And here I am again with practically the whole class laughing at me, and I secretly wish the brown-haired girl would come down with a horrible case of laryngitis. "God, get up! What are you, a wimp or something?" I decide it's probably best to keep my mouth shut and focus my burning, brown eyes on the highly-polished wood floor of the gym.

Miss Wiig finally comes over and tells me to get up and get back in position so we can resume the game: skinned knees do not count as an injury. I go back to the center line, but quickly learn that isn't right. Apparently, you only go to the center line at the start of the game. God, I'm such a loser! I decide to put myself into a kind of a running daze and start running haphazardly, figuring it's better to zig and zag than stand in one spot. I stop, though, when my side starts to hurt and I can't catch my breath. Sweat droplets are streaming down my cheeks, the back of my neck. I've never run so much in my entire life. I look down and see that the ball is in my hands. I'm right by the basket, so shooting makes sense. I miss, of course, but guess what? The joke is on me—again. If the ball had gone through the basket, I would've scored for the other team. The Trio is laughing, laughing, laughing while my team is becoming more and more incensed. They're complaining to Miss Wiig that it isn't fair to have me on their team. And I guess it probably isn't. I don't want me on my team, either.

Besides the lovely games we get to play, the other super wonderful thing about gym is the good ol' locker room. Whoever came up with this idea must hate kids. To remove my clothes and expose what I already know is the grossest body on the planet to twenty or so other girls is mortifying. I do not look at anyone else. I keep my eyes focused on the floor, wet with sweat and water from the girls who take the time to shower. Mom's words come to me in bursts—and I know she's right, I AM fatter than everyone else. I try to change clothes quickly, but one of the blondes from the Trio's locker is nearby, providing her with a birds-eye view of my gross atrocities. If it isn't my thighs or my stomach, it's my underwear or my bra. And if it isn't any of those, it's my mother-like clothes or nerdy shoes. Nothing I wear comes close to what the Trio, or any of the other girls for that matter, wear.

Mom did all my clothes shopping and, lucky me, she bought me exactly what she wears: matching polyester shirts and slacks from the ladies' department at JC Penney. Mom calls them pantsuit sets, and she was kind enough to get one in every color—I have a pale blue set, a yellow, a pink, and a weird lime green. It's not lost on me that I look like a miniature bank employee, but what am I supposed to do about it? I don't have anything else to wear. She didn't know what size to get me, so the pants and tops are at least one size too big. I have begged Mom for one pair of jeans, just one pair—it doesn't even have to be a pair of Levi's—but her answer is that I should be thankful for what I have, it's her hard-earned money that bought it.

And if the clothes aren't bad enough, there's the shoes. Somewhere along the way, it was decided that I have wide feet. Apparently, no one else in the whole wide world, or at least in New Brighton, requires C-width shoes, because most stores don't stock them. The only place to find wide shoes is at Connco Shoes at Apache Plaza Mall. That was a winner of a shopping trip.

"Here, Joanie, try these on," Mom said, handing me a box of shoes. As I looked inside the box to see what she found, I gasped—Girl Scout green shoes with bright gold imprints on top. Mortified, I protested.

"Mom, I can't wear these! They're green! There must be something else!"

"Nope, this is the only pair in your size. It's too bad you don't have normal feet or narrow like mine: there are a whole bunch of narrow shoes," she replied. Reluctantly, I tried them on, and of course, they fit, so those were awarded the position of being my everyday shoes. Next, I searched and searched the rows of tennis shoes: there had to be a pair of white ones that would fit me. There just had to be. But no, a pair that looks like something my Grandma Tighe would wear was the only pair in the whole store in wide. A sickly tan color and, on the back of the heel, a blue and yellow daisy. So ugly.

"Mom, no! I need a white pair! Everyone I know has white tennis shoes! I can't wear these old-lady shoes!" I protested, to no avail. With the tennis shoes and everyday shoes chosen, we had to find one more pair—something that could be worn in the shower during swimming class to prevent planter's warts, whatever they are. Mom found the winning pair, and I couldn't even look at them. How could a shoemaker create such an awful pair of shoes? The base of the clogs is made of white plastic, and a super wide elastic ankle strap holds them on. The ugly part is this: the shoes are topped off with red polka-dot fabric that looks like it could double as a picnic tablecloth. Mom instantly deemed them to be my shower shoes. So now I have a green pair of everyday shoes that look like something you would only find at a Girl Scout store, old lady tennis shoes, and a pair of shower shoes that look like something a toddler would wear. In fact, Gloria insisted on trying them on, and though they were about six sizes too big, they were adorable on her.

Today the blonde girl focuses on my underwear, which is quite possibly two sizes too small. The pair I have on today has a hole on the side of one leg, where the elastic stuff meets the fabric, and blonde girl notices.

"What's that? A hole in your underwear? Look at that! Hicks has a hole big enough for another leg! Well, it would have to be a skinnier leg, but still!" I try to dress as quickly as possible, before she draws the attention of her leader, the brown-haired girl. But suddenly, it's too late, or I'm too slow, because there she is, perched on the bench next to me, glaring at my legs.

"God, wow! Hicks, what's the deal? Why didn't you get some underwear at the same garage sale you got your shoes at?" Oh, she thinks she is so funny—she's cracking herself up at her joke, and the blonde is joining right in. Luckily, the other girls are scrambling to get dressed to get to their next class, so no one else signs on for this show. I feel my face flushing red—in anger and embarrassment. I don't move, hoping they won't find anything else to add to the spectacle. When the locker room finally empties, I finish dressing. Now I'll be tardy for home ec, but at this point, I could care less.

The school day finally came to an end, and, on the bus ride home, I think about how glad I am that Sharon and Elise haven't caught on to the fact that I'm a big fat loser. It's probably because we don't have any classes together—if we did, they'd figure it out super quick. What if Sharon or Elise meet the Trio and they tell them how dumb and fat I am?

As I come through the door, I see Mark and his new girlfriend sitting on the living room couch. I haven't met her yet, so he tells me her name. I imagine they were necking before I came in, so my plan is to hurry to my room as fast as possible. As I bend over to untie my laces, my brother takes note of my shoes.

"Are those GREEN shoes?!" Mark cries out, in disgust. In an instant, my face turns beet red; I freeze in place—I suppose I look like a cherry Popsicle. "You're wearing green shoes to school? They look like something out of the Girl Scout catalogue!"

I'm stunned into silence. I don't think he meant to hurt me, and he has no idea what's going on at school, so he couldn't know that he is adding oxygen to a fire. But still. I look up at him, tears forming at the rims of my eyes. I am speechless, dumbstruck. What could I possibly say right now? How could my brother, of all people, have said that to me—and right in front of his girlfriend? I catch her eye, but can't read her face—I have no idea what she's thinking. She could be a big sister of one of the Trio for all I know. Mark is looking at me, his arm slung over the girl's shoulders, waiting for an answer. I understand he's trying to look cool in front of this girl. I slip my shoes off and run at breakneck speed, past them and into my room.

I throw myself onto my bed, squeeze my eyes shut, and try to stuff the tears back behind my eyelids. There is no way I want Mark's girlfriend, who probably has figured out by now what a weirdo I am, to hear me bawling. But it's so hard—the tears are trying to force their way out. My chest lurches for the sobs I'm holding back. My body is shaking, but I know it won't be enough to shake off the fat, the pimples. And it certainly isn't going to help the clothing or shoe situation.

In the silence of my room, I finally fall into a sort of trance. I have so many questions about this stupid life I have. Why do I have to be the person in this world that is such a loser? Mark has been cool his whole life, and now that he's a senior in high school, he's way cooler than anyone I know. Who can beat a guy who has long, brownish-red hair (it's even curly), has light blue eyes, plays the piano AND guitar, and has about a billion friends? The summer between his sophomore and junior year, he told Mom he wanted to go to Arizona to visit some friends. Mom told him he couldn't go. The next thing you know, he's off to Arizona. He hitchhiked the whole way there and back. I was positive he wouldn't come back, but apparently New Brighton, Minnesota was better than wherever he was in Arizona, so here he is. I wouldn't even know how to go about doing something like that.

Other than Sharon, the only two people that still think I'm somewhat normal are Gloria and Bernice. They are also the only people that I talk to anymore. I still don't know why Bernice likes me so much. Every single day, when I go over to pick up Gloria, Bernice has a hug for me. Sometimes I think it's because she feels sorry for me, but other days I think it's true what she says—for some odd reason she likes me—just the way I am.

Gloria's only three—still so young, that she can't understand what a sorry sight her big sister is. In fact, she thinks I'm the best thing ever. We have so much fun when it's we are on our own, that sometimes I forget I'm a loser—it's such a freeing feeling to be normal, even if only for a few minutes. At night, when I put her to bed, she tells me she loves me—and of course, I tell her the same.

If someone, anyone, were to ask me what I want, I know what I would say. I want to ask the brown-haired girl, who is so very pretty, how she gets her hair so silky-looking, and how she gets it into a braid. I want to tell the blonde-haired girl that my mom doesn't have any money for new underwear, and that is why I have what I have. I want to tell the Trio that when they smash me up against the lockers in the hallway, and my back or arm connects with the lock mechanism, it hurts, and I have bruises from it. I want to tell them that if they keep physically hurting people, they could end up being like my dad. I want to ask the girls where they buy their jeans, because as soon as I have enough lawn mowing money saved up, I plan on buying a pair.

I want someone to give a shit about me. I want Mom to ask me how my day was. I want a teacher, or anyone for that matter, to say to me: "Hey, I saw what just happened, are you okay?" I want the blonde-haired girl to go home and tell her mother about the disgusting girl with the too-small, holey underwear and have her mother tell her to treat that girl with kindness. I want someone to ask me why I stopped brushing my teeth, taking a bath, and washing my hair. I want a teacher to ask me why I never do my homework. I want Miss Wiig to offer to teach me how to play basketball. I want my brother to teach me how to be cool.

Someday, I hope I find the courage to speak out, say what I want and what I need. But right now, I can't. I'm too afraid. My bottom teeth are practically cemented to my top teeth, clenched so tightly my jaw hurts. My lips are sealed with what feels like super glue. My vocal cords are paralyzed with fear.

THE OLD SINGER

GLORIA'S NOT UP FROM her nap yet when I arrive at Bernice's, so I head downstairs to see what Bernice is up to.

Bernice has one of the best sewing machines money can buy, and this is where I find her when I enter her family room. "Hang on a minute, Joanie. Gotta finish this hem!" Bernice says with a smile, a few sewing pins sticking out of her lips.

Bernice's basement is a crafter's haven, and I wander around while I wait. Starting with the macramé corner, I see a multitude of colored rope piled up, waiting to be fashioned into hanging lamps and planters. Next to the macramé, I find an old chair in the process of being reupholstered. I know from her past projects that it will look like a brand-new chair when she's done with it. In the middle of the room, there is a long table. This is where we sit when she hosts her famous fish fry dinners. But right now, it is covered with a white tablecloth that she is decorating by painting pink flowers along the border. Amid the crafts, I find an empty Schmidt beer bottle. Behind the bar, I pop the bottle into an empty beer box and turn on her Hamm's beer sign. I take a penny out of the dish on the bar and set it on the top of the battery-operated bank. It's fascinating to watch the white-gloved hand come out to grab the coin and pull it inside. Soon, I head to the sewing machine, and, after she puts out her cigarette in an overflowing ashtray, she holds up today's finished project: a pair of jeans for one of her sons.

"What do you think?" she asks me, while she's looking over her work. "Oh, bull feathers! I missed a spot on the waistband. Give me one more minute." Once fixed, she holds the jeans up for inspection; instantly, I'm impressed.

"Wow! You know how to make jeans? Jim and David are so lucky!" I exclaim. And then, I get an idea. "Hey, Bernice, do you think you could teach me how to sew? I want to make myself a pair of jeans."

"Sure! I can teach you how to sew. But to be honest, I don't know how to make girl clothes, so I don't think I'll be any good in the girls' jeans department. But you're smart, so you can probably figure it out once I teach you the basics."

We have a sewing machine at home, but it's nothing like Bernice's. It's in my mom's bedroom, and I guess it was Grandma Tighe's before she got a more modern one. The black Singer, embedded in a beautiful oak table, is about twice the size of Bernice's. I'm hoping that once I learn on Bernice's machine, I can teach myself how to use the Singer.

ॐ

Over the past couple of weeks, I spent an hour or so with Bernice every day. She taught me what a pattern is, how to lay it out on a piece of fabric, how to pin the fragile paper onto the fabric, and how to cut the pieces out. She gave me the lowdown on fabric—how to tell which way the selvage goes, what "cutting on the bias" means. She has been very patient: she didn't seem to mind if she had to show me something more than once. Over the past few days, she showed me how her sewing machine works: how to thread the machine, wind the bobbin, set the tension, and choose a stitch length. And finally, today I'm going to sew my first seam.

"Okay, Joanie," Bernice says while I settle myself on her sewing stool. "Can you feel the pedal on the floor? You need to press that with your foot to make the machine sew. The harder you press down, the faster the machine will go. When you want to stop, lift your foot off the pedal."

Bernice hands me two pieces of scrap fabric and shows me how to line them up for what she says is the standard seam width, 5/8 of an inch. "Perfect! Now, before you sew, lock down the presser foot—okay, now as you push your foot down, gently guide the fabric through."

I'm a little nervous: I don't want to break her beautiful machine. As I press my foot down on the pedal, I'm shocked at how fast the fabric surges through! As I ease off on the pedal with my foot, I look up at Bernice, hoping she isn't disappointed in my attempt. Bernice's brown eyes meet mine, and she starts to giggle. And then we're both laughing, causing her roly-poly tummy to jiggle.

"Wow, Bernice! This thing has tremendous power!" I finally say.

"Yes, well, it takes some practice to get the speed right. I think you pressed your foot down a little harder than necessary. Let's try it again."

Once I have the foot pressure down, and I've successfully sewn a bunch of 5/8" seams, Bernice deems me trained. She sends me home with a pile of scrap fabric and wishes me well on learning to sew on the old Singer machine.

When Mom walks in the door, I tell her about my accomplishment.

"Mom! I have great news!"

"My God, can't you at least wait until I have my shoes off before you start hounding me?" Mom's reply stings a little, but she's right—by now I should know better than to talk to her right when she gets home. I guess my excitement took over, and I forgot.

Later, after supper, I try again. I try to keep my voice quiet, so she doesn't think I'm overexcited or trying to brag about myself.

"Hey, Mom? Remember when I told you Bernice was going to teach me how to sew?" I start out, quietly testing the waters.

"Yes, I remember. What about it?" Her reply seems calm, so I don't think she's angry at me any longer.

"Well, I'm all set to try sewing on the old Singer. Bernice taught me the basics, and I sewed four seams on her machine today!" I show Mom the scrap fabric that Bernice gave me and start talking about patterns and stitch length—but Mom has already heard enough.

"I don't sew, and I don't care to know how. No need for you to give me a rundown." I don't know exactly how to take this response, but I want her to help me move the old Singer out of her bedroom and into the family room so that I can start sewing on it, which means I can't stop talking quite yet.

"Okay, got it. No more talking about sewing. But I need help moving the machine out into the family room. Do you have time to help me tonight?" Much to my surprise, Mom agrees, and soon the old Singer is in the family room, behind the Duncan Phyfe, on the wall by the refrigerator. I am so excited to get started, but Mom informs me that I can only sew when she's not home, because the noise may interfere with her television watching. I guess she doesn't know the old Singer doesn't make a sound.

⟳

After a few days of practicing, I've got the machine down and am ready to start my first real project. It took a few tries to figure out how to thread the machine (I'm surprised to discover it's easier than Bernice's) and to fill the bobbin. The foot pedal, which Bernice says is called a treadle, was the hardest to master. The power of the machine comes from a rocking rhythm of your feet on the treadle. I learned that the constant rhythm must be coordinated with a bit of extra pressure here and there to keep it moving.

For my first project, I'm making a dress for Gloria's doll. She's very excited and watched my every move while I planned it all out. I let her pick out the fabrics from Bernice's pile, and she picked a purple print. She stood by my side as I measured the doll and made a pattern out of paper grocery bags. And today, when I sew the last seam, she squeals. As for me, I'm surprised to see that the finished product truly looks like a dress!

"Time to show Bernice!" I say to Gloria. "Let's race!" I exclaim as we start to cross over the alley into Bernice's yard.

"Beautiful!" Bernice beams as I show her the little dress. "Joanie, you are amazing. Just amazing," Bernice concludes, giving me a tight hug.

I AM WOMAN

I'M SO SICK I don't know what to do. Tomorrow is February 13th, 1975—my thirteenth birthday—and even though we don't have any plans to celebrate, I don't want to be sick for it.

When I got home from school yesterday, I was so dizzy I could hardly walk, and it's only gotten worse since then. I must stay as still as possible: the slightest movement causes my head to spin. Mom doesn't believe in missing school or work, so she is surprised when I wake her up to tell her there will be no school for me today.

"What do you mean, you can't go to school? I thought you were just dizzy?" Mom said.

"Still dizzy, but I also threw up about six times during the night," I tell her. "Probably have a fever, too. Do we have any of that baby aspirin stuff?" Mom feels my forehead and agrees that it feels warm. She gets up, finds the aspirin, and gives me four of the little orange-flavored chewable tablets.

"I have to go back to bed," I say. "Can't stand up any longer."

"I'm off to work," Mom says from my doorway a little while later. "Make a soft-boiled egg for yourself later, okay?"

A soft-boiled egg is my mom's answer to all ailments. Earache, headache, stomachache, fever, or any other illness—a soft-boiled egg is the cure. But today, the thought of the mashed egg/butter mixture turns my stomach.

After she leaves, I try to go back to sleep. It's impossible, though, because just as I start to drift off, I have to run to the bathroom. Now it isn't just throwing up; it's also diarrhea. Sitting on the toilet is the worst—my head is spinning out of control. My tummy feels like it has fire in it, and I wonder if this is what it feels like if you are a circus performer who swallows flames.

I have no idea how much time has passed when I find myself waking up from a nap. The dizzy, spinny feeling seems to be gone, but my head is pounding with pain! How is it even possible that something could hurt this bad? I try to open my eyes, but when I do, a stabbing pain pierces through my brain, from my eyes to the back of my head. I try to roll onto my side, thinking that will help, but no, that is not the right thing. It seems the only thing I can do to prevent the pain from getting worse is to stay flat on my back and be as still as possible. Oh, God, now I feel the urge to throw up again.

In the bathroom, the retching makes the pain inside my head even fiercer. As the last of the fluid inside my stomach forces its way out, I realize I'm extremely hot. Sweat is trickling down my forehead. Sitting back, I press it against the bathroom wall— the cool, pink tile feels good for an instant, but then a wave of pain comes back. It feels like a knife has been jammed into my left eye.

Once I'm settled back in bed, I start shaking uncontrollably. I'm so cold and can't get warm. I lean over to grab my blanket— try to fold it over so it is a double layer—and a surge of pain that supersedes what I felt moments ago causes me to cry out in anguish. What is wrong with me? Probably a brain tumor. What else could cause such pain? Great, now I'm crying, which only makes the pain worse. But I guess I need someone to cry for me as I die. Almost as suddenly as it started, the shaking stops. And now it's time for another trip to the bathroom.

Sitting on the toilet, I lay my head on the marble vanity. As my insides empty out, the pain in my head changes—instead of a knife through my eye, it feels like there's a hammer inside my head trying to pound its way out. The coolness of the marble offers no relief.

Washing my hands, another sure sign of death appears: the toilet bowl is full of blood! What's wrong with me? Then I think, could it be possible the headache is causing me to see things that aren't there? I look again, but the blood is still there. And then it dawns on me—my first period. Great.

I search around the bathroom and Mom's bedroom to find where she keeps the pads but come up empty. We haven't discussed it, but how could there not be any pads in this house? Holding my head in my hands, willing it to stop throbbing, I sit back down on the toilet to think. Finally, I decide I'm going to have to call Mom to find out where the supplies are. I have never called the bank before, but I need help, and I have no other way to get it.

"First State Bank of New Brighton. How may I help you?" I'm not sure what to say.

"Hi, um. Is Mrs. Hicks available?"

"Sure, may I ask who's calling?"

"My name is Joanie? Her daughter? I know she's busy, but I need to talk to her for a quick second," I say, hoping the lady can convince Mom to stop working for a minute.

"Oh, sure. Hi, Joanie, I've heard a lot about you. Hold on a minute." The lady who answered sounds so nice, I thought whoever answered would be irritated to have a kid call the bank. I hear a clicking sound, and then Mom's voice comes on the line.

"Lyla Hicks speaking. How may I help you?"

"Um, Mom? It's me."

"Joanie? What is it? Why are you calling? I'll be home in a few hours."

"I need help. I'm getting sicker: my head is pounding, and I think I got my period. I can't find any pads. Can you tell me where they are?" My stomach is roiling as I wait for her response. After a moment of silence, I hear Mom sigh.

"There are none. I wish you would've told me to get some. I'll have to stop on my way home from work and pick some up," Mom says, and I guess I have pissed her off.

"What am I supposed to do in the meantime?" I ask, a little pissed off myself.

"Use one of the old towels from the bathroom. I'll see you in a few hours," Mom grumbles. And just like that, the conversation is over.

I choose a hand towel from the cabinet, fold it in half, and then kind of roll it. As I climb back into bed, I place the roll in between my legs. This is SO gross!

Suddenly, the pain rears up as though I've been kicked in the head by an angry horse. I can't believe this pain. A hot flame encompasses my body, and I realize my temperature is ratcheting up again. I close my eyes. I am exhausted, but I doubt I'll be able to sleep through the pain.

I'm in a sort of half-sleep when I hear someone come into my room. Trying to open my eyes, I realize I'm still boiling hot. Is it possible Mom is home from work already?

"Joanie?" I recognize the voice, but can't quite place it.

"Who's there?" I ask.

"It's Mrs. Kewatt, stopping in to check on you." I'm stunned. How in the world did Mrs. Kewatt even know I was sick? And why would she think to check on me? She hasn't been in our house since the famous birthday party I threw for Mom a few years ago.

"Nancy said she called you and she couldn't understand a

word you were saying. She told me you weren't in school today, so I thought I'd come over and check on you. Is that okay?" This makes absolutely no sense to me.

"Yeah, it's okay. I don't remember talking to her," I say, starting to cry. This extreme act of kindness is too much for me. My emotions are taking over. I can hardly speak. At the same time, I realize what a disaster my room is—there are dirty clothes all over the floor. "Sorry my room is such a mess; I didn't know you were coming over."

"Oh, no worries, I have two girls myself, you know," she says.

"I'm so sick I think I'm dying," I tell her, in between sobs. "I don't want to die. Plus, tomorrow's my birthday."

"Oh, that's right, tomorrow is the thirteenth—your golden birthday!" Mrs. Kewatt gently lays the back of her hand on my forehead. "My goodness, you're burning up. Do you have a thermometer? We should check your temperature." I tell her the thermometer is in the medicine cabinet in the bathroom.

Soon she's back in my room. Sitting on the edge of my bed, she puts the thermometer in my mouth and takes my hand in hers. Gently, she strokes the top of my hand. When she takes the thermometer out, her suspicion is confirmed. My temperature is 102.5.

"I found the aspirin in the bathroom; let's get some into you. Do you have any idea how much you weigh, honey? I need to know so I give you the right amount." I'm embarrassed to tell her my weight.

"I weigh about 110 pounds."

"Okay, then you would take four of these. Now, what have you had to eat or drink today?" I tell her about the throwing up and the diarrhea, and she seems concerned that I haven't had anything to drink since yesterday at school. She tells me it's probably okay to drink some water but to take small sips to try to prevent more vomiting. "I'll go get you a glass; you just keep resting."

While she's in the kitchen, I thank God for her. He must have sent her; truly He must have. I didn't even pray for it, didn't even ask God for help this time—and yet, here she is. Like a fairy godmother, or a guardian angel.

When she comes back, she has me sit up to take a sip of water, and I tell her how bad the headache is. "It's worse when I move around. The worst of it is right behind my eyes, and it either feels like a hammer pounding or a knife being pushed into my brain."

"Oh, my. You are one sick young lady. I'll put a cool cloth on your forehead; that might help a little. Also, the aspirin is going to help with the fever and the pain, so you should feel better soon. You can take it again before you go to bed tonight. I'll leave it here by your bedside: that way, you don't have to get up to look for it. How does that sound?" And I want to tell her that it sounds great. Her voice is like a lullaby—so soothing and comforting. I want to ask her if she'll come back to see me again, but I don't want to be a bother. I know this is one of the kindest things that has ever happened to me, and I'm guessing it might not ever happen again.

"That sounds good, Mrs. Kewatt. How can I ever thank you?"

"All I want is for you to get better, okay? You've got a birthday to celebrate! I'm going home now—try to sleep for a bit until your mom gets home."

And it's hard for me to believe it, but my head already feels a little better. More like a thudding than a pounding.

❧

When I wake up, Mom and Gloria are next to my bed; my sister is whispering my name.

"Hi there," I say, weakly.

"How are you feeling?" Mom asks, as she removes the now

warm cloth, and feels my forehead.

"Maybe a little better. The headache is more like a thudding feeling now, no more hammering. I might still have a fever, though. Mrs. Kewatt came over a while ago and checked it—it was 102.5 then," I report to Mom. She takes the thermometer, puts it in my mouth, and tells me my forehead feels a little warm.

"Okay, it's down to 100 degrees. That's better. I think you're going to have to take a bath, are you up for that?"

After Mom helps me in and out of the bath, she gives me a belt and a box of pads. I wasn't planning on a belt. I thought I would get the new pads that stick to your underwear, but when I ask Mom, it's clear she's not going to get that kind.

"I'll tell you what, Joanie. Back in my day, no one said anything to me about my period. I had to use rags and had only an outhouse to use for a bathroom. My brother, your Uncle Earle, would yell over the wall of the outhouse and tease me. So how about if you just be grateful for what you have, okay? I don't get my period anymore, so you can use my old belt and these pads until you have your own money to spend on something fancier."

I have a hard time thinking that anything to do with having a period could be considered fancy, and I would like to point out that no one has ever talked to me about this disgusting process, and think it is quite preposterous to place any blame on Uncle Earle for any of this miserableness, but I decide to keep my mouth shut.

"Welcome to womanhood," Mom says, as she exits the bathroom.

After she leaves, I try to figure out the belt and pad system. I guess I should have paid attention back in fifth grade when we had that stupid mother-daughter class. Mom couldn't come because she had to work, so for me, it was a daughter class. I begged Mom to come; the teacher had made it clear that it was important. Knowing she wouldn't want to take any time off from work, I asked Mom if she could use her lunch hour, but she pointed out the obvious—how would she be able to eat lunch that day? The moms all sat in their daughter's desks that day, the girls on the floor. As I sat on the floor next to my empty desk, I imagined my mom out for lunch with her bank friends—probably at The New Brighton Diner or somewhere—having a BLT, coffee, and a cigarette. By the time I started paying attention to the filmstrip, it was almost over, and I hadn't learned a thing. When I brought the pamphlets home, I threw them right into the garbage—there was no way I wanted Mark to see them! So other than reading *Are You There God? It's Me, Margaret* two times through, I have no idea what to do.

Finally, I get the long tabs of the pad through the belt. I pull the whole apparatus up, only to find that Mom's old belt is too big for me. I tighten it up as much as it will go, but it still won't stay on my waist. I guess my too-small underwear will have to help hold it up. It's only slightly more comfortable than the rolled-up towel was.

My head has started its hammering again, and I figure since I'm not going to be having supper, it's basically bedtime. I take another four St. Joseph's Baby Aspirin, drink a large sip of water, put on my "Sound of Silence" record, climb into bed and hope for the best.

Welcome to womanhood, indeed.

SINKING

I'M HEADING TO GYM—we're finally nearing the end of the basketball section, and I couldn't be happier. Volleyball is next, followed by health and then swimming. I know nothing about volleyball, but Sharon is on the school team and loves it. I'm not worried about swimming, because I've been swimming at Long Lake every summer for practically my whole life. But right now, my goal is to get through these last few days of basketball.

As I turn the corner and approach the stairs that lead down to the locker room, I see the brown-haired girl from the Trio standing at the top railing, bouncing a basketball. It seems a little weird: she should be in the locker room getting ready for gym. As I put my foot on the top step, she calls out to another Trio member, who, as it turns out, is standing on the landing below me.

"Hicks is here! She's on her way down!" At this, the girl on the landing looks up to the girl at the railing, and I realize they have something planned—for me. I hear the top girl tell one of my classmates they can't go down the stairs and it dawns on me that she is directing traffic—no one else is allowed on the stairs right now. I stop where I'm at, stare down at my feet, hug my books tightly across my chest and contemplate my next move. Keep going? Stay put? Step back into the hallway? I decide to head down the stairs; the locker room seems like a safety zone to some degree. As I near the landing, the two girls start communicating with one another.

The girl on the landing is apparently the coordinator of whatever is going to happen, and as I try to pass by her, she grabs me and holds on tight. "Shoot!" she screams up the stairwell. In the flash of an eye, the brown-haired girl pitches the basketball with a powerful force and a precise aim. As the basketball connects with my back, I fall, landing on my hands and knees. My books scatter across the landing and down the next set of stairs. I hunch my back, tuck my arms under me, wait for them to pass by me. But they're not done yet.

"Again!" I hear. And I realize, too late, that the top girl has at least one more basketball. I know I should try to get up, try to move. But my back hurts so badly that I'm afraid to, and I'm guessing the girl that's standing guard over me won't let me up anyway. I can hear other voices at the top of the stairs—the rest of my class is now watching the spectacle. When the second ball strikes my back, a bit higher up than the first time, I scream, then try to roll myself into a tight ball and scoot as far into the corner as I can. I'm crying, which I know won't help anything. In contrast, the two girls, happy with their performance, are laughing. They got me. And they are proud and happy of their achievement.

The girl at the top rescinds her traffic control duty, and the rest of the class starts to file down the stairs. I stay rolled in my ball, crying quietly. I peek out of my huddle and watch as each student makes their way down the steps, trying not to bump into me, trying not to step on my books. The last to come down is the brown-haired girl, gloating over her ability to lob the basketballs at me.

"How's that, Hicksy? THAT's how you throw a basketball!"

She emphasizes her self-prescribed authority by giving me a little kick as she makes her way down to the locker room.

I know I bumped into her on the first day of school, and I know I suck at softball and basketball, and I know I'm dumb and stupid and ugly and have all the wrong clothes—but what I can't figure out is if they hate me so much, why don't they just ignore me?

I wait for the bell to ring, then slowly unroll my tucked body. The stairwell is empty now. I try to move, try to stand. My back is killing me, and I think it probably should be looked at by someone. Standing up, my knees lock in pain—guess I landed on the gleaming cement harder than I thought. I gather my books and head up the stairs to the office.

"What can I help you with?" The lady behind the desk peers at me through her wire-rimmed glasses.

"I need help. I, um, got hit with a basketball and I need someone to look at my back," I say, trying to hold back my tears. "It hurts pretty bad."

The lady tells me to have a seat; someone will be with me in a minute.

I sit in one of the plastic chairs; I hope it doesn't take too long, because the hard surface is making the back pain worse. I look down at my knees and see little bits of blood seeping through my blue polyester pants. God, it's hard not to cry.

"I understand you are here about a fight," A lady, much younger than the one behind the desk, says as she approaches me. A fight? Where did she get that idea?

"No, I want someone to look at my back, and maybe my knees. I got hit with a basketball and fell onto the concrete." At this, she directs me into her office. Once inside, she closes her door. She wants to know exactly what happened. And I tell her.

"So that's why I want someone to look at my back, I think it might be broken," I say, finishing up my story.

"Okay, well, here's the thing. I'll need to know what you did, or they did, to instigate the fight. And then, if you want to file a report, I'll need to call your parents, and of course, the other girls' parents. And just so you know, whenever I do that, it seems like it gets worse. So—what do you want to do? File a report at the risk of getting beaten up worse? Let it go? It's totally up to you."

"What I want is for someone to look at my back and get a couple of Band-Aids for my knees," I say, feeling like I'm repeating myself. If I don't get some help for my stupid back soon, I'll probably die. Why is this so hard for her to understand? "I'm not sure if you know how hard basketballs are? When they slam into you, they hurt." But if I feel like I'm repeating myself, she's a true broken record, skipping away like my 45's when they have a scratch. By the third time she asks me what I want to do, my blood is boiling and I'm ready to scream. My heart is pounding: it feels like Randy, the drummer in Mark's band, is playing a solo right under my ribs, inside my chest cavity.

"I hate to tell you this, but your smart mouth will get you nowhere. Do you want to narc on them or not?" Hmm, this lady, who sits before me, apparently thinks she has power and has control of the situation at hand.

"So let me get this straight. You're telling me that the only way I can get my back looked at is to file this report thing?" I finally ask.

"Right, and of course the first step to do that would be to call your parents."

Call my parents. The statement makes me laugh. This lady knows nothing about me, and I hate her almost as much as I hate the Trio. There is no "call my parents." She has no idea my dad is in and out of my life so randomly that no one knows when to expect him. That when he's in, he has no capacity to hold down a conversation, let alone help make a report. And she thinks she's going to call my mom at the bank? About me getting hit by a basketball and now complaining that I have back pain? Mom would eat her alive, right over the phone line. I want to tell this lady, who seems to hold all the power of the school in her office, that I know exactly what my mom would say. "Tell those idiot girls to knock it off! And for God's sake, learn how to run that damn school without my help!"

But Mom has enough on her plate—she doesn't need to get involved in this. The only reason I came here was to have someone to look at my fucking back and tell me whether I was going to live or die. Now I don't even want that.

I stand up and lean over her desk. Tears brimming on my lids blur her face, but I try to focus, try to look her right in the eyes. "Fuck you!" I yell.

And then I run. I run out of her office, into the hall, and keep going until I'm all the way out the door. I make a plan that if the bitch tries to follow me, I will deck her.

Once I'm outside, I run some more. I run all the way to the end of the sidewalk, where it meets County Road D, the road they built this stupid school on. I look behind me, but no one has followed me. It's cold outside, and the shock of the air hits deep into my lungs—shocks me back into breathing, or maybe shocks the breath out of me, I don't know. My heart is still pounding, and running wasn't the greatest for my back. I don't have my coat, but I'm not going back into that hateful place to get it. School, what a joke. I know I don't belong here. I belong somewhere else, wherever it is that losers live out their lives, that's where I belong. But I doubt a place like that even exists, and how would I get there anyway?

Finally, I sit back against the school fence to think. The coldness of the chain link feels somewhat soothing against my back.

I know I'm not going to live much longer and I don't see any reason to prolong the inevitable. Some people live until they're

seventy, even eighty years old, but I've known for a long time
that I won't be one of them. I've thought about the end of my
life many, many times—but now, the possibility of dying looms
before me. I was hoping to make it to sixteen, but that hope
is dashed and seems completely unrealistic now. I feel like I've
given this life thing all I can. I've tried my hardest to be a good
and true person, a person that people would like to be around, a
person that God would be proud of. I've tried to be as invisible as
possible in the hallways at school—I always walk with my head
down, my shoulders caved in, hoping that the Trio and the other
kids who hate me won't notice me. So much for that plan.

I've tried hard to do good in school. The only class I can get
an A in is English—but even my English teacher had to have
a talk with me yesterday. She says I'm daydreaming too much
in class. I didn't have the heart to tell her that when my mind
wanders, the thoughts I'm having probably wouldn't fall into
the typical daydreaming category. My social studies teacher told
me that if I don't do well on the next test, my C- will drop to a
D. I've tried to memorize everything he hands out—but I truly
don't give a crap as to where France is. Germany. Australia. I
just don't. If I could be smart like Mark, I might have a chance.
He's read every volume of our World Book Encyclopedias at
least twice and has every fact memorized. I can't even read a
paragraph about France and write a decent report about it.

The truth is, I'm tired. Not the kind of tired like I need
sleep, but the kind that tells me there isn't anything left inside
of me. Chest cavity, abdominal area, skull—all are empty. Soul,
collapsed like a deflated balloon. Today's episode on the stairs
purged my last remaining spark of life right out of me. It's all
sitting on the landing. Right this minute, kids are trampling on
the jumble of me as they make their way to and from gym. This
is not a situation that will be solved by a pair of jeans or the right
tennis shoes. I made it to thirteen; I guess that will have to do,

because there is no reason to continue living at this point.

I know about so many ways I could make myself die. I've thought about cutting open my skin—I do seem to bleed easily, so that would probably work. But what to use to make the cuts deep enough? I've contemplated running, or riding my bike, in front of a car, a bus—or maybe a train, though I'm not sure where to find a moving train. I checked out the school buses one day, and the thing with that is you would have to get hit exactly the right way—there's so much extra room under them it would be possible to get run over and not die.

I look over at the softball field, covered in a pristine layer of snow. The sun shining on the whiteness temporarily blinds my eyes. I suppose I could lie down and try to bury myself in the snow—it's cold enough out here that I would probably freeze to death. But then again, I've been out here for how long now? And I'm still alive. So maybe it takes longer to freeze to death than I think.

Of all the ideas, the best one seems to be the oven at home. I've known for a long time now that if you turn the knob (to any temperature), and you don't light the pilot light, the kitchen will fill with deadly gas. I think it only takes about an hour, so if I turn the oven on right when I get home from school, I should be dead long before Mom gets home from work. I think this is the best option—it will be fast, and there will be no blood or anything for anyone to clean up.

Now that I've made up my mind, I feel calmer. Peaceful even. I feel the muscle of my heart, deep within my chest, softening. My heartbeat slows into a relaxing, steady beat. My brain cells are no longer flurrying around inside my skull trying to figure out what my next move should be, how to defend myself, how to live.

I think my body knows it isn't going to have to last much longer. My heart is beating even slower now, and it is softer, more like the bass guitar holding a rhythm than the drummer pounding out a solo. I can't explain it, but even the cold air on my skin feels good—maybe the pimple on my chin will freeze off and I will die with a clear complexion. My breathing also subsides. I close my eyes. It's possible I may fall asleep.

The sound of a school bus turning onto the circle drive wakes me up, but I'm staying put until mine arrives. Finally, Bus 43 rounds the corner and I hoist myself up—my knees and back are still sore, but the fiery, piercing pain seems to be gone. The cold weather stopped my knees from bleeding, but the fabric is stuck to the dried blood and pulls at my knees as I walk. The winter wind cooled me down: my hands are frozen solid.

On the bus, I think about where my soul will go when I die. I know there isn't any guarantee it will rise all the way to Heaven, but I don't think I qualify for Hell. I hope God can put my tired soul in a quiet, private place for a while. Maybe it could rest on the top of a puffy cloud or something, because I want to be alone. I don't even want to meet Steven or Cecelia right now. I can't handle meeting anyone, not even a soul or an angel.

If Sharon and Elise were on the bus, I would say goodbye to them. But they stayed after school for band practice. In fact, Sharon has something after school almost every day. Volleyball, gymnastics, something for band—there's no way to keep track of everything she's involved in. I wouldn't tell my friends that they weren't going to see me again, but I would thank Sharon for greeting me each morning at the bus stop with a smile. For sharing her sense of humor with me. For being a good friend. And I would thank Elise for teaching me more about sewing than what I already knew. She's tremendously talented, and I'm guessing she'll probably be a famous wedding dress maker someday. I hope that when they find out I'm gone, they will still be able to feel me somehow.

In the house, this 509 where I've always lived, I take a

moment to say goodbye to my room, my records, even my stupid old games. I call Bernice to tell her I won't be able to pick up Gloria today. I ask if she can keep her until Mom gets home— and she says that won't be a problem.

Bernice, my cheerleader.

I don't think Mom will miss me all that much. Maybe a little, but she'll probably be somewhat relieved. I do believe that Mom and Dad are my true parents, something that took me a long time to be certain of. After Gloria was born, I started asking Mom about my birth story. For a long time, her pat answer was that she couldn't remember. She would become irritated, agitated even, when I would ask her. How could she be expected to remember every little thing from her life? And I would be left with the thought that she never had me—revert to my own made-up stories about how she found me at church, picked me up from the side of the street, obtained me through some fancy bank deal. The fact is she carried me in her belly for nine months, resulting in the birth of her first living daughter. Is it possible for someone not to remember something so significant? Then, one day, she told me a story that, such as it was, certified me as a true daughter of Lyla and John.

"You were in the nursery. Your father and the doctor were watching you through the window. Both were smoking. You stopped breathing, and they both ran in. The doctor got you breathing again."

Despite this remarkable lifesaving event, I'm left to wonder what my parents thought of me. Did they hold me? Did they notice my eyes, my eyelashes, my fingers, my toes? Did they kiss me and cuddle me? Did I cry, smile, laugh? Did Mark hold me? Like me? These questions cannot be answered.

If I am their true daughter, that Mom's egg and Dad's sperm joined to create me, then I guess I have a lot of other people in me, too. On Dad's side, I have the Hicks lineage in me. Grandpa and Grandma Hicks, neither of whom I even remember. Dad's many sisters and brothers—my aunts and uncles who are mostly unknown to me. I understand that two of his brothers took their own life, and one of his sisters starved herself to death, according to Mom. So I have all that in me. And Dad, of course, is in me. Part of my blood, part of who I am came from him. But he is lost to me, now. Off in some other world that he alone has created, that he alone lives in. The only emotion left in him is anger.

On Mom's side, I have lots of aunts and uncles, but I rarely see them. My Aunt Sharon, who seems to be very close to Mom, has a hard time liking me, I know that. I can't help it, and I don't have the energy to care about that anymore. My Aunt Charlotte and her family have lived in places I'll never see—New York, Ohio, and now Florida. My Aunt Sharlene, her husband Allen, and my cousin Debbie live right here in New Brighton, go to St. John's and everything, but I hardly ever see them. Aunt Sharlene is quiet, sweet as pie—nothing like my mom or Aunt Sharon. My Uncle Earle is a lawyer and owns a restaurant. He lives in Redwood Falls. but they don't travel much, because both of his boys have cystic fibrosis. What I know about Uncle Earle is that he swears, so maybe that's what I got from him: the ability to curse like a sailor. I know Grandma Tighe pretty well. She's stern and strict but has been generous in letting me come to her house to stay for a week every summer. Plus, she took me to Milwaukee. Grandpa Tighe died about a month before Gloria was born, but I do remember his sweet smile, his cowboy-style hats.

So, for what it's worth, I have bits and pieces of these people in me. And yet I feel very alone, empty.

I'm sitting on the floor of the kitchen now, right next to the oven. My mind drifts back to Mom. I can't think what I got from her, what part of her blood is in me. I suck at math, so I'm surely not going to be a banker. I didn't seem to get any of my physical characteristics from her—she isn't why I have pimples, fat thighs, and a big stomach. As hard as I try to please her, to find a way to bring her happiness, I let her down time after time. I know I do, and I'm out of energy to keep trying to please her. This will give her some relief in her life, one less thing to worry about, to have to deal with.

I open the oven door and turn the knob until I hear the telltale hiss letting me know the gas is coming through the little opening at the bottom of the oven. I take a whiff of the air in the oven to verify that the gas is on. I slide my back against the cabinet, sit on the floor next to the open oven door.

My thoughts turn to my sister. Will Mom tell her she loves her a hundred times a day like I do? Will she take over tucking her in at night? Make sure Gloria's had a bath, had her hair combed out so the curls aren't tangled in the morning? Who will babysit her on Friday nights? Bernice can't, because she and her husband head to Lake Mille Lacs every weekend to go fishing, even in the winter. Will Mom bundle Gloria up in her snowsuit and take her sledding in the winter? Take her to Hansen Park in the winter to learn how to ice skate? Take her for stroller walks in the summer? Make her French toast with lots of syrup on Saturday mornings? Read books to her and teach her math so she becomes smart like Mark? Swim with her at Long Lake in the summer? What if, as my dear, darling sister grows up, Mom tells her she has fat legs and ugly hair? Who will be there to counter those remarks—to tell her she's a beautiful and smart young girl, capable of anything she wants to be? Who will help her, if, God forbid, some idiots at school try to make fun of her? The thoughts course through me, and despite my tired mind, my exhausted heart, my nearly empty soul, they sadden me tremendously; tears start pouring down my face.

Gloria, my sunlight.

I could turn the gas back off. But—what then? I have no energy left to face the miserableness in my life. I don't want to see the Trio ever again. I don't want to go back to Johanna ever again. I don't want to ride the bus ever again.

But—do I want to die? Not see what the future holds for Gloria? For Mark's rock band?

But—to live? Like this?

If I do live, then I need to change. I cannot let people push me around anymore. I don't want to be scared to death of everything anymore. But—how? I've only ever been me, and that's the only person I know how to be. Who in this godforsaken, desolate world of mine can help me through this?

I watch my hand raise and turn the dial to the off position. My hand drops back into my lap. "Well," I say to myself.

I raise myself up off the floor and stand for a second. As I close the oven door and reach for a Kleenex to dry my eyes, the back door opens and, with a whoosh of cool air and a quick burst of sunshine, my brother breezes in.

"Hey," Mark says, taking off his shoes.

"Hey."

"What's up? You look like you've been crying or something," Mark says.

"Yeah, well. I guess I had kind of a rough day."

"Hmm. I guess that happens once in a while. I'm going to make some chocolate milk—want a glass?" Mark asks. If soft-boiled eggs are Mom's answer to anything that ails you, chocolate milk is Mark's.

"Sure, that'd be great," I say, as I make my way to the table. Once our milk is gone, I stare at the clumps of Nestle Quik that have settled into the bottom of my glass. For some reason, it feels like I might start crying again. "Hey, Mark? Can I ask you something?"

"You can ask me anything! I've read every volume of our encyclopedias, you know!" Mark says, proudly.

"Well, this isn't exactly a fact kind of question. I was

wondering—do you think Mom drinks too much beer?" I ask.

"Oh, that's easy! The answer is yes—yes, she does. It's one of her three B's."

"Three B's?" I'm not sure what he's talking about.

"Mom's life revolves around the three B's: the bank, beer and the boob tube. That's just the way she is," he says. As I ponder Mark's theory of the three B's, he decides to change the subject.

"Hey, Randy and the guys are coming over for band practice tonight. You can come down and listen if you want," he says. I am so shocked at this invitation that I don't even know what to say. The coolest person on the planet is inviting me into his personal space, with his friends no less.

"Oh, I don't think you and your friends want a little sister hanging around during practice. Randy, for sure, wouldn't want me down there. Remember that time you and I were fighting, and I slammed the gate right on his one of his drums?" I say.

"Oh, that was back when you were a little kid. My friends think you're cool! I mean it, come down for a bit. You can bring Gloria down, too, if you want."

"Well, okay. Maybe for a few minutes," I say. My mind is spinning. Could this be true? My brother and his friends like me? Mark—he's been my teacher, my role model. Who knows— maybe they'll play my favorite, "Sunshine of Your Love." "Are you going to play 'Sunshine of Your Love?'" I ask.

"Your request has been granted! It'll be the first song on the playlist tonight!" Mark says. And with that, he heads downstairs.

Mark, my idol.

Rising from my seat at the table, I decide to head over to Bernice's to pick up my sister. We have a band practice to attend!

REVENUE

"JOANIE! COME HERE FOR a minute, I need to talk to you about something," Mom shouts from the doorway as she comes in from work. Gloria and I are in my room listening to records, and Mom's request surprises me. Usually, she doesn't speak to us until we sit down to eat supper.

"Be right there!" I call out, turning off the record player. "Come on, Gloria, let's go see Mom."

As I sit down across from Mom, I see she is in a good mood. She looks up at me, smiling. Is it possible she got another promotion at the bank?

"Okay, well, guess what? You have a job!" Mom says, her smile spreading across her face. Mom's eyes have a sparkle to them that I haven't seen in a very long time.

But a job? When do I have time to work? At thirteen, I can't even drive, so how am I supposed to get there? Mark's had a bunch of jobs, but he has a car and is almost eighteen.

"You mean like a paper route?" I ask. Sharon and Elise both have paper routes, so I know that's something kids can do to make money.

"No, not a paper route. You're going to work at the bank!"

Me, work at the bank? They allow kids my age to work at the bank? Not to mention that I'm no good at math. "Oh, I don't think that's a good idea," I say. "I barely have my multiplication tables memorized."

"You're not going to be around money. My friends, Jack and Arlene—you don't know them, but Arlene works at the bank with me—are the ones that clean the bank after it's closed. Their daughter is getting older now and can't help them every night like she used to. I told them you were available, and they thought it was a great idea! Jack will even pick you up, and bring you back home. On Tuesdays, he'll be here at 4:30 p.m. and you'll be home by 7:00. On Friday's, he'll pick you up at 7:30 p.m. and you'll be home around 11:00—that's because they do a more thorough cleaning on Friday nights. They're going to pay you six dollars every week. Isn't that great?"

I have no idea whether this is great or not, but what comes to mind are the janitors at Johanna Junior High—one of them is a creepy, old man and there is no way I want to hang out with someone like that twice a week. "So I'm going to be a janitor? Like, clean the toilets and stuff?"

"Well, sure, you'll have to clean the bathrooms—but there's more to it than that. You'll be vacuuming, emptying the ashtrays, dusting the desks, cleaning the teller windows. That kind of thing."

"Who's going to take care of Gloria?" I ask, hoping this will turn the tide back in my direction. I don't think I want a job.

But Mom tells me she has that all worked out, I am not to worry about Gloria. Bernice will keep her on Tuesdays until Mom gets home, and on Fridays, I'm to take Gloria over to Mrs. Kewatt's house before this Jack guy picks me up. I must hand it to Mom, she thought of everything. It seems that this arrangement, brokered without my knowledge or input, has been finalized.

"Mom, I don't think I want to be a janitor? I want to stay home, if that's okay? Am I not doing a good enough job taking care of Gloria? I can do better, I swear."

"It has nothing to do with that. They need help, you need money, and that is that. You start this Friday."

I guess it's true; I do need money. While I used to pester Mom about getting a pair of jeans, Levi's are not on my current needs list. What I've been nagging Mom about lately is that I need tampons. In my opinion, tampons are a necessity; in Mom's opinion, they, along with the pads with the sticky backing, are a luxury. Therefore, she will not pay for them. I had to sit out the first few days of swimming, and, once the Trio saw me sitting out, they capitalized on it. One day, they followed me into the bathroom, and one of them peeked under the stall to verify that I did, in fact, have my period. I hoped that there was some deadly germ on the floor so that she'd get super sick, but of course, she survived her disgusting expedition.

Mom and I have talked about tampons about a hundred times now, and the conversation ends the same every time.

"Mom, I have my period again, and I need tampons, so I can go swimming at school," I start. "If I don't swim, everyone at school knows I have my period."

"This again. If I've told you once, I've told you a thousand times. I don't have money for tampons! They're considered a luxury item. If you want tampons, you'll have to pay for them yourself." And then she usually works in a reminder about how her brother teased her relentlessly at the outhouse when she had her period, which makes my issue a non-issue in her book.

Once I mentioned that I thought beer and cigarettes would fall into the luxury category.

"What I do with my own money is my business! This is my point exactly—when YOU have YOUR own money you can choose to buy luxury items. Buy a whole store's worth of tampons if you want!"

So I guess it's all settled. Two days from now a man named Jack is going to pick me up, and I will start my career as a janitor at the bank so that I can buy tampons. And maybe a pair of jeans.

At the bus stop the next morning, I tell Sharon about my new employment, and she's curious how much I will make. She tells me her paper route pays a bit more than that and I wonder what I've gotten myself into.

৶

So now, here it is, Friday, the day I start my job at the bank, a place I have a love-hate relationship with. After I make supper and play with Gloria for a while, I take her over to Mrs. Kewatt's house as planned, then sit on the front step and wait for Jack the janitor to arrive.

When his car rounds the corner, I walk down the sidewalk. He drives a square-style car, light blue. The windows are rolled down, allowing the spring air to flow inside. As I approach, he leans towards the passenger side and yells out the window.

"Hi, you must be the famous Joanie I've been hearing about! I'm Jack! Come on in—are you ready to work?"

"I guess so," I reply as I get inside. "I'm not sure what I'm supposed to do, though," I tell him. He leans over and puts his hand out. As I reach over and shake his hand, I notice he has a twinkle in his eyes that would make any Santa jealous.

As we drive, he babbles on about how I will follow him around for the first few times, then be set free with my own vacuum and cleaning cart. Their plan, he informs me, is that once I'm fully trained, I will be responsible for cleaning the entire lower level of the bank. As he's talking, I glance over to get a good look at him. His hair is all white, somewhat thick on the top, but shaved close at his neck. He's on the skinny side but has a little bit of a belly poking out over his belt, and his skin seems tan. He's wearing a white tee-shirt and blackish-gray pants, the same style Bernice's husband wears to work. As he turns out of the neighborhood onto Seventh Street, he tells me about what he calls his day job. He's a driver's license evaluator; he takes people on road tests to certify they can get a driver's license.

"You've got a couple years to go before that happens, right?" Jack asks.

I tell him that I'm thirteen, so I haven't even thought about it. "My brother drives, though! He aced his test—100 percent! He drives an ugly black station wagon, but at least he has a car!"

Jack looks over at me and gives me a quick wink.

It only takes about ten minutes to drive to the bank, so we arrive before closing time. Jack parks right next to Mom's green Chevrolet, and we hop out. He pulls out a keychain with about fifty keys on it and unlocks the door marked *Employees Only*, which is at the back of the bank next to where the drive-thru starts. Inside the entrance, Jack points out a bathroom that only the employees know about and the janitor closet. He unlocks the closet door and gives me a quick tour. It's kind of boring, so I lean against the door frame and watch as he points out the various cleaning supplies, the janitor sink, and so on. There is one supply, however, that I'm guessing would not be found in your typical janitor closet: a small cooler filled with beer that Jack brought in from the car.

"A little juice to get me going!" Jack explains, as he pops open a can, takes a long drink, then nestles it into the pile of rags on the top of his cleaning cart.

"Oh yeah! Gotta have that!" I say with a chuckle. Jack gives me another wink.

Jack told me that since the bank is open until 8:00 p.m., and since customers can walk in right up 'til the stroke of 8:00 (a practice he clearly does not believe in), we have to be quiet and somewhat discreet until all the customers, and then all the employees, are out the door. Arlene, I'm told, will join up with us sometime after 8:00—when her bank duties are complete.

I follow Jack around as he cleans the surfaces not being used by a customer or employee, backtracking when necessary. I see Mom at her desk, but I don't wave or anything, because I have no idea if that's appropriate, and I don't want to embarrass her. The last customer goes out the door around 8:15, and soon after that, Arlene arrives on the scene.

"Joanie, nice to meet you. I'm Arlene," she says. The first thing I notice about Arlene is her sparkling blue eyes. Her reddish-blonde hair is styled like Mrs. Cleaver's on the *Leave it to Beaver Show*—but a little higher. Her eyelids are decorated with blue eyeshadow, and she's even wearing mascara. It seems weird, but she has the same twinkle in her eye that Jack does! A Mrs. Claus, I guess. Arlene has changed out of her bank uniform and is wearing jeans. Jeans! She's as old as the hills, probably older than Mom even, and here she is, wearing jeans! I'm jealous of her and in awe of her, all at the same time.

"I'll just take a quick sip before I get started," Arlene says, as she leans into the nest of cleaning rags and finds Jack's beer.

Throughout the night, I learn the ins and outs of all the cleaning details. I follow Jack around upstairs, then Arlene downstairs, to get the full scope of the job. The only thing I'm worried about is making sure I set everything back on the employee desks the right way—some of them are very particular, I guess. One person complained when their stapler was on the right side of the desk instead of the left, for example. Yikes!

Around 10:00 p.m., the three of us do a final inspection and walk through the whole bank to make sure every surface is bright and shiny for Monday morning. Once we all agree on that, we head out the employee door.

As we get in the car, I notice Jack has a can of beer with him. Apparently, he didn't finish it before leaving the bank. Arlene lights up a cigarette and, after she sets it in the ashtray, takes a sip of Jack's beer.

On the way home, Jack and Arlene tell me what the plan is for next week. When I come back next Tuesday, I'll start out following Arlene around downstairs, and then she'll leave me to myself while she helps Jack upstairs. Next Friday, I'll be completely on my own. As we approach my house, they ask me if I have any questions.

"Just one," I say from the back seat. "When do I get paid?"

Jack and Arlene both chuckle. "We'll pay you every Friday, how does that sound?" Arlene asks.

"Great," I say. "That's perfect."

When I walk into the house, I find Mom in her usual spot on the couch, watching television.

"How was your first night of work?" she asks me. And as I recount my evening for her, I feel that she's truly interested. We finally have something in common.

"Well, that's great!" Mom says, and I notice that she is slurring her speech a bit.

"Jack and Arlene drink beer, too. The same kind as you do," I mention. "Jack keeps a can on his cart, and he and Arlene share it. He didn't quite finish his last can, so he brought it in the car with him. It was kind of weird to have them drinking while they were working and in the car."

"Oh, they've been doing that for years," Mom says.

ॐ

I've been working for three weeks now, and I have eighteen dollars saved up. I figure that must be enough for tampons and a pair of jeans, and, since it's Saturday, Mom has agreed to take me shopping. I'm feeling quite proud of myself that I've earned enough money to buy myself these luxuries, and I can't wait to walk into school on Monday morning with my new pair of jeans!

We head to the grocery store first. While Mom is doing our weekly grocery shopping, I go straight to the aisle where the tampons are. I have no idea how many of the lifesaving devices to buy. Finally, I grab two boxes, which leaves me with twelve dollars; I hope that's enough for a pair of jeans.

At JC Penney, Mom and I search around for the jeans department, but all we can find are polyester pantsuits. Mom finds a saleslady—of course it's a customer from the bank, so the two of them have to chat and get caught up on what's new with this and that. I want to interrupt, but the last thing I need is for Mom to get mad today, so I don't say a word. Finally, Mom asks about the jeans, and the lady directs us to the back of the store.

"Hurry up, I'm getting tired," Mom says while I start looking through the racks. But I can't find what I'm looking for—there are no jeans on these racks.

"Mom, I don't think this is right—there aren't any jeans here. I think we need to ask for help again," I say.

And as much as I tried to prevent her from getting upset, this tips the apple cart, as they say. I can tell she's had enough of this scavenger hunt through JC Penney.

"My God, why would it be so hard to find jeans? Why do you need them today anyway? Let's go home and come back some other time," Mom says, as she sinks into a chair sitting near a mirror. "Your sister is tired, and my feet are killing me. I've had about all I can take for one day."

I need Mom to hang in here with me. I'm SO close to having a pair of jeans.

"Mom, it's okay. I'll go ask. You stay here, okay? Do you want me to take Gloria with me?"

"Ten minutes," she tells me. "We're leaving in ten minutes, whether you have a pair or not. Gloria can wait here with me."

I run off and find Mom's friend exactly where we left her.

"Where are the jeans—like Levi's—for kids my age?" I ask,

trying to help her figure it out. Apparently, she's never been asked to find jeans in the store before. Finally, she seems to understand what I'm looking for, and walks me over to a different area of the store.

"I think I found them," she finally says. "Are these what you're looking for?"

"Yes! Thank you so much!" Jeans are now within my reach.

The next problem is deciding what size to buy. My polyester clothes either say large or size fourteen on them. The jeans on the rack are all in odd sizes, from three to thirteen. There are only four pairs in size thirteen, and none of them are blue. How is it possible that none of them are blue? Ugggh. Every pair of jeans at Johanna are blue; I'm certain of that.

"You're down to two minutes," Mom says, coming up behind me.

"Yeah, I know. I don't suppose there's any chance of going to a different store, is there? Maybe after you rest for a bit?" I ask. "I guess they don't have jeans that are blue here." I know it's dumb to even ask her, but what have I got to lose? Nothing, absolutely nothing.

"No. C'mon, let's go then. It'll have to wait for another day."

But I have convinced myself that today is the day, and whether they are blue or not, I'm bringing a pair of jeans home. I pull a copper-colored pair off the rack and examine them quickly. The back pockets are embroidered with a cute bumblebee, and I decide that's the pair.

I'm so excited my hands are shaking a little. I can hardly count out my money. Mom is standing by, making sure I do it right. Finally, the transaction is complete, and the lady hands me my first-ever shopping bag.

"Congratulations," Mom says, as we get in the car to go home. "You worked hard for those. You should be proud of yourself."

And I am.

FROM JOANIE TO JOAN

I'M TRYING TO GET my courage up to talk to Mom tonight about something, and I'm not doing very well. What if she says no? What if she tells me she doesn't have time for questions tonight? My stomach is all knotted up at the thought of asking her my question, but I know I must.

During supper, I try to set a happy mood.

"So how was your day, Mom? How are things at the bank?" I ask, trying to sound cheerful.

"Oh, it was fine. Same old, same old. Do you remember Mr. So and So? He came in today. It was good to see him, get caught up." I don't know who she's talking about, but nod my head as I eat. Tonight, we're having one of my least favorite meals—tuna on toast.

"Thanks for the great supper!" I say, hoping the compliment will perk her up a little. "Um, I was wondering if you could help me with something tonight?" I ask, hopefully.

"Depends on what it is. Bernice is coming over for cribbage tonight," she answers. But she's kind of smiling, and she didn't say no, so I keep going.

"I don't think it will take too long. I need you to show me how to use a tampon," I say, talking faster than I ever have before. "I want to make sure I know what I'm doing before swimming tomorrow."

Mom sets her fork down and gives me a look that lets me know I've gone too far. I watch her smile fade, her eyebrows scrunch towards her nose. "What do you mean, show you how? You just stick it up there," she says.

"Well, that's the thing—stick it up where? How do you know where to put it?" I have no choice but to push for the answer. There is no way that I'm missing one more day of swimming, and this is the only Mom I have, so I have to make her tell me.

"Joanie, for Heaven's sake, you take it out of its wrapper, and you stick it in! That's all I can tell you," Mom yells.

"Okay, God, Mom—I'm just asking! The nurse at school said I had to ask my mom, and that's you. Excuse me for bothering you!" I scream as I stomp my way to the bathroom.

I wish the school nurse would have helped me with this—I didn't even know we had one until some girls were talking about asking for a pass to go to her office. During math, I asked my teacher if I could go see the nurse, and he gave me a pass. It took all the bravery I could summon up to ask her for help. Her answer was not helpful in the least—she could give me a tampon, but it's up to my mom to teach me how to use one.

Sitting on the toilet, I try to do as Mom instructed. But I can't make it go in. What are these things made of, anyway? It takes me several tries, and four tampons, before one goes in. Heading back out to the kitchen, I hear Bernice's voice—cribbage is about to begin.

As I cross through the living room, I suddenly experience an intense, burning type of pain. I stop walking for a second and catch my breath a little. I had no idea tampons caused pain. By the time I arrive at the table, I can hardly walk.

"Hi, Bernice," I say, wincing in pain.

"Hi there. You don't look so good—are you feeling okay?"

I glance over at Mom. She will be utterly embarrassed if I tell Bernice that it's my first time using a tampon. But she's already pissed off at me, so what does it matter?

"Yeah, well. I'm using a tampon for the first time. I had no idea there was so much pain involved. I don't like this whole womanhood thing," I tell Bernice.

Both Mom and Bernice tell me there should be no pain, no burning.

"You're sure you put it in the right place?" Mom says. What am I supposed to say?

"I have no idea," I say. "It went in, that's all I can tell you. Maybe I'm allergic to the cardboard or something?"

Now I can tell that Mom has her answer as to what's wrong, but I'm still in the dark. Her face lights up; she looks over at Bernice. And then Mom starts chuckling a little.

"Don't tell me you left the cardboard in? Oh, my God, Joanie! Didn't you know you're supposed to take the cardboard out?"

As my face flames into the brightest red of embarrassment it has ever been in, and as my mom lifts her chuckle to full-blown laughter, I fly to the bathroom.

Sitting on the toilet, I try as hard as I can to get the fucking thing out of me. It hurts so badly that I'm pretty sure it could ruin my insides for life, possibly even kill me. I suppose I have third-degree burns. What have I done to myself?

Finally, after I've gotten everything out, I take a deep breath. I looked at the box earlier for directions and didn't find any. I pick it up again—turn it over and over—there must be some way people learn how to use these stupid things! Finally, I decide I'm just going to have to try again. As I pull out another tampon, I see a piece of paper in the bottom of the box. I reach in and pull it out. Directions. What idiot would put the directions in the bottom of the box?

When I come out of the bathroom, I grab my coat. I know I'm going to cry, but it won't be in front of Mom.

"Oh, Joanie!" Mom says, still laughing, as I approach the back door. "I can't imagine how you wouldn't have known that!"

"I'm heading out for a while!" I scream as I go out the back door. "And don't call me Joanie anymore! From now on, I only answer to Joan! And that goes for you, too, Bernice!"

Outside, I run for a bit. When I can't catch my breath, I slow to a walk, then stop and sit down on the curb.

My God! How can my mom be so mean? To laugh at your own child? Your own daughter? And embarrass me in front of Bernice?

And then I make a promise to myself. If I ever have a daughter, I will tell her and show her everything about becoming a woman—everything. I will buy her the latest and greatest products available—even if I have to work three jobs to do it. I will make sure she knows what she's doing, every step of the way.

As I come back in the house, I don't ask how the cribbage game is going, don't say a word—just turn and head straight to my room.

THE SUMMER OF '75

WHEN SCHOOL ENDED IN early June, I don't think anyone on the planet was happier than me. None of the Trio live in my neighborhood, and I don't think they know where I live, so I'm Trio-free for three whole months.

It's been a busy summer so far. Mark is taking classes at Brown Institute—he should be a full-fledged radio announcer by the end of the summer. I'm babysitting Gloria full-time this summer: the only time she goes to Bernice's or Mrs. Kewatt's is on days I work at the bank. Sharon comes over almost every day, and we take Gloria for walks, play games, run through the sprinkler, and have a ton of fun. Occasionally, I get together with Nancy and her sister, Patti Jo, as well. But Nancy continues to have an interest in boys, so we kind of go our separate ways most of the time.

Gloria has a new playmate—a little girl who moved into the house that Brenda used to live in. They are the same age, and the two of them have become best friends. I'm glad she has a friend, but it's a little tricky, because the Mrs. of the house hates me— for absolutely no reason, too! What happened was that Rhonda and Connie were hired to babysit and they came up with the idea to have me come along to help them. They had already checked with the Mrs., and she said it was okay. I couldn't imagine why it would take three babysitters to take care of the little girl and her baby brother, but Rhonda promised I would get paid fifty cents, which didn't sound too bad. Mom said that if the Mrs. was okay with it, then it was okay with her.

On the night the three of us babysat, I spent the whole time in the living room, playing with the kids. We read books, played with toys, and sang songs. At bedtime, Rhonda and Connie gave them a snack. After the kids went to bed, Rhonda gave me fifty cents, and I went home. Easy as pie, right?

The next day, right after Mom got home from work, the Mrs. called. By the time Mom got off the phone, it was clear that something bad must have happened.

"Mom, what did she want?" I asked.

"Well, that's the end of your babysitting over there!" Mom glared at me, eyebrows curved in, mouth formed into its straight-lined angry look. "Drinking wine! What were you thinking!"

"Wine? I don't even know what that is!"

"Oh, don't be so naïve, you know what wine is. And Mrs. So and So who lives next door to them saw you!"

"What is it, Mom? I mean it! Is it like beer or the stuff you drink on Saturdays and Sundays?"

"No, it's not either of those things. It comes in its own bottle, you pour it in a glass and drink it. Mrs. So and So saw you through the window, sitting in the kitchen drinking it. So don't even try to deny it! You're not to ever go in that house again, do you understand?"

"Mom, why would you believe Mrs. So and So? I did NOT drink wine! Swear! I played with the kids in the living room the whole night, never even went into the kitchen," I screamed. "How would Mrs. So and So see into the kitchen anyway? Call her back, Mom. Let me talk to her. I'll tell her I didn't do it."

"We are not calling her back. What's done is done. So make sure you never go over to that house again!"

I tried for a few days to convince Mom to call Rhonda or Connie—they would be able to verify that I did not, in fact, drink wine. Or to call the great Mrs. So and So to see exactly what it was she saw. But no, Mom is going with what was reported. So now, if Gloria is playing at her friend's house, I can't go all the way into the yard to get her—I must stand on the edge of the yard and call her name. And I know that if one Mrs. thinks that I drank wine, so does every other Mrs. in the neighborhood. There goes any chance of me becoming a neighborhood babysitter. Stupid.

歾

While it's true that boys are of no interest to me, there are two amazingly cute guys that work at the bank right now. Apparently, there is a summer program for high-school kids, and these two guys got the job. Last Tuesday I barged into the lunchroom thinking I had the place to myself, and there they were! As I started emptying ashtrays into the overflowing trash bins (bankers are kind of sloppy), someone started talking to me.

"Well, hi there! You don't look like a banker!" one of them said.

"Oh, hi. Sorry, I didn't think anyone was in here."

"My name's Tim, and this is Jeff. We're high school interns— we work afternoons in the mailroom. You look younger than us!" Tim is tall and thin and has short, brown hair. Jeff wears glasses, is a little shorter than Tim, and has blonde, curly hair.

"Oh, well, it's nice to meet you," I said, feeling my cheeks turn a little pink. "I'm one of the cleaners. I help Mr. and Mrs. French. You might know Arlene? She works as a banker during the day. My job is to clean the downstairs on Tuesday and Friday evenings."

"No, we haven't met Mrs. French yet. But like wow! You look awfully young to have a job. What's your name?" Jeff asked.

"Oh, yeah. Well, I'm thirteen—my mom kind of got me the job. I didn't even know about it until it was all arranged. My name is Joan. Joan Hicks. You might know my mom? Lyla Hicks?" I said.

"Wait, your mom is Mrs. Hicks?!" Tim asked. "Far out! We were both scared to death when we had to interview with her! She is one classy lady! You must be very proud of her."

"I sure am!" I said, beaming with pride for my mom. "She's worked here for about twenty years, or something like that."

"Okay—we better get back to work—nice talking to you! See you around!"

"Yeah, same here," I said.

I have my cleaning routine down now—after I get the lunchroom done, I work on the bathrooms, then the dusting (which we only do on Fridays), and then finish with the vacuuming. Typically, once I start vacuuming, I sing to my heart's content. Since the bank is empty, my poor singing voice doesn't bother anyone. I have a long list of songs in my head to choose from, but my favorite songs right now are "I Shot the Sherriff" by Eric Clapton, "Cats in the Cradle" by Harry Chapin, and "I Honestly Love You" by Olivia Newton-John.

But, only one week after I had met them—the boys heard me singing! Apparently, there was more mail yesterday than usual, so they worked a little overtime to get caught up. I had no idea they were still there and stopped singing as soon as I saw them. Oh, my God—I was so embarrassed—my cheeks got incredibly red—redder than ever before! But then, to my amazement, they both smiled at me and went on their merry way—headed up the stairs to leave. I'm absolutely amazed they didn't make fun of me!

⁓

Today is Friday, and Jack is downstairs with me, inspecting my work. I like Friday nights better than Tuesdays, because sometimes Jack and Arlene take me out for pizza after work. We either go to Carbone's, which is kind of by my house or to Big B's, which is by the bank. We always order two large pizzas—one for Jack and one for Arlene and me to share. Mom hates pizza, so until I met them, I had never been out to a pizza place. The pizza at both places is way better than Totino's frozen pizza, but I can't decide if I like Carbone's or Big B's better.

"Well, Joanie. Your work looks great. I think we're all done for the night! Would you like to go out for pizza?" Jack asks as I carry the vacuum up from downstairs.

"Yes! Yes!" I say, smiling.

"Well, who can resist a smile like that? Arlene, what do you think? Are you up for some pizza?"

"Let's do it!" she says, with a huge smile and a wink, and I can't help but giggle. "But first, I think we better pay her! If we forget her pay, she might not come back next week!"

On the way to Carbone's, Jack comes up with an idea.

"Say, how about we get the pizza to go? Then we could take it over to your house and share it with your Mom? Do you think she's still up?"

"Yeah, she's probably still up. She usually watches *The Tonight Show* before she goes to bed. But I don't think it's such a good idea. She doesn't like pizza at all," I say from the back seat.

I don't want to take pizza over to my house. It's not that I don't want to share the pizza with Mom, but I like having Jack and Arlene all to myself. They talk to me like I'm a real person and it appears that they might possibly like me. Plus, Mom will have had way too many beers by now, and probably won't be stable on her feet. Her speech might be a little off. I don't want

Jack and Arlene to see her like that.

Despite my protest, Jack and Arlene decide to give it a try. Even if Mom only has one piece, they think it will be worth it.

When we get to my house with the pizza, I open the back door very slightly and call out to Mom, to alert her to the fact that Jack and Arlene are with me.

"Mom? Surprise! Jack and Arlene are here—they brought pizza for all of us!"

"What? Oh, my goodness," Mom says. I see her grab her beer and head for the refrigerator—she looks startled, and I understand she wants to put her can of beer in the fridge so Jack and Arlene won't see it. "I wish you would've called first!"

Jack and Arlene follow me through the door and see Mom's beer. "I'll have one of those if you have an extra, Lyla!" Jack says. "And one for Arlene, too, if you have enough."

"Oh, okay," Mom says. "I've already had a couple!" As she takes another step towards the refrigerator, she stumbles a little.

"Mom, why don't you have a seat at the table. I'll grab beers for Jack and Arlene," I say—thinking they won't notice that she's a little tipsy if she's sitting down.

Once we're all seated, we start in on the pizza. I have never seen Mom eat pizza in my whole life, and I'm shocked when she helps herself to a few pieces of both kinds.

"Mom? You like pizza?" I ask.

"Oh, you know—sometimes pizza hits the spot!" Mom answers, with a little giggle. "That Canadian bacon and pineapple is delicious!" Though I'm glad to see her eat pizza, I have to wonder where my real mom is tonight.

"Lyla, you've got quite the young lady here. She's a great worker; we're so glad to have her on board!" Jack says, sending one of his winks my way, as our pizza night comes to a close. "We have absolutely no complaints—and she's quite the singer, too!"

"My goodness, I don't think the lower level has ever been so clean! It has taken such a load off us, even if it is only two days a week," Arlene adds. "And that smile of hers—it just can't be beat!"

And at that, I can't help but smile. I'm a little embarrassed to hear their compliments, but proud of myself at the same time. I guess working for a living isn't so bad after all.

"Well, that's good to know!" Mom says. "I'm glad to hear she's doing a good job for you guys."

Once Jack and Arlene are gone, Mom and I clean up the pizza boxes, throw away the paper plates and head to bed.

"Hey, Mom? Since you like it now, do you think we can go out for pizza once in a while? Maybe take Gloria and Mark with us to Carbone's?"

"Oh, no. I wouldn't go so far as to say I like it

Just another mystery about Mom, I guess.

PIE DAY

WE'RE THE ONLY FAMILY on our block with an apple tree, and, despite the rule of nature that states it takes two apple trees to have a good crop, our tree proves the exception. Every spring, right around Memorial Day, hundreds of small pink-tinged buds open into white-petaled flowers, delicately bordered in a blushed-rose color. It seems to me that the annual springtime beauty of the tree is to be expected but, every year, Mom appears to be surprised. "My goodness, look at that tree! Take a deep breath, Joan—can you smell it? Gloria, doesn't it smell pretty? The apples are going to be delicious this year!"

Mom is as protective of the apples as she is of the piano. They belong to her and no one, other than family, should dare to pick even one apple. I'm certain some sort of internal sensor connects her straight to the tree, alerting her instantly if a neighbor kid is picking an apple—or worse, climbing the tree to take more than one. One night a few weeks ago, she was in her bedroom—the room furthest from the backyard—when she heard someone in the tree. I was sitting at the dining table, right in front of the window that looks out over the backyard, and had no idea we were being robbed. Mom came flying into the dining room from her bedroom, notifying me that someone was in the tree. As she slid the window open, she yelled sternly at the criminal: "Get out of my apple tree! Out!" And upon hearing Mom, the offender dropped to the ground and ran for his life. As I watched him (it was one of Rhonda's brothers) run down the alley, I saw that he had succeeded in getting one of the apples. "Just unbelievable that kids would steal apples from us! Unbelievable!" Mom lamented, lighting up a cigarette to try to calm herself down. "We need every apple we can get for pie day!"

The flowers spent the summer months maturing into hundreds of apples, and it looks to me like they have been ready for picking for a week or so, but it's not for me to decide. Mom is the official apple tester, and, since about August 15th, she has conducted a daily review—picking an apple, turning it over in her hands to make sure the color is right, and then taking a bite to determine the taste. Yesterday, the apple she tested was "not quite right," but a day later, it seems the apples are at their peak.

"The apples are perfect today!" Mom declared this morning. "Look at the color—perfectly marbled with red and green," she continued. As she took a big bite from the flawless apple, her taste buds helped her conclude her review. "And the taste— honey flavored, with just a hint of tartness!" I know exactly what this means, but she confirms my thoughts with a final proclamation: "It's pie day!"

Mom and I have been making pies every year for the past eight years or so, but this is the first time that Gloria will be helping, and she instantly senses a celebration at hand. At four years old, she asks more questions than we have answers for. Today, her questions are all about the apples and how to make the pies.

"First, the two of you need to pick the apples!" Mom claps her hands in excitement. "Are you ready, Joan? Let's head outside!"

By the time pie day arrives each year, the lower branches are so heavy with mature fruit that some of the apples are within arm's reach—these are the ones that Mom picks. As Mom relieves these branches of their excess weight, they slowly rise back to their original positions.

While Mom obtains a bag or two of apples from the lower branches, Gloria and I tackle the rest of the tree. Mark used to be the one to climb up the center of the tree, but as he grew older and had other things to do, I took over. Today, my plan is to see how high Gloria can climb—if she's not too scared, then I can stay on the ladder.

"Okay, Gloria, see all the apples way up high? Do you think you can climb up there and pick them?" I ask.

"I can do it!" Gloria says, with confidence and a great amount of energy. I give her a boost into the center of the tree and watch as she climbs up towards the blue sky. Gloria has the kind of skin that tans instead of burning, and, as she climbs, the white bottoms of her feet are almost shiny in contrast with the rest of her dark brown skin. "It's kind of like being on the jungle gym at the park!" Gloria squeals.

"Yep!" I say. "Be careful—make sure you get one of your feet in between the branches before you let go with your hands."

She's moving fast, with no fear whatsoever.

"Okay, that's high enough. Now start picking. When you get one, hand it down to me before you pick another. When you can't reach any more, move side to side instead of up—otherwise, you won't be able to reach me," I instruct, standing on the top rung of our ladder, which I've wedged in between the branches she just climbed. The paint-speckled wooden stepladder is quite wobbly, and Mom holds the bottom while I try to steady a paper grocery bag on an angled branch. As soon as we fill one bag, I send it down to Mom, trying desperately not to drop it as this will bruise the apples. Once Mom has the full bag, I head back up the ladder with another empty one. Mom saves her paper grocery bags all year long for this purpose.

"See the apples just below you? Come down a little to get those." I tell Gloria, guiding her down to the next level of fruit.

"Wow! There's lots of apples!" she says, and she's right. We've already filled about eight bags, and there are still a lot of apples within view.

Once we're done with the inside of the tree, we attack the branches that lean on the high, white wood fence that divides our yard from the neighbors. We climb all the way up and all the way down the fence, adding four more bags of apples.

"How about some Kool-Aid for my hardworking girls?" Mom thankfully offers, as we come down off the fence. "It's a little warm out here today!"

It's true—the temperature is probably around ninety degrees, and it's a little humid. But I for one am glad it isn't raining—I hate picking apples in the rain.

"Okay, time to get up on the garage," Mom announces, as we finish our snack.

"Can I go up? Can I?" Gloria asks. She's a little dynamo, full of vim and vigor.

"Yes, but let's have Joan go first," Mom says. I'm not sure Gloria's old enough to go on the garage, but once Mom says it's okay, my little sister starts jumping up and down with excitement.

I move the ladder so that it's under the overhang of the garage, and Mom holds it while I climb up. There's a gap between the top step of the ladder and the roofline, and I have to jump-hop onto the asphalt shingles.

"Mom, it's ungodly hot up here. The shingles are burning. I think Gloria better have shoes on," I recommend, as I try to get my footing on the steep slant.

In a flash, Gloria runs into the house and retrieves her sandals, which Mom helps her put on. When she gets to the top step of the ladder, I reach down, grab both of her hands and tell her to jump. She's not scared—but I am—and once she's all the way up,

I breathe a sigh of relief.

The long, stiff branches on this side of the tree graze the roof of the garage, so I stand on the edge of the roofline and pluck apple after apple. My fearless sister is now afraid she will fall off the edge of the garage, and I can't blame her, so I tell her to stay in one place and hold the bags. Once I've gotten all the apples I can reach, Mom hands up the apple picker, which is a wire basket attached to a broom handle. The wire on one side of the basket pokes out a bit, and I maneuver it under an apple and snatch the piece of fruit off the tree. The basket can hold about six apples, but negotiating the heavy basket from the tree back onto the sloped garage roof is a balancing act—I feel like a tightrope walker with an unbalanced bar. By the time I'm done, the only apples left on the tree are on the highest branches near the power line.

Mom is satisfied with our bounty, and once we have the twenty or so bags of apples in the house, we have a quick lunch. Now it's time to make the pies.

"We've got a lot of apples to peel, Joan!" Mom exclaims, as though it was the best activity anyone could be doing on a Saturday afternoon. "Let's get started."

Mom uses a paring knife, and it's quite amazing to watch her, because she can peel a whole apple in one long, continuous strip. I use an apple peeler, and, despite this being my tenth year or so, I still can't create an unbroken ribbon of skin.

"Okay, Gloria, climb up in my lap and help me peel the apples," I say.

"Why?" she asks.

"Because," I say, with a wink. I already know where this is going, and so does she.

"Because why?"

"Because, because, because!" I say, getting ready for the finale, which involves me making a buzzing sound and tickling her. "Bzzzzz . . . bzzzz . . . " Her laughter is as contagious as ever, and Mom and I both start laughing as well.

Once we have a good start at peeling, Mom starts creating the pie crust. Incredibly, the only ingredients required for pie crust are flour, water, salt, and butter. She doesn't need a recipe for the crust—but stops her kneading when it feels "just right."

"How many pies are we making today, Mom?" I ask.

"Well, I've got thirty pie plates, so that's my goal. Gloria can help you deliver the pies to the neighbors this year."

Mom can bake four pies at a time, so once she has lined the bottoms of four tins with crust, I start slicing until each plate has a large mound of fruit in the center. After sprinkling a quarter cup or so of a cinnamon-sugar mixture over the top of the apples, Mom places dots, as she calls them, of butter on top. As she starts to roll out another set of crusts to drape over each pie, I go back to peeling. From my spot, I watch Mom pinch the edges of each pie with her thumb and index finger, then hold each one up in the air so she can trim off the excess crust. Using her paring knife, she makes a few slits in the top, and then, right before they go in the oven, she dusts the top of each pie with a smidgen of the cinnamon-sugar mixture.

"Okay, the first four are in! Let's get going on the next batch!" Mom says happily. On pie day, Mom has almost as much energy as Gloria does.

When the first four pies come out of the oven, the next four go in, and we start the process all over again. As soon as a set is cool enough, Mom wraps them in foil and sets them aside for delivery. The smell of apple-cinnamon fills our hot kitchen, and the once-a-year aroma sinks deeply into my lungs.

"Can you smell the pies? Don't they smell delicious?" I ask my sister, who is squirming like crazy on my lap.

"Yes, but when can we eat some?" Gloria asks.

"As soon as you girls are done delivering, we'll have a slice!" Mom promises. She is as anxious for a sample as Gloria and I are.

"Okay! Let's get started!" I say. "We better wash up and change our clothes first—we're a mess!"

Mom sends us off with two pies at a time, and at each house, we are greeted with ear-to-ear smiles from our neighbors.

"Oh, we were wondering if your mom was going to make pies this year," more than one of them tells us. "Be sure to tell her thank you!"

"Mrs. Johnson said to say Thank you! They're going to have their pie right now!" Gloria tells Mom as we come back in the house.

Once we are done with our deliveries, Mom comes through with her promise. She slices into a warm pie and puts a big slice on each of our plates. I add a scoop of ice cream to each—and then we dig in. Sliding my fork through the crisp, flaky crust, I lift the first bite into my mouth and let the cinnamon-sugar-apple mixture settle on my taste buds before swallowing. An extravagance, I think, to have such a delicious delicacy right here in our own home.

"Good job, team! A job well done! Thanks for all of your help," Mom says. "What do you think of pie day, Gloria?"

"The best part is eating it!" she says, with a giggle.

"Joan, can you put the rest of the pies in the freezer? Won't it be nice to have a fresh apple pie this winter?" Mom says.

"I hope they last that long!"

"Hmm, well look at this," Mom says. And again, I know what's coming. "We seem to have a lot of apples left over." Every year Mom seems surprised that we have an excess of apples, but I figured out a long time ago that ten bags is more than enough for the number of pies we make. "Joan, why don't you take the extras around to the neighbors, see if anyone wants some apples?"

And so, as pie day ends, I go around and offer bags of apples to any neighbor who wants them, including the families of the kids who Mom was so mad at for trying to steal them.

FROZEN

MOM ARRIVES AT BERNICE'S, and, as we walk home, Mom wants to know exactly what Dad said. She seems a little agitated. I try to recall the conversation as best I can.

"That's all he said?" Mom asks.

"Well, he also asked how old I was, but that's about it."

Walking up the sidewalk, we hear the phone ringing. When we get inside, Mom answers and I can tell it's Dad.

"What do you want, John?" she asks. Whatever it is, Mom denies his request and slams down the phone. In an instant, the phone rings again. Mom answers, and basically the same scenario plays out. By the time Mom is finished frying up our pork chops for supper, Dad has called about twenty times.

"Let's leave it off the hook for a while," Mom suggests. And so, the receiver of the phone is put on the ledge while we eat. The last time Dad pulled the phone out of the wall, Mom decided to upgrade to a more modern style, so now we have an ivory-colored receiver with the dial thing right in the center of it. When it's off the hook, it makes a strange sound for a bit, then an operator comes on announcing that "the call cannot be completed," and then silence ensues.

When I finish up the dishes, I get the okay from Mom to use the phone to call Sharon. I put the receiver back on the cradle to reestablish a connection, and it instantaneously starts ringing.

"Why don't you try talking to him?" Mom suggests. When I answer, my voice is shaky and wobbly, but Dad doesn't seem to notice.

"Joanie! What's going on over there! Who've you guys been talking to for the last hour? I called and called, but all I got was the busy signal!" Dad's voice sounds animated—like a salesperson trying to sell a used car on television. I guess he's excited that he got through to us again.

"Oh, I was talking to a friend," I lie, sensing that Dad wouldn't appreciate us having taken the phone off the hook to avoid his calls.

"Well, let me talk to your beautiful mother, will you? She's there, on the couch, right?" And, though just about anyone could predict that Mom would be on the couch after supper, I'm a little taken aback by his comment.

"Yeah, she's right here," I say, handing the phone to Mom.

When she's done talking to him, she hangs up the phone, and I am not surprised when it rings again. This time she decides to let it ring, instead of answering or taking it off the hook. And it rings. And it rings. After what seems like about fifty rings, we are both almost out of our minds. Mom finally picks up the receiver, and I think she's going to answer it, but instead, she hangs it up as fast as she can. And as fast as she hangs it up, it rings again.

"I don't know what to do. He won't tell me where he is, and he's not making any sense," Mom says, obviously disturbed by the constant phone calls. It takes a lot—and I mean a lot—for Mom to cry, but right now, she looks as if she's is going to let loose. She's also had about six beers, and I'm worried she's getting a little tipsy.

"Do you think he's drunk, Mom? At a bar or something?"

"I don't know. I'm trying to think of a place where he could have constant access to a phone. I don't even know where he's living right now. I can't imagine where he is."

ଚ୬

By the time bedtime rolls around, we're all tired of listening to the phone ring. I finally counted how many times it rings before he either hangs up and redials; the magic number is forty. Each time, right after the fortieth ring, there is a brief pause before the ringing starts again. I don't even want to look at the phone anymore, let alone listen to the ringing.

"Okay, Gloria! Time for bed!" I say, scooping her up. "Let's get your jammies on—then you're going to brush your teeth, okay?"

"Are we going to do a three-way hug tonight?" she asks, hopefully—and I can see the joy of anticipation on her face. The incessant ringing of the phone has not affected her spirit!

"I think so!" I answer. "Mom, Gloria's ready—and she wants to do a three-way hug!" I shout. I pick Gloria up, and she puts one arm around me, one around Mom; Mom and I do the same, and soon we are assembled into a kind of huddle. Gloria is already giggling as we give each other good night kisses—by the time we start with our "crazy kisses," where we kiss each other faster and faster—all three of us are in a full belly laugh. Finally, Mom and I pretend to drop Gloria to the floor, giving her the signal that it is officially bedtime. Gloria, still giggling a little, hops into bed.

"That was fun!" Gloria proclaims as Mom and I tuck her in, turn off the light and shut the door.

Back in the family room, Mom and I continue to listen to the phone ring. She tries taking it off the hook, but as before, as soon as she hangs it up it starts ringing again. Dad has been calling the house for over five hours now, and it's taking a toll on both of us.

"I think we should put the couch in front of the door tonight," Mom says.

"Yeah, I think so, too," I agree. Though I don't know for sure that Dad made any threats, I know that if Mom suggests moving the couch, she must feel it's possible he will pay us a visit later tonight. Mom and I each take an end of the couch, lift it up and put it in the back doorway—making it impossible for him to break in. It works, too. The last few times Dad tried to break the door down, he was stopped in his tracks—giving Mom time to crawl over the couch and call the police while Gloria and I stayed in our rooms. One time, I heard Gloria wake up, so I took her into bed with me, so she wouldn't be too scared. Each time the police came and scared Dad away, and we went back to sleep—safe and sound.

Once we get the couch in place, Mom takes the phone off the hook and we work our way over the couch and head to our rooms. I'm feeling jittery—something about this whole night seems weird. I decide to read for a while—try to calm my nerves down a bit.

৩৬৩

I'm not sure how long I've been asleep when I wake up to the sound of Dad pounding on the back door. I wonder how long he's been at it? Even from my bedroom, in the back of the house, I can hear him yelling. I wait a few minutes, waiting for the police to arrive, waiting for the silence of the house to return. I haven't heard Mom on the phone—maybe she called the police before I woke up? But soon, I decide something is wrong—the police should've been here by now. Once, I had to wake Mom up—Dad's pounding and yelling weren't enough to wake her. I wonder if that's the case tonight.

The pounding continues as I nervously sneak out of my room to investigate. Creeping slowly down the dark hallway, I stop in

Mom's room and find her bed empty. Where is she? I briefly wonder if Dad broke in already, but the pounding on the back door assures me he is still outside. Walking through the living room, I call out to Mom.

"Mom, are the police on their way?" No response. I repeat my question, a little louder this time. Still, no response. I'm scared, not sure what to do—the police must be called—but where is my mom? Why isn't she answering me?

I walk cautiously—I'm tiptoeing, though it occurs to me that my footsteps could never be louder than the noise Dad is making—through the dark living room and kneel near the piano bench. Peeking around it, I look up at the window on the back door and see Dad's face. He's staring into the family room. He's pounding constantly with both fists. His eyes have that blue ice fire look to them. "Lyla, let me in! You will let me in, or I will come in!" My God, he is strong—pounding the door so hard that the wood is moving, almost buckling with each punch. Then he starts kicking the door, and I see the couch start to move—Dad is moving the couch from the outside. Crouching down, I get right next to the couch, then leap onto it and run across it as fast as I can, hoping with all hope that Dad will not see me. I was unsuccessful, however, and when he sees me, he becomes even more enraged.

"Open this door, Joanie! Open it now! Be a good girl, not a bitch like your goddamned mother! Goddamnit, open this door!"

As I bolt the rest of the way through the kitchen, he repeats his requests, adding more profanity, and continues pounding and kicking. I'm calling for Mom, but still she doesn't answer. Where is she? Finally, I see her. She's huddled beside the refrigerator and, though she is out of his line of sight, I'm sure Dad knows exactly where she is. Mom is holding the phone receiver, sitting quietly on the floor, legs splayed out in front of her. In the darkness, I can see the phone cord, which is at its stretch limit—pulled so tight it looks like a misplaced clothesline. Sliding under the cord, I crouch down next to Mom. There is a stillness about her—she does not look up at me or speak to me as I enter her hiding space. Her eyes are looking down into her lap; her chin is almost touching her chest. Her face is a shadow, slightly lit by the dim bulb in the receiver of the phone. I hear the repetitive "whaa—whaa—whaa" sound we listened to earlier. My body is shaking; I can feel tremors in my arms, feel unsteadiness in my legs. My breathing is fast. How am I going to break Mom out of this bizarre trance?

"Mom, did you call the police?" There is no response. She doesn't even lift her head to look at me. She appears to be frozen in place.

"Mom! Answer me! Did you call the police?" I scream. I put my hands on her face, try to get her to look up at me. I peek around the refrigerator to look at the back door—it's open a tiny bit, and the couch is slanted. Time is running out. My breathing speeds up even more; my heart feels as if it will leap right out of my chest.

"Mom!" I'm furious with her now, but she will not respond to me. I must break her out of this spell—must melt the ice off her! I want her to answer me, but more than that, I *need* her to.

"No," she finally murmurs, so quiet I can't be sure what she said.

"No? You didn't call the police? What do you mean? Mom, you must call right now! Dad's going to get in any minute! Can't you see that? Call right now, Mom!" I twist my body so that I can look into her face. "Mom, call now! Dial the number! Can you hear the pounding? The door is already open—it's going to break, Mom. You have to call right now!"

"I can't," she says. What is wrong with Mom? I can't imagine why she wouldn't want help. Frantically, I try to take charge, try to get the phone away from her.

"Give me the phone, Mom! I can call! Give it to me!" But she will not. In fact, her grip tightens around the receiver as if she means to hold onto it forever. I try to pry her hands off, but it's no use.

"If you won't give me the phone then you must dial, Mom! Right now! Do you hear me, Mom? Right now! 633- . . . !" But Mom is still under the influence of the frozen spell; she doesn't move, doesn't make any attempt to put her finger into the rotary dial.

And then, it's too late. In an instant, the couch goes all the way up, and the door flies open. Dad scrambles over the couch, runs in, and stands in front of us. Mom moves her head down farther into her lap—I put my body around her as best I can to try to shelter her, to block Dad from being able to get to her.

"Dad! No!" I scream as he reaches around me and grabs the phone out of Mom's hands, pulls the cord, our lifeline, out of the end of the receiver, throws the destroyed contraption across the room.

"Called the police, did you? They are going to save you, ha? Think again, bitch. And you, Joanie. You couldn't see straight enough to let your dear old Dad into his own house? Who do you think you are?"

He moves away from us, pulls the base of the phone off the wall. He makes it look easy, as though he is merely taking a picture frame off a nail. In a flash he's back, looming over the two of us. He grabs Mom out from under me, lifts her up a little while he drags her to the middle of the floor. Mom looks like a rag doll—looks as if she has no muscles at all. I watch as Dad lands a punch on her face and then throws her down onto the kitchen floor.

"Dad, no!" I scream again, sobbing. But it appears that Dad has no idea I'm there anymore. It's all about Mom now.

In his escalated rage, Dad kneels and straddles his body over

Mom, puts her arms up above her head and holds them there with one hand, while he uses the other hand to strike her. "You think you're so smart! What kind of a fool do you think I am? This is my house! Why can't you understand that?"

I know we need help, but how to get it? Oh, how I wish Mom would have called the police! I think it's possible Dad might succeed in killing her this time! I've got to do something, but what? How? To get out of my spot, I will have to go around the two of them or jump over their combined bodies somehow. My heart is beating furiously in my chest, in my ears, everywhere. I can't do it. But I must. I can't do it. But I must. Finally, I talk myself into it. I jump from my spot, leap over their outstretched bodies and head to the open doorway.

Outside, I scan the neighborhood to see if anyone has lights on, but all the houses are dark. Everyone but us apparently asleep. I run into the street, try shouting—"Help! We need help!" My frantic screams empty out into the dark night sky; no lights come on.

I could run to Bernice's, but if I do that, I won't be able to see our house. I decide to run to Nancy's, directly across the street. I hop their chain link fence, run to the back door, fling open the screen door and start knocking. When no one answers, I pound even harder and scream as loudly as I can, "Help! Wake up! We need the police! I think my dad is going to kill my Mom! My God, someone, anyone, please wake up!" I'm just about to give up when I see their kitchen light come on. It worked! They're awake!

Mr. Kewatt, the rest of the family behind him, opens the door and I frantically try to tell them what has happened, what is happening. My speech is too rapid, though, my words so garbled they can't understand me.

"Slow down, Joan," I hear Mrs. Kewatt say. I try as hard as I can to breathe, to talk a bit slower, and finally, they understand.

"You have to call the police," I beg. Then I see Mr. Kewatt

looking up the phone number in the New Brighton phone book—he doesn't have it memorized like we do, and, though I had recited the number to my mom, I cannot remember it now. I start to panic—"Hurry, Mr. Kewatt," I beg. "Hurry!"

I run to their living room, and look out the little window on their front door so that I can watch our house. Mrs. Kewatt, Patti Jo, and Nancy are standing right behind me—the four of us all trying to see out the tiny window. I see Dad's dilapidated van parked in front of the house—so I know he's still there. Mr. Kewatt finally comes in the living room and tells us the police are on their way. "Oh, my God. Oh, my God," I say, starting to cry. "I've got to get back over there! I've got to save my mom!"

But as I start to open their front door, Mrs. Kewatt steps in front of me, blocks my path. Then she wraps me in her arms.

"You can't go over there right now," she tells me. "It isn't safe; you're going to stay right here with us for now." Mr. Kewatt, standing behind her, nods in agreement and I know there is no point in arguing. Sobbing, I stand at the window with the Kewatt family, who are also weeping, and watch for the police to arrive.

Finally, we hear sirens—two police cars come screeching around the corner, their lights flashing, waking up the night that surrounds my dark house. The five of us are stunned into silence as we watch two officers jump out of their cars and sprint to the side door.

A moment later, a beam of light shines onto our back step, indicating someone has turned on the kitchen light. I plead with Mr. and Mrs. Kewatt to let me go—trying my hardest to convince them it must be safe now that the police have arrived and are in the house. Finally, they relent, and I run out the door.

As I fly across the street, I notice I'm wearing Nancy's pink robe. How in the world? I almost trip on the hem as I meet one of the police officers and my dad on our front sidewalk. Suddenly, I realize that the officer is escorting Dad to his van. Dad is not

going to jail? He gets off scot-free in this? I listen as the officer
scolds my dad.

"Now, John, we don't want any more trouble tonight, okay?
You got somewhere to go to cool off? I think that would be a
good idea. Let's leave well enough alone for tonight, okay?"

At this, I freak out. My hands fold up into themselves, making
tight fists. My arms raise up, and I know my fists are ready to hit
something, someone. I try as hard as I can not to hit the officer,
but I cannot stop my rage altogether. For the second time that
night, I scream out into the dark night and let the police officer
have it.

"Who do you think you are putting my dad into his own car,
letting him go free?! He is so drunk he can hardly walk! And
he almost killed my mom! For God's sake, put him in jail! I'm
begging you!"

"Okay, young lady," the police officer replies. How can he be
so calm? "I think it's time for you to get back in the house. Your
dad already told me he is going to go somewhere and cool off for
a bit. He promised there wouldn't be any more trouble tonight.
You go on in the house now."

"Go cool off? And just where do you think he will do that?
He'll probably go around the block and be back here as soon as
you guys are gone! Can't you see that? For God's sake, any idiot
could figure that out!"

I lose the battle; my screaming does no good. Dad looks over
at me. In the flashing of the police lights, I see that the blue ice
that was in his eyes has melted away. Oh, and he is smiling. He
is satisfied with himself? I watch as he climbs into his rat-trap
van and drives away.

Now, my anger shifts to Mom. Storming back into the house,
I can feel my body, my heart, my everything, fuming. I'm ready
to unleash my anger at her, tell her how disappointed I am with
her for not calling the police. I want to know why she couldn't

dial the phone, why she put our safety at risk. By the time I come through the broken-down doorway, I am ready to burst.

But—then. As I come in, I see Mom sitting in the only chair that's not overturned, near the Duncan Phyfe table that's laying awkwardly on its side. A police officer, dabbing at her face with a small piece of white cloth, nods in my direction. "I'll be fine," Mom says to the officer, holding her arms across her chest, wincing a bit as her wounds are being tended to. She is alive.

I don't know what to do, what to say. The anger I felt towards Mom a fraction of a second ago is gone, but it hasn't been replaced with anything. I'm empty.

And then . . . to my horror, in the still-dark living room, I catch a glimpse of Gloria. How could I have left her? What had she heard? What, at her young age, had she seen? I should have known better! I had left her, and now here she is, sucking her thumb, standing near the piano. My sister looks as though she's rooted there, planted firmly in place like the old ash tree in our front yard.

I turn to Gloria and extend my arms toward her—she instantly jumps up into them. Her little legs, fully encased in feet pajamas, grip my waist; her arms encircle my neck. Her darling head, curls strewn randomly, cuddles itself in the hollowed-out shell of my shoulder.

"I couldn't find you," she whispers into my ear, tears now trickling down both sides of her face. We both cry. Our tears roll down our cheeks, flow down the slopes of our necks, sneak under our pajamas, and finally pool near our hearts. Closing my arms around her in a tight embrace, I feel like the two of us are one person, inseparable from here on. As I hold her, our collective gloom overtakes me. My stomach starts to quiver; my arms are shaking so hard, I think I may lose the strength to hold her. The deep channels of my heart and soul slowly fill with disbelief. *Why? Why did this happen again?*

"You can sleep with me, okay?" I tell Gloria as I carry her into my bedroom.

I climb into bed, robe and all, scooping Gloria in with me. I lay on my side and tuck her small, trembling body into my own. I gently drape the covers over us and tighten them at the edges so that we are wrapped together, cocooned. She keeps asking me where I had gone, and truthfully, I don't know how to explain it; I don't want her to know I had forgotten about her.

"Where did you go when Daddy was being mean to Mommy?"

"I had to go get help, sweetie. I had to go find the police officers. And then I came back to you."

"But where did you go?"

"I went over to Mr. and Mrs. Kewatt's house. Mr. Kewatt called the police for us. I had to stay there for a while before I could come home."

"I couldn't find you."

"I know. I had to wait for Mr. Kewatt to tell me it was safe to come home so that I wouldn't get hurt. When he told me it was safe, I came right home to you." I squeeze her tighter. I try to wipe her tears, but the best I can do is smear them across her cheeks.

"Go back to sleep, sweetie. I'm right here. I promise I won't leave you again."

Finally, her thumb finds its way into her mouth and she settles into what I can only assume is going to be a troubling sleep.

As my sweet sister drifts off, I find myself crying again. Sobbing. Moaning. At some point, it lets up a little, but then it starts right back up. My pillow is sopping wet with tears. I try as hard as I can to stop crying, but that just makes me feel sick— like I'm going to throw up. My body is trembling so powerfully I'm sure it will wake my sister. It feels like the time I had the chills when I was sick, but I know that I am not sick now.

My body finally settles itself. I'm not shaking anymore. I don't think I'm going to throw up either. As these bodily reactions subside, however, I switch into some sort of high gear, I feel electrified! My eyes burst open in the dark bedroom and thoughts start racing through my mind. *I can't count on Mom to call the police; I better come up with a way to keep us safe.*

My dad is out there somewhere, and that, combined with the dismantled phone and the door hanging by its hinges, fills me with fear. If he comes back tonight, he will have instant access to the house. I need to figure out a way to keep my family safe.

I'll need to spring into action immediately if Dad enters the house. But how can I get us out of the house with Dad in it? The best escape plan I can think of is to use my bedroom window. My plan: if I hear Dad arrive, I'll open my bedroom window, swiftly kick the screen out and jump to the ground. I made the three-foot jump once before when Mark banished me to my room, so I know it isn't a big deal. After I'm safely on the ground, I'll tell Gloria to jump into my arms. But what to do once we're outside? Even our shadows are going to need to be under cover to stay hidden from Dad's ice-blue eyes. I try out a few scenarios, then decide on the best one. I repeat it over and over in my mind, to memorize it.

Wake up Gloria and tell her to stand at the window and be quiet—no crying allowed. Open window. Kick screen to the ground. Tell Gloria (again) to stay by the window. Jump out of window. Immediately turn around and tell Gloria to jump into my arms (tell her not to be scared). Pick her up and run towards the alley (think fifty-yard dash from school). Climb over the fence (one at a time). Pick Gloria back up and run to Bernice's. Knock on Bernice's door until someone wakes up. Tell whoever does to call the police.

This plan will hopefully get us through tonight, but then what? I need a bigger plan, something that will keep us safe in the future. We need someone to help us, but who? I haven't been praying much lately, and supposedly God doesn't answer prayers on the spot, but, at this point, anything is worth a try. *God, if there is anything you can do to keep us safe, please do it.*

I wonder what good it would do to call the New Brighton Police. I don't believe they are the ones who can help us with this. They are good for an instant scare tactic, someone of authority that can tell Dad to go cool off or whatever, but it doesn't seem they have a way to stop his behavior. They have no way of knowing where he is or predicting what he's going to do.

Even if I could find a way to call Mark, what could he do? How far away is Spearman, Texas from New Brighton, Minnesota? I have no idea.

The clock ticks, the night is tilting towards morning, and I still don't have a plan.

What happened to Mom tonight, anyway? Mind frozen like a block of ice, body as limp as the wilted celery in our refrigerator. If she isn't going to call the police to come when Dad's in one of his rages, then I don't think Gloria and I should stay here. It obviously isn't safe. But maybe it was a one-time thing or something? Maybe she had some sort of episode that made it so she couldn't think right? Maybe she needs to see a doctor of some kind?

If I could figure out what's wrong with my dad, that would help. If I knew what was wrong with him, maybe I could cure him. I don't know if he's an alcoholic—I'm not even sure what that is, other than someone who drinks a lot. If that's all there is to it, then a lot of other people in my life are also alcoholics, including Mom.

Maybe there's something wrong with Dad's brain? Mom recently told me about a young man who came to the bank to get a loan for a brand-new car. "That man was not playing with a full deck, if you know what I mean," she said.

"Actually, I don't," I said. "What does it mean?"

"Well, he didn't have any collateral, hardly any money for

a down payment, and he comes waltzing into the bank to get a loan. Any idiot knows you need both of those to qualify for a loan. I think he's missing his Ace of Spades," Mom concluded.

So maybe Dad is missing his Ace of Spades? Maybe it was taken out and replaced with the Joker? Is the Joker creating havoc—running wild in his brain? The only card game I've played that involves the Joker is War. Is Dad at war with us? With himself?

Maybe Dad has been taken over by the Devil? If that's the case, how can I get Satan and his ugly, slimy, fork-tongued snake to take care of this once and for all? The Devil certainly has the power required for the situation, but how can I tap into it?

Never moving or releasing my hold on Gloria, I close my eyes tightly and try to bring the Devil right into me—ask him to tell me his thoughts on the matter at hand. And then, I hear him—his words are in me, coming fast. I try to listen closely, but he's talking so fast it's hard to keep up.

"There's a baseball bat in the basement—the one Mark tried to use against Dad when he was six. Move it to your room so it can be used as a weapon. Dismantle the brakes on your Dad's rat trap van, so that he will have a major car accident, make him sail right off a bridge like on Hawaii 5-0. *Start the house on fire the next time you're home alone. No house, no break-in . . . "*

Visuals of each of these scenarios flash before my eyes like scenes from a horror film, and I quiver. I had no idea it was so easy to talk to the Devil. But now, watching these snippets of horror in my mind, I start to feel woozy: my stomach is acting nervous again. I see blood spray across the kitchen wall as the baseball bat connects with Dad's head. I see Dad's van jet off a bridge and crash into the water below. I see bright-orange flames leaping into the sky during the fire, feel their heat even.

But in the end, every one of the schemes ends in futility. I open my eyes a little and realize that a thirteen-year-old girl could never carry out the plots and schemes Satan is proposing. It's been proven time and again in gym class that I can't swing a bat, so how would I ever do it right—so that I hurt my dad? I don't know where the brakes are on a car. Destroying the house with fire would leave us with no place to live. I try summoning Satan again, modifying my request: please send me a plan that I can carry out. But apparently, the situation is too much to handle, even for him—he gives me nothing more.

෨෨

My eyes snap open. My God. What's wrong with me? What kind of a kid plots out how to kill their own father? What a horrible person I am! A sinner, certainly, but more than that, a horrible, horrible person. I could go to confession every day for the rest of my life and never get over this transgression that has stained my soul.

෨෨

At around 6:45 a.m., I unwrap my arms from around Gloria's slumbering torso and peel away the layers of bedding. I have fifteen minutes to get to the bus stop. As I choose some clothes from the floor and start to put them on, Gloria stirs. I bend over her, smooth a strand of hair away from her face.

"I have to go to school. Go back to sleep; Mom will wake you up when it is time to go to Bernice's," I tell her. A few minutes later, as I slip out of my room, I notice she has already fallen back to sleep.

As I pass by Mom's room, I wonder if she's asleep. It occurs to me that she might have lain awake all night, too. Is she feeling better now? Her way of thinking and reacting back to normal? I could peek in at her, but I'd miss the bus for sure.

Getting out of the side door to run for the bus is going to be tricky. The inside door is jammed into its frame—I lift it and pull it towards me far enough to create a narrow opening. As I squeeze through the gap, the screen door falls, crashing onto the top step. I cannot set it back into its frame, so I lean it awkwardly against the house. I'm running late, and make it to the bus stop just in time.

About halfway to school, I look down at my lap and am horrified to discover it is empty. I brought nothing with me. Normally my lap would be full—but today there is nothing. I can't even remember where I left my math book, science log, or social studies textbook. I don't have my vocabulary assignment for English, which is due today. Then I realize I forgot to wash my face, brush my teeth, comb my hair. I can just imagine what my face looks like after a long night of crying. The Trio and their followers are going to love this.

ை

The next thing I know, I'm back on the bus, on my way home. I have no idea what I did all day. I try to think, but my mind is like a blank sheet of notebook paper. I have absolutely no idea what occurred—I can't even remember what we did in gym class. Did I get into trouble from any of my teachers for not having brought the requirements of the day with me? Did one of the Trio trip me down the stairs? Was I called on in class? As the bus pulls into our neighborhood, I realize that it's possible that all—or none—of this occurred. All my quaking, quivering, and planning from last night took its toll, I guess, put me in some sort of hazy fog. I don't feel like myself, and it is strange for me to think that I spent seven hours at good old Johanna Junior High but can't recall a thing.

As I step off the bus, I'm greeted by Rhonda. She goes to Mounds View High School now, and her bus gets home before mine. I haven't seen her in a while: she doesn't come over that much anymore since Mom still hates her.

"I heard the police were at your house last night," Rhonda says, as I start walking up our front sidewalk.

"Yeah, it was kind of scary. My dad broke in," I reply, wondering how Rhonda would have known about last night. Maybe Nancy told her?

"What happened?" I don't know what to say—or even how to say it. I finally settle on what I think is the least of Dad's actions.

"Well, he ripped the phone out of the wall, so I have to wait for the phone repair person to come over this afternoon."

With this, her eyes light up. "Can I see it?"

"What do you mean?"

"I mean . . . can I see the phone? I have never seen one ripped out before," she says, and I start to wonder where this is coming from—it kind of seems like her excitement over this is a little weird. And yet, I don't want to walk into the house alone. What could it hurt to show her the phone?

As we approach the back door, Mother Nature puts a new light on the damage. The sun, now glinting off the varnish on the door, reveals signs of Dad's entrance: various dents on the lower part of the wooden door, a hole near the top. The doorknob is hanging listlessly, like a button on a shirt hanging by a thread. How to open this used-to-be door? How in the world did I get out of it this morning? I finally decide to push it open by slamming my whole body against it. With this, the door gives way—we are in.

As we enter the family room, I realize there is more to see than a broken phone, and instantly I regret my decision to let Rhonda come in. At the same time, having her with me as I view the damage first-hand gives me something to hold onto, a sort of lifeline. Rhonda and I have our arms linked together as we walk the short distance to the family room. The drapes are still pulled shut, blocking sunlight from entering the room. The eerie darkness makes the family room feel like what I imagine the inside of a cave, or maybe a haunted house, feels like. At the spot where the dining table should be, we stop—seem to lock in place—and take a visual tour. I start to breathe fast and my stomach feels queasy as my mind takes stock of the destruction:

- Couch sitting awkwardly in the space between the kitchen and family room, a few cushions on the floor
- Phone wall unit completely ripped from wall, sitting upside down on the floor; a multicolored web of spidery wires hanging loose from the wall
- Phone receiver torn away from its cord, laying on far side of couch
- Globe-sized hole on wall near refrigerator, where Mom and I were crouched last night
- Dining room table turned over and leaning haphazardly against the couch
- One dining room chair sitting upright, the other three tipped in various positions

"Well, I guess I better get home; my mom is probably wondering where I am," Rhonda finally announces.

"Yeah, okay. I'll see you," I say, helping her out the door.

With Rhonda gone, I push the door into place as best I can—it won't seal tightly. I decide to leave all the drapes closed so that if my dad comes, it will look like I'm not home.

Back in the family room, I walk around to take a closer look. The hole in the wall is in about the same place as the one Dad made back when I was four. But I can't remember him doing it last night. Was it while Mom and I were still sitting there? I put my hand inside of it—I could put both of my hands in if I wanted to.

When did he topple the table and chairs? After I ran out of the house, I guess.

The phone, thrown haphazardly on the floor, draws my attention away from the rest of the room. Dad went above and beyond this time; every wire is disconnected. I'm scared to touch the phone, so I kick it with my foot to turn it over. More wires—all broken, ends frayed.

The last time Northwestern Bell came to fix the phone, the repairman was friendly but curious.

"Hi there, are your parents here?" the repairman asked as he came in the door.

"No, my mom is at work. She told me you'd be coming."

"Oh, okay. Let's take a look . . . hmmm, well now, I haven't seen anything quite like this before. How did this happen?" At that point, I got nervous. I didn't want to say my dad pulled it out of the wall.

"Um, well, I'm not exactly sure. You'd have to ask my mom," I hesitantly replied. He gave me a puzzled, questioning type of look and I had the distinct feeling that he thought I had done it.

But the destruction of the phone this time is much worse. What in the world will Northwestern Bell think about this? The entirety of the phone system is utterly destroyed. I doubt the repairman will believe me this time if I say I don't know what happened.

While I wait, I set the Duncan Phyfe into its upright position and place the chairs around it. Retrieving my schoolwork from my bedroom, I sit down and try to catch up on my homework—maybe if I look through the textbooks, I can figure out what we did today. I try algebra, but that requires too much brainpower right now. I try reading out of my social studies book, but after about ten tries I realize it's hopeless. I can't keep my mind on track, can't concentrate.

All I can think about is what's going to happen to us. How are we going to stay safe? And alive?

CALVARY

"PACK UP YOUR STUFF, we're going to Bernice's," Mom says in a hurried voice, as I help her through the broken doorway.

"Are we invited for supper? I've been waiting for the phone repairman. He hasn't come yet."

"I said, pack up your stuff. We are going to Bernice's. NOW!" Mom instructs.

"Okay! I'll finish my homework when we get home."

"We're going to stay there—overnight. For a few days. Here, take this grocery bag and pack your school stuff, pajamas, and a few items of clothing. I'll pack Gloria's stuff. We're leaving in five minutes."

It takes a minute for this to sink in, but when it does, I'm elated. We are moving to Bernice's house! This is the best news! Suddenly, I'm full of energy again. I feel the knots in my stomach slowly start to untie themselves. Suddenly, the full impact dawns on me; we are going to be safe from my dad! If anyone can take care of Dad, it is Bernice's husband, Lawrence.

As Mom and I ease our way out the back door, she does not bother to make sure the door is shut all the way.

"Don't worry about the door right now, let's just get over to Bernice's," Mom advises. "I talked to a lot of people today and decided that it isn't safe for us to be home right now," Mom informs me as we make our way down the back sidewalk. "I went to the police station and filled out what's called an Order of Protection. This means your dad is not allowed on our property," she tells me.

Walking past Bernice's garage, I see Lawrence inside, standing at his workbench. Lawrence works on cars every night—neighbors, friends, and family bring their cars to get oil changes and other services from him. My dad is tall and thin; Lawrence is taller and bulkier.

"Hello," he says, shuffling to the open garage door as we walk by. As always, a cigarette dangles out of the corner of his mouth, an open bottle of beer sits on the workbench. He's wearing a baseball hat and overalls—Bernice makes him wear the overalls when he works on the cars, so he doesn't get his jeans dirty. Considering he has grease from head to toe, I can see why. As a rule, he doesn't talk much—he has kind of a mumbling, grumbling way of speaking. "I'll be in," he tells us, which I would say counts as a complete sentence in his case.

As we come through Bernice's door, she announces dinner is ready. She helps Gloria fill a plate and tells me to help myself. She hands Mom a Hamm's and tells her to sit down at the table. Suddenly, I'm starving. Bernice takes Gloria and me downstairs where she sets up a couple of TV trays for us to eat at, and then goes up to eat with Mom and Lawrence.

"Did you know we're staying overnight at Bernice's tonight?" I ask my sister.

"We are?! That makes me happy!"

"I think it will be fun. I think we're going to stay for a few nights. Dad won't be able to hurt us here," I tell her.

Once we're done eating, Gloria watches television while I

try to work on my vocabulary. Soon, it's bedtime, and Mom and Bernice come down to get us ready for bed.

"Okay, you two! Up the stairs to the bathroom—get those pearly whites brushed!" Mom says.

"Once you're ready, come back down—the two of you are going to sleep down here tonight," Bernice says.

As we come back through the living room to head downstairs, Lawrence is seated at the kitchen table. He must be done with his car work for the night.

"Hello. I mean, I guess I should say goodnight," he says gruffly, and I am flabbergasted to hear him string so many words together!

"Goodnight!" Gloria and I exclaim at the same time before scuttling down the stairs.

Bernice unfolds the couch into a kind of bed, and Gloria and I climb in. As we snuggle in, Mom leans over and kisses us goodnight.

"Sometimes it gets cold down here," Bernice says, covering us up with an extra blanket. "Sleep tight, girls!"

"Don't let the bedbugs bite," Mom shouts as she turns to go back upstairs.

It's weird to feel so calm. Is it possible the knots in my stomach are going to uncoil completely while I sleep? My arms and legs are as still as can be—no trembling at all. Even the constant pounding in my head seems to be gone. I'm so glad Mom isn't frozen anymore. Cocooned together, Gloria and I drift off to sleep.

ଚ୨

The smell of bacon wakes me up, and while Bernice cooks up breakfast, I take a shower. One of the cool things about showering here is that Lawrence works for a trucking company that delivers shampoo. Whenever a box breaks, he gets to take it home—so they have about four different shampoos to choose from. There is also conditioner, which I have never used before. As I comb my hair out in front of the bathroom mirror, I think it looks more shiny and radiant than usual—kind of like the old days when Mom did the vinegar rinses.

On the way to the kitchen, I hear Mom cough from the spare bedroom. She coughs a lot, and it worries me. I've pretty much memorized the seven warning signs for cancer put out by the American Cancer Society. One of the signs is a cough that never goes away, and so I'm worried Mom might have lung cancer. I taped the list of the seven warning signs inside the cupboard door where she keeps her cigarettes, hoping she would read them, stop smoking, and see a doctor immediately. That was about a year ago, though, and she still hasn't seen a doctor—or quit smoking.

"Okay, Joan, here's the deal," Bernice advises as I eat the eggs and bacon she prepared for me. "You come here straight from the bus this afternoon, okay? I don't want you to cut through your yard or anything, walk straight here. I'll be watching for you."

"Yep, okay, got it," I answer. I don't believe I've ever felt so safe.

"If you need anything from your house, we'll make a list and Lawrence will go get it for you," she adds. "So there's no reason for you to go home right now, okay?"

"Okay, see you after school!" I answer, heading out her back door.

There's a bus stop on Bernice's corner, but I decide to go to my same bus stop, hoping the other kids won't catch on to the fact that I'm not living at my house right now. I don't want to have to explain it to them. It's weird, but I'm kind of looking forward to school today.

๛

On the way home, I silently beg the boys at the back of the bus to not spit in my hair. They started this gross hobby about a week ago, and it would be SO embarrassing to have to tell Bernice about it. Whether they heard my silent plea or had something else on their minds, my hair is nice and dry when I get off the bus.

Walking to Bernice's, I look over at my house. It appears that 509 is under construction—Lawrence and at least one other guy are in the house. Peeking through our neighbor's yard, I see some lumber and a paint can along the side of the house.

As I finish the last steps of my walk, a hymn that I learned in third grade comes to me: "Whatsoever You Do." Our classroom had two chalkboards, and Mrs. Treleaven wrote each verse on the black expanse until she had the entire song written out. Even though she used a chalk holder, I couldn't believe how well she wrote in cursive—from the very top all the way to the very bottom of the chalkboards.

Mrs. Treleaven didn't just want us to memorize the song; she also wanted us to know the meaning behind it: that God expects us to treat each other with love and kindness and that even the littlest thing could mean a lot to someone else. If someone forgot their cold lunch from home, for example, we could lend them a hot lunch ticket, or give them half of our own.

Once we had the whole song memorized, Mrs. Treleaven arranged for us to sing the hymn for the rest of the school at our weekly mass. I still have every word of it memorized and look forward to singing it in church whenever it's one of the chosen hymns. I don't know if Bernice and Lawrence have ever heard the hymn, but they sure know how to live it. Climbing the steps to Bernice's door, I start humming the tune.

Whatsoever You Do

Whatsoever you do to the least of your brothers, that you do unto me.

When I was hungry you gave me to eat. When I was thirsty you gave me to drink. Now enter into the home of your Father.

Whatsoever you do to the least of your brothers, that you do unto me.

When I was tired you helped me find rest. When I was worried you calmed all my fears. Now enter into the home of your Father.

Whatsoever you do to the least of your brothers, that you do unto me.

When I was lonely, to me you did speak. When I was troubled you listened to me. Now enter into the home of your Father.

Whatsoever you do to the least of your brothers, that you do unto me.

When I was homeless you opened the door. When I was naked you gave me your coat. Now enter into the home of your Father.

Whatsoever you do to the least of your brothers, that you do unto me

When I was laughed at, you stood by my side. When I was happy, you shared my joy. Now enter into the home of your Father.

Whatsoever you do to the least of your brothers, that you do unto me.

⸎

Our temporary stay at Bernice and Lawrence's is coming to an end. We've been here for three nights, but after supper, we're heading back to our house. Bernice wants our last night to be special, so she's making her famous chicken noodle soup for dinner.

"Man, oh, man! It smells good in here!" I say, coming through the door after school.

"Making some soup and biscuits," Bernice says as if it's no

big deal. Gloria's not up from her nap yet, so it's just me and Bernice.

"Guess we're headed home after supper," I say, munching on some potato chips while watching Bernice cut the thinnest noodles anyone has ever seen off a stack of homemade pasta dough. Once sliced, she lays the noodles out on paper toweling to dry out.

"Yep! I'm sure going to miss having you girls around! Your Mom and I played cribbage every night!" Bernice giggles. "Did you know she skunked me last night! What kind of friend is that?!" Bernice takes a break from slicing the noodles to wipe the sweat off her forehead; her small kitchen heats up like a sauna when she's cooking.

After supper, Mom and I pack up our stuff. Mom has a few tears in her eyes as she thanks Bernice for the past few days.

"I don't even know how to thank you—" she starts, as Bernice envelopes her in a big bear hug.

"Don't give it another thought," Bernice answers. "It was great having you here. I'd do it again in a heartbeat!" At that, she lets go of Mom, leans down and tweaks Gloria's cheek, tells her she'll see her in the morning. "And you," she says to me. "If you get any taller I'm not going to be able to hug you!"

"That's okay; I can lean down!" I say as I bend over to capture Bernice's sweaty embrace.

At the garage door, Lawrence pops out and says he's going to walk with us. "Just to be sure," he says, taking the lead.

Walking up the back sidewalk, I notice that we have a new set of doors. The screen door is no longer wood, it's metal or something but painted white. This door has a lock on it, and Lawrence unlocks it with a tiny key before opening it. The inside door has also been replaced, the old wooden door with the memories of Dad's punches and kicks is nowhere in sight. Lawrence unlocks this door as well, and we all step in.

Inside, a few other things have changed. We have a new phone on the wall. This receiver has a push button dial in it instead of the rotary dial. Mom also had Northwestern Bell install a phone in the bedroom hallway, right outside her door, so that we can call the police from there if we need to. The Duncan Phyfe table, wobbly as ever, is back in its spot, as is the couch. The hole in the wall has been repaired, but if you look closely, you can tell something happened in that spot. Not all the evidence can be erased, I guess.

"Joan, come over here for a minute," Lawrence says, as I watch him carry what looks to be a piece of lumber over to the side door. "I want to make sure you know how this works before I leave."

Standing next to him in the entryway, I watch as this gruff man, cigarette hanging out of his mouth just like always, proceeds to place one end of the piece of lumber against the frame of the basement door, and wedge the other end under the doorknob of the back door. He shows me how he has sawed off the end that goes under the doorknob so that it's angled, allowing it to make a perfect fit.

"This here brace has to be jammed into place every night before you go to bed," he instructs. "In fact, I want you to put it in whenever you're in the house. The door can't be kicked in if this is in place—I tested it to be sure. Do you understand what I'm saying?" At that, Lawrence, who has been staring at his lifesaving invention the entire time, looks directly at me. Our eyes meet for the first time ever, and in his eyes, and on his face, I read the message he's trying to impart. This man of very few words, this truck driver, husband of my mom's best friend, wants us to live. He wants us to survive. And he wants to give us a means to do it.

"I do," I say, tears streaming down my cheeks.

"Okay, well, one more thing. I need to see you do it; I need to make sure you can handle it." And with Lawrence's guidance, and Mom standing by, I remove the piece of lumber and then replace it exactly how I was taught. I push as hard as I can with the heel of my hand to get the wood under the doorknob. It hurts a bit, but I succeed.

"Great! I knew you could do it, such a strong, smart girl you are!"

I am struck by this compliment; I think it's possible that he's referring to more than my ability to force the wood under the doorknob. And as the compliment sinks in, a mixture of feelings overcomes me; a mix of graciousness, love, and tenderness. I know instantly that someday I will be a Bernice, a Lawrence; I will be someone who helps others in their time of need.

Lawrence asks me to follow him into the living room and proceeds to show me the wood brace he made for the front door—this one is a little trickier, because it has to angle a bit from the base of the front closet to the doorknob, but I get that one set as well. "Okay, ladies. I'm heading home. Call the house if you need anything."

Once Lawrence is gone, Mom and I reset the wood brace and start the process of putting Gloria to bed. Mom decides it's a three-way-hug night, so we go through that ritual. I sing the Lawrence Welk song, and before I'm done, Gloria is snoozing on her pillow.

"Let's go sit at the table," Mom says. "I have to tell you a few things."

"What's up?" I say as I take my place across from her.

"Okay. First, here is your set of house keys. The small one is for the screen door; the other one is for the inside door. From now on, we must keep both doors locked at all times. That means you have to take the keys with you to school, so you can get in the house when you come home."

"Okay, sounds good," I say.

"And then—I don't quite know how to say this," Mom is

talking quietly. She's not looking at me, but staring at the cigarette in her ashtray instead. "I met with a lawyer today. A lawyer that specializes in divorce. Do you know what a divorce is?"

I'm not quite sure how to answer. I kind of do know, but I kind of don't. I guess the parents on *The Brady Bunch* were probably divorced before they got married. And I suppose my Uncle Earle got divorced, because he has a new wife, my Aunt Barb, now.

"Sort of," I finally say.

"Well, this idea of telling your dad he can't be here isn't working anymore. He keeps coming back, or I let him come back, and then everything is okay for a while, and then it's not again. I filed for a divorce—and I'm trying to make it so the three of us can stay in the house, but I can't be sure how the judge is going to go on that. The bottom line is that your dad won't ever live with us again."

All this talk of lawyers and divorce is spinning in my head. I'm imagining Perry Mason, in his court of law, standing before a judge who proclaims that John Russell Hicks is no longer married to Lyla Marie Hicks and that Mr. Hicks is not allowed to ever reside at 509 again.

"It's not that I don't love your dad. I love him very much—that's why I married him. But we can't live with him anymore. This is the only way to do that," Mom concludes. And for the first time in my life, I see Mom cry. Really cry. "I will miss him; he's the love of my life." I head over to Mom, kneel next to her and hold her as she cries, as she weeps for herself, for her husband.

"So is it, like, done then?" I finally ask. "The divorce, I mean? Does Dad know about it?" Mom explains to me that it's not quite that simple. He has to be served some papers, but they can't locate him—no one seems to know where he's living or working. Once that's done, a court date will be set and the lawyers and judges will finalize everything. "I'll let you know when it's all done. We're going to be a team from now on—you, me and

Gloria—a team, okay?"

"Yeah, okay, Mom. We'll make a great team!" I say, holding Mom's hand in mine, trying to reassure her she's making the right decision. "I think everything's going to turn out alright."

"By the way, where did you go the other night?"

"What do you mean?" I'm not sure what Mom is referring to.

"The other night—I saw you come in through the side door while the police were still here. I didn't even know you had left. Where did you go?"

"I ran over to the Kewatts'. They called the police for us," I answer.

"I was wondering how the police got here," Mom says, quietly. "Okay, well, goodnight."

In bed, trying to fall asleep, I think about what Lawrence said, about what Mom told me. I think about what a powerful feeling true love must be—that Mom could still love Dad after all he's done to her, to us. I can't imagine me ever loving him again—he terrifies me. Mom seems to be a different person—more courageous than before—she certainly isn't frozen in place like she was the other night. I'll do everything I can to help her through this, that's for sure.

Before I roll over and tuck myself into my covers, I pray for everyone. For Mom, for me and Gloria. For Bernice and Lawrence. For Dad. Is there a chance that peace and quiet are coming our way?

JUSTICE

I STILL HAVEN'T TOLD anyone, not even Sharon or Elise, that Mom and Dad are getting a divorce. It seems like something that should be kept private, not shared with too many people.

One thing about Dad right now is that he's not happy about this divorce thing. He calls me after school almost every day to tell me how miserable he is. If I don't answer the phone, it rings and rings, which is extremely annoying. So I figure I might as well answer it, let him get whatever is bugging him out of his system. Sometimes he tries to tell me everything is Mom's fault; sometimes he just talks nonsense. But always, he talks. And talks. And talks. I can even put the phone down and go to my room to grab something—and when I pick the phone back up, he'll still be talking.

"Joanie? Are you there? Are you there, Joanie?" Dad randomly asks.

"Right here, Dad. I'm listening," I say, even if I haven't been.

"Well, your dear old Dad wants to make sure you know what a mean person your mother is. Kicking me out of my own house. It's not fair!"

"Where are you living now?" I ask, trying to steer him off the topic of Mom being a mean person.

"Well, where do you think I'm living?" This response is immediately followed by more rambling, more nonsense. Soon enough, he'll repeat the same questions again.

I've told Mom about some of the calls, but I haven't told her he calls every day. I'm hoping that once the divorce thing is settled, they'll tell him he can't call us anymore. Mom hasn't given me any updates yet, but I'm hoping it'll be taken care of soon.

The good news is that Lawrence's invention has worked well. Dad has only come to the house once since the big fiasco last month, and though he got the screen door open, he was not able to move the inside door even a fraction of an inch. Mom called the police from the hallway as soon as she heard him pounding— they came and told him to leave, and that was that.

❧

Today Mom, Gloria and I are headed to Madelia for Thanksgiving dinner. I can't believe it's already that time of year! Mom made her famous baked beans for the occasion (not one of my favorites, to be honest, but the rest of the family seems to look forward to them) and she's also bringing an apple pie from the freezer. Gloria has already fallen asleep in the backseat. She loves to lay with her legs up in the air, so she has her feet resting up on the window.

I guess Mom has been busy with the lawyers and stuff; as we drive down the highway, she gives me an update. "My lawyer called the other day with some news," Mom starts. "You and your sister are going to spend some time with your dad."

"What?!" I say, instantly alarmed. "What are you talking about? You mean he's going to come to the house after all? I thought he couldn't because of the Order of Protection or whatever!"

"Well, this is something separate from the protection order. He's going to come over, pick you up and take you girls somewhere."

"You mean just the two of us? By ourselves?"

"Yes. It's called visitation. That means the parent who doesn't live with the kids gets to have some time alone with them. And the judge decided that your dad deserves time with his girls," Mom finishes.

I'm seething with anger. His girls? When have we ever been considered his girls? I cannot believe this is happening! I can feel the insides of my stomach turning into furious little balls of fire-knots.

"Mom, think about this. This is not a good idea. He can't even talk straight. What if he tries to hurt us?"

"Yeah, well. I don't have any say in this. The judge has decided, and when a judge rules on something it has to be followed."

Who is this judge? Does he know what Dad is capable of? Does he know I'm only thirteen? That Gloria isn't even five yet? What kind of judge would think this is a good idea?

"I'd like to meet the judge," I finally say. "Or talk to the Governor or somebody who's in charge."

"I bet you would, but that's not going to happen," Mom tells me. "It doesn't work that way. The lawyers are the ones who get things decided. They listen to what I want, what your dad wants and then write it all up in a sort of plan. They present it to the judge—and once he finalizes it, that's it. That's how the justice system works."

And Mom's lawyer agreed that it would be best for my dear old Dad to have visitation or whatever it's called? Did Mom tell her lawyer what Dad is like? How about if the lawyer spends the day with him instead of us?

"You told the lawyer what Dad's like, right? The lawyer knows what he did to you? To our house?" Mom assures me that she did, and I am silent for a bit.

"When is this supposed to happen?" I finally ask.

"A week from Sunday. He'll pick the two of you up at 1:00 p.m."

"And where is he taking us? To a movie or something?" I ask. But Mom doesn't have the answer to this question. Apparently, it's completely up to him where he takes us. The only rule is that we must be home by bedtime.

"And what if he doesn't bring us home? What if we never come back? What if he hurts us and we can't walk or talk or something? What if he kidnaps us? How would you ever find us if you don't even know where we were going?" My mind is spinning with questions—I feel like Gloria's *See 'n' Say* toy, winding up over and over with another query for her.

But Mom is silent. She can't, or won't, answer any of my questions.

When we arrive at Grandma's I say hello to everyone, try to be my usual polite self. It's a smaller crowd than usual. My Aunt Sharon and Uncle Lee couldn't make it this year, and I think Uncle Earle is with his new wife today. Aunt Sharlene, Uncle Allen, and my cousin Debbie are here, and soon enough, we all head to the table for dinner.

I'm not in a very good mood, not very hungry, so, even though the feast has just started, I ask to be excused from the table. Gloria seems content to sit and visit with the adults, so I settle into Grandma's favorite chair in the living room and check out her latest *Reader's Digest* magazines. I make it look like I'm reading—turn a page occasionally, that type of thing, but I can't concentrate at all. A whole bunch of awful feelings have consumed me—anger, rage, sadness, fear, dread. What am I going to do? There must be something I can do to prevent this from happening.

ᏻᏬ

Over the past week, I've tried everything to convince Mom that we shouldn't go. I even suggested that I go by myself, leave Gloria home. But it all boils down to the fact that the judge has made his decision. Justice trumps the safety of my sister and me.

"I want you to keep a close eye on your sister. Make sure she doesn't run off or anything," Mom says to me as we watch out the window for Dad's rat-trap van to appear.

"And Gloria, you mind everything Joan says," she tells Gloria while helping her get her coat on. "Whatever she says goes, okay? I need you to listen to her very carefully today."

I'm praying as hard as I can that Dad will not come—he'll forget, have a flat tire, run out of gas—anything to will stop this madness from happening. But right as rain, Dad's van pulls up in front of the house exactly at 1:00 p.m. God, I hope I'm up for this.

"Brought you something, Lyla. A little gift. Can I bring it in?" Dad says, standing on the front step.

"I guess so," Mom says, hesitantly.

"Okay, girls, why don't you get in the van while I bring in your mom's gift," Dad says, cheerfully. The cool fall finally gave into winter; it snowed yesterday, and the cement is slippery. As we follow Dad down the sidewalk, I take Gloria's hand—the last thing I need is for her to slip and get hurt.

"Joanie—right up front for you! Gloria, hop into the back of the van—you can sit anywhere you like!" Dad says. He is so cheerful, like the chimney-sweep guy in *Mary Poppins*. A major contrast to the doom and gloom Dad I talk to on the phone almost every day. The van is high off the ground, and Gloria can't quite make it, so I give her a little boost before I get in the front passenger seat. Dad shuts our doors, and I turn to look back at Gloria. I am stunned to see there are no seats in the back. The metal floor is covered with garbage, clothes, boxes—and what looks like plain old junk.

"I don't know where to sit," Gloria says, standing in the middle of the floor. As I try to figure out the best place for her, Dad opens the huge back doors of the van.

"Alright, here it is," Dad announces. "I got your Mom a little refrigerator! I think she's gonna like it!" I watch as Dad pulls a small gold-colored refrigerator out of the pile of junk. He lifts it up, carries it to the side door. Another oddball gift from Dad—a miniature refrigerator. I can't imagine how he thinks that's any kind of a gift for Mom.

While Dad's in the house, I try to get Gloria settled. I could let her sit on my lap, but I want to keep her as far away from Dad as possible. Finally, I spot a pile of fabric—it's white with paint stains on it. But at least it looks somewhat soft.

"Grab that blanket-like thing," I tell her. "Pull it so that it's kind of behind me, but where I can still see you."

"Okay, sit down—cross your legs like a frog," I suggest. "Make sure you stay super quiet, okay?" It's clear by the look on her face that Gloria is scared into silence. I don't think she'll be pestering me with one question after another today.

Soon enough, Dad's back in the van. He starts it up, and off we go. I have absolutely no idea how to act, what to say. I haven't been alone with my dad in years, let alone in a car, let alone in a rat-trap vehicle like this. Mom has told me that I show my emotions on my face—everyone knows if I'm happy, sad, scared, or whatever, because my face paints the picture. I concentrate on making my face look happy; I don't want Dad to know I'm scared to death.

"Sorry to say the heat doesn't work in this old van!" Dad announces, laughing a little, right about the time I realize I'm freezing. "You'll get used to it!" Everything seems to be a joke to Dad, like we're doing some sort of comedy routine for Laugh-In.

"Oh, okay. Well, hopefully, we're not going too far—wouldn't want Gloria to catch a cold," I say, smiling over at Dad. It's hard to smile and be nervous at the same time. "Where are we headed, Dad?"

"Well, here's what I thought we'd do—drive on over to Rosedale! Do a little shopping! Have a nice lunch at The Bubbling Kettle! Treat you girls to a special day!" I've never heard so many short, happy sentences in a row. Listening to Dad is stranger than reading a Dr. Seuss book.

I try to think of a way to stop, or at least change, this plan. I don't know my way around Rosedale and don't have any idea how to walk home from there. It'd be better if we went somewhere that I'm familiar with. I have Apache Plaza memorized and am sure I could find my way home from there.

"Hey, Dad. Rosedale's cool—but how about going to Apache? Gloria can throw some pennies into the fountain and then we could have lunch at The Mad Hatter?"

"Nope, no Mad Hatter for my girls! You can do that any old time. We're headed to Dayton's—you girls can pick out some pretty dresses and then we'll have a fine lunch at The Bubbling Kettle," Dad confirms his plans.

I look back at Gloria. She's sitting exactly like I told her, cross-legged on the white fabric. She hasn't said a word since we got in the car. I reach my hand behind my seat, and she grabs it tightly. Our eyes meet, and I give her a small smile.

Watching out the window, I try to look for clues that will tell me where we are, but nothing looks familiar. Dad's driving funny—it seems like he's going too slow, and having trouble keeping the steering straight. If Gloria wasn't in the car, I'd try to jump out of this trap and run for my life, but there is no way I'm leaving my sister, and there is no way for us to jump out together. I feel like Hansel and Gretel without the breadcrumbs; I have no way to leave a trail to get us back home.

As Dad pulls into the mall parking lot, I try to memorize what I see. We park kind of by JC Penney, next to a blue car. I help Gloria out of the side door and tell her to hold my hand at all times.

"Never let go, okay?" I say. "Do you understand me?"

"Yes," she says. Her lower lip is pushed out a little, and I hope she doesn't start crying.

Dad comes around the side of the van and starts to herd us to the mall entrance. Once inside, he wants to hold Gloria's hand. Something tells me that would be a bad idea.

"Oh, we have this rule that Gloria always has to hold my hand," I tell Dad. "She's used to it, so I think we should keep it that way, okay?" I try, hoping Dad won't freak out.

"Gotcha! Well, you two are quite the sisters, aren't you?!" he says, as I breathe a sigh of relief that he believed me. "Okay, let's find Dayton's!"

I've never shopped at Dayton's, but Mom has. When they first got married, Mom worked at First National Bank in downtown Minneapolis, and a Dayton's store was right across the street. She told me she used to go there and buy high-heels, dresses, nylons. Then, one day, Dad decided they needed to move to Detroit, so she had to quit her job. Mom didn't want to move to Detroit, but Dad said they had to because he got a new job. She packed everything she could into their car and hired movers to move their furniture. When she tells me the story, she always makes me promise to never move to Detroit, because it's filthy. Apparently, every surface in their apartment was covered with soot. Mom would clean it off every day, but the coating of fine black dust would be back the next morning. They only lived in Detroit for about a month—the day their furniture arrived from Minneapolis, Dad came home from work and informed Mom the new job hadn't worked out after all. They moved back to Minnesota, but Mom couldn't get her job downtown back, and that's when she started working at the First State Bank of New Brighton. Since she wears a uniform and buys her pantyhose by mail, I don't think she shops at Dayton's anymore.

As we walk down the hall, Dad starts talking funny—like he does on the phone sometimes.

"Well, Joanie! Meanwhile, back at the ranch! Ah, the good ol' days, back at the ranch! Much ado about nothing! The sun shining, horses running. Joanie! The ranch! Can you SEE it?" Dad asks. His voice is getting a little loud.

I have no idea what he's talking about. He's said this ranch phrase about a hundred billion times, but I still don't know where it is, or if it's real. Maybe the ranch is the farm he grew up on?

Dad doesn't notice that I'm not answering him—all the while he continues with his babbling. That's when I realize he isn't talking to me or anyone else. He's talking to himself! My God, I'm so embarrassed—my cheeks are turning red. I squeeze Gloria's hand and try to slow down our pace so that we fall a step behind Dad. He doesn't seem to notice that, either—it's possible he's forgotten we're with him. Now, instead of talking, he's singing. I don't know the song. Maybe he made it up? I do know that people don't normally sing while walking through a mall. Now I'm terrified.

I look around—try to see if there are any familiar faces walking near us. I try to meet the eyes of every adult that passes by, hoping they will notice that something's wrong—but everyone walks right past us. My stomach is upset now, and I hope I don't throw up. My arms and legs are doing their shaking thing. Must stay alert. Must keep my eyes wide open. I try to slow my breathing down, try to stay focused on keeping us safe.

Finally, we find Dayton's. Stepping into the store, Dad yells out, "Can we get some help here? Hello, hello? Can we get some help?" He spots a saleslady off in the distance. "How about you? Can you help us?" he says, pointing right at her. He's agitated, upset that someone isn't helping us yet, even though it's only been about one minute. The lady he pointed to waves at Dad, walks over.

"Welcome to Dayton's! What is it you're looking for today?"

"These are my girls—Joanie and Gloria. I want them to each get a new dress. Cost is of no concern! Whatever they want, they can have!" Dad says, waving his arms over us like a fairy godfather.

The lady doesn't seem to know what to make of the three of us but finally decides to help us. "Okay, well, let's see. What size do they wear?"

Dad looks confused.

"A thirteen/fourteen chubby for me, 5-6x for my sister," I say.

We start in the junior's department, and I choose the very first thing I see—a blue corduroy skirt. In the fitting room, I realize it's way too big. Doesn't matter, the most important thing is to find something and get out of here as fast as possible. The lady comes in the dressing room area to check on me, see if I like the skirt.

"It's perfect," I answer from behind the curtain. "Can you find something for my sister? We're kind of in a hurry."

"Sure, I'll find a few things. It'll just take me a minute," she says. While we're waiting, I tell Gloria that the first thing that fits is what she's getting—we don't have time to try a lot of stuff on. Luckily, the lady brings in the cutest jumper-style dress: strawberries embroidered on blue and white striped fabric, and it fits perfectly. I take Gloria out and have her model it for Dad.

"Great!" Dad exclaims. "Now my girls each have a special outfit from their dear old Dad!"

While I help Gloria get her clothes back on, the saleslady comes in and asks for the jumper and skirt, so she can start ringing them up. Almost instantly, I hear a commotion.

"Shhh . . . " I say to Gloria, though she hasn't made a sound. I lean out of our little cubicle, try to hear what's going on.

"Check it again!" I hear Dad say—not quite yelling, but close. "I'm good for it!"

"Sir, I'm sorry. That account appears to be closed or something.

We're not able to accept your check." It appears Dad doesn't have a way to pay for the clothes. Gloria and I stay in the small room while the lady and Dad figure out what to do.

"Okay, then, try this!" Dad yells. When that doesn't work, he demands to see her boss. "Who do you work for, anyway?! Is it one of the Daytons? Well, get them down here, then!"

I'm not sure what to do. Stay in the dressing room? It seems like a safe enough place for Gloria and me to be. But then, maybe if I went out there I could calm Dad down? Tell him we don't need the clothes?

"Umm . . . Dad? You know, we don't need the clothes today—we could come back another time and get them," I try. Holding Gloria's hand, I move her behind me, out of Dad's reach, just in case he goes into a rage or something.

"We're not leaving here without those clothes!" Dad yells as the manager walks up to the counter.

"Sir, what seems to be the problem?" The manager, an elderly lady about Mom's age, arrives on the scene to take charge. While Dad and the manager work things out, I try to catch the eye of the saleslady. I want to make sure she remembers us. If kids go missing nowadays, they put their picture on a milk carton—I imagine if we go missing, they'll put both of us on the same carton. The more people who see us, the better the chance of someone saying: "I saw them at Rosedale!" I've been keeping my eyes open for the missing children for years, though have yet to spot one.

I don't know how, but somehow Dad purchased our dresses—both are packed up in a fancy Dayton's bag. Dad carries it proudly, satisfied with his success. But as we go up the escalator to the restaurant, I hear Dad mumbling about what a stupid store Dayton's is. He can't believe that Dayton's has the reputation it does when they treat good-paying customers like shit. "Shit and Shinola!" Dad yells to the rooftop. Though I'm probably cutting off her circulation already, I squeeze Gloria's hand a little tighter.

Once seated in our booth, I order the least expensive item on the menu—a bowl of soup. "Gloria and I can share it, Dad. I mean, we already ate, so we're not that hungry," I say, hoping once again that he believes me. Dad continues to talk during lunch, not babbling like he was in the hallway, but not talking to us either—which is fine with me. At least he isn't singing. Or yelling. I start to panic when the bill comes; I wish I had some money with me. But as it turns out, Dad has some cash in his wallet, and it's enough to cover our soup, so there is no reenactment of the travesty that occurred earlier.

"What would you girls like to do now?" Dad asks as if he has all the money in the world in the palm of his hand. There is only one thing I want to do, and that's go home.

"Oh, I think we should head home, Dad. I have some homework to get done before tomorrow, and it's getting late. Plus, we want to show Mom our new outfits! Don't we, Gloria?" I say, giving her hand a little squeeze. But Dad wants to walk around the mall some more—we might have missed something on our first walk-through. Gloria and I stay a step behind him, watching as he weaves a bit while he walks. When I see JC Penney, I try again to get Dad to take us home.

"Well, if I didn't know any better, I'd think you didn't want to spend time with your dear old Dad! Joanie, what kind of daughter are you?" Dad asks. And so we walk around the mall again. We don't go in any more stores, just walk. Finally, Dad says he's ready to take us home.

"You're sure you don't want some ice cream before we go?" Dad asks as we approach the exit.

"Nope, that soup filled us up!" I say. "We're good."

When we get to the van, Gloria settles in on the white fabric, and once I'm seated, we resume our handholding. I watch out the window to make sure we're headed in the right direction, but

I can't be sure—nothing looks familiar. At one point, Dad slows way down while driving—he's staring off into the distance, but I have no idea what he's looking at.

"Everything okay, Dad?"

"You betcha! Never been better!" he answers, glancing over at me with a bizarre-looking smile on his face.

When Dad finally pulls up to 509, I breathe a huge sigh of relief. We made it.

"Okay girls! It was great seeing you today! I'll probably see you again next Sunday!" he says.

"Yeah, okay," I say, nervously.

"We are NEVER going with him anywhere, ever again!" I scream at Mom once we're in the house with the doors locked, wood braces secured. "Never! I don't care what you, the lawyers or even that stupid judge says—we are never, ever going anywhere with him again!"

Mom wants to know what happened, and as I tell her, she seems to agree with me that the visitation day wasn't such a good idea.

"Never again, Mom. The justice people can put me and Gloria in jail, at least we'll be safe there!" I tell her.

"Okay, okay," Mom says, holding Gloria on her lap. "Try to calm down. Take a deep breath; it's going to be all right. I'll call the lawyer on Monday. Try not to worry," she says. Mom walks over to my chair, wraps her arms around me. "I'll see what I can do, I promise," she says as I rest my head in her arms.

In my room, I put some of my records on, slide under my covers and try to disappear into the music. Mom better take care of it—I hope she keeps her word. I wish I could call Sharon to tell her what happened, but I can't get the courage up to do it. And I know he's been gone a long time, but I wish my old dog TNT was here right now. He'd probably smile at me with his crooked teeth to cheer me up.

UNEXPECTED VISIT

THANK THE LORD! EIGHTH grade is over, and I'm still alive! Summer is here, and I am in the clear for any pushing, shoving, or tripping for at least another three months. Oh, and no more globs of spit landing in my hair, either!

Gloria and I are having the best summer! She has a new swimsuit, purple, and loves to run through the sprinkler with her friends. I think she could do it all day if I let her! Fridays continue to be our favorite day, because Mom works late, so we get to spend the entire day and evening together.

Today was an extra fun day, because we went swimming at Long Lake. Gloria's butt is so tiny we can both fit on the seat of my ten-speed. She held on tight while I pedaled and steered us all the way there. We had a blast swimming together. She giggled at the games I played with her and loved being thrown up in the air so she could splash down into the water. As if the beach day wasn't enough fun, Mrs. Kewatt called right when we got home and invited us to go out for supper with them.

"Hurry up, Gloria," I say, as we head out the door to dinner. Mr. Kewatt is already in the driver's seat of the car—ready to go.

Nancy and her sister, Patti Jo, are standing in their front yard, waiting for us.

"Hi, girls!" I hear Mrs. Kewatt say, as she comes through their front gate. "Are we all set?"

"Ready as we'll ever be!" I say, cheerfully. Then, out of the corner of my eye, I see Dad's rat-trap van come around the corner. I quickly pick Gloria up, and we all watch as he parks in front of 509. What is he doing here? He has never come to the house during Mom's work hours.

"Hello! Hello!" Dad greets all of us with a huge grin. "What's going on, Joanie? Going somewhere with these folks?"

"Dad, um . . . yeah, we're going out for supper," I say, pulling Gloria tighter.

Dad's eyes are that weird color of blue. I back up a little as he crosses the street, comes up and stands on the grass right by us. Is there something wrong with his legs? He looks a little off, like he might trip over himself or something. Drunk, I suppose.

"Oh, I don't think so! You girls are coming with me tonight. Come here, Gloria—come to your dear old Dad." He opens his arms, thrusts them towards me and tries to tempt Gloria into going to him.

"Dad, no. You aren't even supposed to be here," I try.

"You girls are coming with me! Don't try to argue, Joanie. I'm here to take my two girls out for a tremendous evening! Now give me your sister and get in the van," Dad's voice has that weird cheerfulness to it, like at Rosedale, and I'm getting goosebumps.

How to handle this situation is beyond me. Dad comes closer to me, so I back up. Dad another step towards me; he's closing in. I squeeze my arms tight around Gloria, an uncomfortable hug, but I can't take any chances. I whisper in her ear, "Wrap your legs around my waist and hold tight. We're going to run."

But as I make my move to flee, Mrs. Kewatt stands beside me, faces Dad. She swings one arm out and places it across my chest, like a human safety belt. To my knowledge, they have never met each other, and I'm stunned to see her stand before my dad. Mrs. Kewatt is short, probably around five feet four inches.

Dad takes another step forward so that his tall frame looms over her, his flaring eyes stare right through her.

I look over at Mrs. Kewatt's face and see her eyes flicker. Her face, normally pale and serene, has the look of a cougar ready to pounce its prey. She appears to be transformed into a woman warrior called into action. Apparently, Mrs. Kewatt is ready to fight what is certain to be an unpredictable battle. She raises her free hand and points at Dad.

"John, I'm sorry to say, but you have to leave. NOW." Mrs. Kewatt sends the command to Dad with a loud, high-pitched voice. "Joan and Gloria are under my care, and they are NOT leaving my sight! Now, I *strongly* suggest you turn around, get in your van, and leave before I call the police." Mrs. Kewatt looks as if she may spit at Dad, instead, she turns to us and orders us into the car.

The four of us spring into action—Nancy and Patti Jo climb in the back seat first, and I follow, holding Gloria with the grip of an eagle. Once we're in, Mrs. Kewatt slides into the front seat and slams her door.

"Step on it!" she yells to her husband. Mr. Kewatt follows his wife's order by stepping on the gas and blasting through the stop sign at the corner. And as fast as a band of bank robbers fleeing the scene, we speed off to Ponderosa. I'm so stunned I don't even know what to do. Or say. Or feel. Mrs. Kewatt stood before my dad and dressed him down like it was nothing—like she does this type of thing all the time. I've never seen anyone stand up to Dad like that. Not Mom, not the police, not even Bernice or Lawrence—and certainly not me. Mrs. Kewatt gets an A+ in my book tonight, that's for sure!

It's a little hard to eat supper—we're all a little rattled. Gloria and I share the chopped steak dinner, and we each manage to get a few bites down. Normally, we stay for a bit after we're done eating—chat about the neighborhood, Mr. Kewatt's cool cars— but not tonight. Everyone is a bit subdued, and the perils of the neighborhood don't seem to warrant any attention.

"Thank you so much for dinner," I say when they drop us off. "And, well, thanks for . . . " But I'm at a loss for what to say. How do I thank Mrs. Kewatt for being brave and courageous?

"Oh, that's okay—glad you had a good supper! Do you girls want to come in for a while?" Mrs. Kewatt asks. "Watch some television or something?"

"No, that's okay. Mom will be home from work soon, so we better get home," I say, figuring they have done enough for one night.

When we get in the house, I make sure all the locks are locked, the door braces both set in place. Gloria and I get our pajamas on and snuggle up on the couch to watch *Planet of the Apes* while we wait for Mom to come home. Typically, she gets home around 8:30 p.m., but sometimes she goes out with the bank crew on Friday nights—usually to Robert Lee's Chinese Restaurant. If she does that, she doesn't get home until 10:00 p.m. or so. When it gets to be 9:00, I put Gloria to bed and assume Mom is out with her coworkers. But then, I hear her knocking.

"Coming! Hold on, the wood thing is stuck under the doorknob," I tell her through the door. "You must've gone to Robert Lee's?" I ask as Mom comes through the door.

"My God, what a night! You won't believe what happened!" Mom says. "Get the doors relocked and the braces put on quickly!" Something has clearly upset her. Maybe they had a bank robbery? I follow Mom to the living room window—three cars are parked outside our house and, after she waves at them, they take off.

"Mom, what's wrong? Why are you so upset?"

"Your dad! Your DAD! That's why I'm so upset!" she screams. "Did he call here tonight?"

"No, he didn't call. He came over here. We were . . . "

"What?! He was here? What time was that?" Mom is frantic now. She opens a Hamm's, and I watch as she drinks practically the whole can in one gulp. When she tries to light her cigarette, her hands are so shaky I think she may drop the match, and then she does.

"Around 5:30 p.m., I guess. We were going to Ponderosa with the Kewatts, and he showed up right when we were leaving," I report.

"My God! I can't believe this!" I think this may be one of the rare occasions where Mom cries, but, on the other hand, she almost seems too upset to cry.

"Okay, Mom, what? What happened?"

"He, well, he. I don't know how he did it, but he must have gone somewhere after he left here—somewhere where there are a lot of phones. Where that would be, I just don't know. He called the bank switchboard, demanding to talk to me. But before Mrs. Murphy could get the call to me, he called again. And again. In a matter of minutes, he had the whole switchboard, every single line, tied up," Mom is breathless, having a hard time getting this all out. "As soon as a line disconnected, he called again—almost immediately. Mrs. Murphy had to send someone over to get me, because she couldn't leave her desk. Your Dad was on every single line. She was so scared—almost out of her mind."

As Mom recounts her story, I try to imagine what kind of place Dad could've been at—one where he has unlimited access to a bunch of phones. The only thing I can come up with is the grouping of pay phones at the mall. But how was Dad using pay phones? Putting in dime after dime in slot after slot—and dialing the bank number from each one? And then keeping each call live long enough to continuously tie up the switchboard? It doesn't seem probable. It's a mystery in my mind, and apparently in Mom's, too.

And to think this was all going on while the bank was open. I wonder what the customers thought—stopping in to cash their weekly paycheck and get a little spending money for the weekend. I wonder if they sensed anything was amiss at their neighborhood bank, one of the most distinguished pillars of New Brighton.

"And then," Mom continues, now on her third beer. "And then, as fast as the calls started, they stopped. It was just a few minutes before eight, all the white lights on the switchboard went out—and no more calls came in." I think about Mrs. Murphy, being beside herself with fear and worry and then suddenly having the chaotic episode end. I hope she took a couple of deep breaths, went home, and had a beer herself.

"In a flash, your dad was at the door of the bank—the door that faces the big parking lot," Mom says, her voice rising in panic.

I realize the terror has not yet come to an end and I feel my legs start to shake. I put my hands on my thighs to try to hold them down, keep them from leaping off the chair. I imagine Dad raging outside the glass doors, the very doors I used to clean.

"Thank God we had already locked the doors on that side. The bank president ran—and I mean RAN—to the other set— the ones by the drive-thru. As he finished locking them—your dad appeared behind the glass. He started banging on the glass, screaming at the top of his lungs. You know what he's like." Mom is winded, her typically strong and commanding voice quiets to a whisper.

"Yeah, I do," I answer, quietly. I don't know if I want to hear the rest. Did Dad break the windows and get in the bank? Did some of her coworkers, her friends, get hurt?

Mom lights up another cigarette and continues the frightful tale. Her coworkers put her in the back corner of an office, so she was out of Dad's view. She tells me about the police arriving and finding Dad's van in the employee lot—not parked in a spot, but parked sideways directly behind Mom's car, effectively trapping it. The police communicated with the president through a private phone line. No one could leave: all the employees had to stay in the bank. The owner of the bank, for whom Mom has worked for the past twenty years or so, was notified and came to the scene.

In my mind, I try to visualize Mom and her coworkers, even the bank president, huddled in a corner, waiting for the police to call on the private phone line to let them know it's safe to go to their cars, go home to their families. Once freed, the president and two other employees followed Mom home.

"That's who was out in the street—one of them followed me into the alley and then drove around front. They said they'd wait to make sure I got in the door okay. Such a good group of people," Mom rightly concludes.

"What happened to Dad?" I ask. "Did he get in his van like always? Do you think he's heading over here now?" It seems to me that Dad was in his worst rage ever and that he could break through our fortifications if he comes over tonight.

"The police took him away this time—but I don't have any idea how long they'll keep him. The officers had his van towed away somewhere—I have no idea where that went," Mom says. "So I think we're safe for tonight, at least."

"Wouldn't this count as a reason for him to go to jail or prison?" I picture Dad in some sort of jail cell, a Perry Mason-type lawyer waiting in the wings to talk to him.

"I'm guessing nothing will get sorted out until Monday."

"I can't believe this, Mom. It's like something out of a horror movie! You must've been so scared."

"I was. But also completely embarrassed. To think he came to the bank, of all places! The president, the owner—all my coworkers—everyone knows about your dad now. I'm completely humiliated. What are people going to think of me now? It's going to be so hard to go into work on Monday," Mom concludes.

Mom tells me she's going to write the number for the private line down on the pad of paper by the phone. From now on, I'm to call her in an emergency.

It appears that the Ponderosa chopped steak dinner is not settling in my stomach very well—I don't feel like throwing up exactly, but my stomach is roiling; things are twisting and twisting inside. My head is pounding, and I hope I'm not getting another one of my headaches. I crawl into bed and pull my bubblegum-pink sheet over my body. But I already know I'm not going to sleep; I'm guessing this night of terror isn't over. It seems like a million years have passed since I held Gloria on the sidewalk and watched Mrs. Kewatt send my Dad on his way—and yet, it was just five hours ago. I guess I never got a chance to tell Mom about what happened to us—her story was the focal point of the night. I wonder what Mom's bosses and her fellow employees are thinking as they go to bed tonight. I imagine they are telling their spouses, children, brothers, sisters, friends—whoever are the important people in their lives—about what happened. It seems no one was spared Dad's wrath tonight.

I can feel tears developing under my eyelids, making little pools between the lid and the eyeball. But I won't let them out. I can't. If I do, I'm afraid I'll never stop crying. I squeeze my eyes shut so tightly they hurt, trying to hold the salty liquid back, to force the tears back into my brain or wherever they come from.

Once again, I wonder what will become of us. I don't know how much longer we'll be able to defend ourselves. Now that Dad has upped his game, it seems we aren't safe outside of the house—and I wonder how much longer the braces are going to be able to protect us.

TEXAS

SPEARMAN, TEXAS, HERE WE come! Mom planned a trip—we're headed to Texas to see Mark! We're going to fly from Minneapolis to Dallas, and then take a smaller plane to a city called Amarillo. Mark will pick us up in Amarillo, and then it's off to Spearman! It is our first time traveling on an airplane, and we are very excited.

I'm still a little upset about being fired from my job at the bank—no more Joan the Janitor for me. One night a few months ago, Jack sent me into the president's office to vacuum—neither of us had any idea that he was still in there working. Mr. President, with his red hair flaming like a bonfire, came roaring at me as if I had tried to rob the place, and that turned out to be my last night of work. About a week later, Mom told me that Jack and Arlene were also fired. The reason? Drinking beer while working. Mom appeared to be shocked at the news—had no memory of me telling her about it on my first day. With the money I'd saved from my bank job, I bought a real-live electric sewing machine. I have wanted one for a while now, because Mom, despite my protests, decided to give the Old Singer to Goodwill. I was so glad when Bernice said she would help me pick out a machine, because I had no idea what to get. So anyway, now I have to rely on mowing lawns to make money. As the trip got closer, I decided to spend a little of my hard-earned money.

First, I had Mom take me to Minnesota Fabrics at Apache Plaza, so I could get patterns and fabric to make matching outfits for Gloria and me to wear on the plane. Mom gave me fifteen minutes to pick everything out, which isn't much time when you are in a store filled with so many luxurious bolts of fabric! I started with the patterns—I couldn't believe it when I found a jumpsuit pattern that came in both of our sizes. Next, I found the grooviest fabric—it reminds me of something Laurie would wear on *The Partridge Family!* The fabric is cream-colored but has a lot of brown shapes all over it—diamonds, octagons, triangles, and so on. Here's the colorful part: the shapes have orange, yellow, and brown flowers inside them. It's so cool! It took about a week to make the jumpsuits—they were more challenging than anything I'd made before—but now they are pressed and ready to wear!

The second thing I spent my lawnmowing money on was a real, honest to goodness, pair of jeans! I skipped right over JC Penney and went straight to the County Seat, where all they have is jeans. I got a GROOVY pair of bell bottoms, and they fit perfectly! They are 100% denim—dark blue—and have super cool pockets. As a bonus, I found a neat belt with a huge buckle on it! I'm in style now!

And last but not least—I decided to get my hair cut! Yesterday, I walked up to McCready's Hair Salon for my transformation. My hope was to come out looking like a cool chick—maybe like one of the groovy girls that dance on *American Bandstand!*

The lady who was helping me with this big change had me look through a few books and magazines to find a style that I thought was cool. As soon as I came across a picture of Dorothy Hamill (I guess she is a famous figure skater), I knew what I wanted—and the hair stylist was all in favor.

"Oh, yes, the wedge haircut is very popular right now! It will look fabulous on you!"

All the ladies that work at McCready's, along with quite a few of the customers, got involved in my haircut. They were all stunned at how much hair was on the floor—the hairdresser told everyone that she was taking about ten inches off the back! The hardest part was to get the bangs right—I wanted one side to droop down towards my eyebrow.

When the beauty operator got done with the cutting and trimming, she gave me a mirror and had me look it over. Once I gave my approval, she showed me how to style it with a blow dryer and curling iron, both of which I purchased. When I got outside, I sashayed my way home as though I was a beauty queen in a pageant! I know I'm not that beautiful, but it felt good to pretend! The icing on the cake was when Mom got home last night and told me she loved my hair!

෧౿

So now, here we are at the airport waiting to get on the plane to fly off to Texas. Gloria and I are kind of in the spotlight at the airport, because of our matching outfits. Everyone who notices wants to know where we got the outfits, and I'm very proud to announce that I made them.

"Well, look at those outfits," a woman says. "The pattern on that fabric is outstanding! What a great idea to make mother-daughter outfits!" The lady finishes.

"Oh, we're sisters!" I correct her. "I made the outfits for our first plane ride."

"Sorry about that! But they are adorable!"

"How dare she!" Mom says, turning to me. "How dare that woman make that comment! I'm the mother! I am!" Oh boy, this is not what I thought was going to happen at all! Mom's hair is pretty much all gray now, and her nails and teeth have turned a little yellowish from smoking, so I guess she looks kind of like a grandma. But there's no way I look old enough to be a mother!

"Oh, Mom," I say. "Don't worry about it. She probably didn't see you sitting there." Geez, I hope Mom calms down—no sense letting something like this ruin our trip.

But after another three or four people say the same thing, Mom is almost out of her mind, and I'm out of ideas of what to say. "Mom, maybe it's because I'm so tall—you're always telling me I'm growing like a weed! Once they take a good look at me, they know I'm just the sister." But I can tell that this doesn't appease Mom in the least; she's sitting in her seat with her lips straight and her eyes glaring straight ahead.

I decide that from now on, if anyone even comes close to us, I'm going to be the first to speak: "How do you like our sister outfits?!"

The plane ride from Minneapolis to Dallas will take five hours, so Gloria and I plan to do a lot of reading—and sleeping. The seats are different than in a car, and everyone must wear a seatbelt, no matter what. Mom's all excited to have lunch on the plane, but when it comes, I'm not too sure I want to eat it. It's kind of like a Swanson TV dinner, but not as good. Gloria lucked out, because the kids' meal was a peanut butter and jelly sandwich with potato chips; she gobbled it right up!

As we get off the plane in Dallas, Mom asks an airport person how we get to our next plane. The answer she receives surprises all of us. The place is so big it would be impossible to walk to our gate; we have to take a train! Even at that, we have a somewhat long walk to get to the closest train stop. Mom is instantly worried that we don't have enough time, which means I'm also worried.

The airport person suggests we can save some walking time by riding on what is called a walkalator, also known as a moving sidewalk. It's so cool! I hop on first, and Gloria and Mom get on right behind me. While we ride on it, we pass by a bunch of stores, restaurants, bathrooms and tons of people. What a place! So much to look at—it's almost like a city in here! And then . . .

"JOAN! Watch out!" I hear Mom yell—at exactly the moment I fall flat on my face! Instantly, I start laughing. I look up at Mom, who is rushing over to me. A few other people stop to look, ask if I'm okay.

"Oh, my!" I say, picking myself up. "Guess I wasn't paying attention!"

"I knew you were going to trip, but there wasn't anything I could do about it!" Mom laughs. "Are you okay?"

"Yeah, guess I skinned my knees," I say. For some reason, neither of us can stop laughing.

Even though I wish I hadn't made a spectacle of myself, it did seem to take away Mom's worrying. She smiles and laughs the whole rest of the way to the train station.

The plane taking us to Amarillo is quite a bit smaller than the one we boarded in Minneapolis. I would say it's cozy—a little too cozy, even. But the ride is short, and before you know it, we're off the plane and on our way to get our luggage. No moving walkways or trains in this place—compared to Dallas, this airport is a piece of cake!

After we get our bags from the suitcase carousel thingy, we step outside to wait for Mark. The first thing we all notice is how hot it is, and while we wait for Mark, Mom announces she doesn't think she's ever been so hot in all her life.

"I see him! I see Mark!" Gloria shouts.

"Welcome to Texas!" Mark says, hopping out of his white Oldsmobile Cutlass. "Whoa! Matching outfits, ha? Did you make those, Joan?"

"Yeah, I did!"

"Wow! Far out!" he says. Gloria and I slide into the backseat of his car, and, once Mom and Mark are inside, we take off.

On the way to Spearman, Mom tells Mark about all the people who thought our sister outfits were mother-daughter outfits. She's getting herself all upset about it again, but I don't care. A lot of people liked them, and so does Mark; if my brother says they're cool, then they are.

Gloria and I watch out the window to see the sights as Mark drives us from the airport to his house in Spearman. Amarillo and Spearman are in what is called the panhandle of Texas, and we have to drive about an hour to get there. I don't know a whole lot about Texas, but by looking out the car window, I can tell it's nothing like Minnesota. First, there are no trees. No plants. Nothing green at all—just a lot of brown, dry-looking land. Even the grass looks brown. And another thing: everything is as flat as a pancake—you can see for miles and miles—but what you see is a lot of nothing. No houses, no farms—there are hardly even any other cars on the road. At one point, I see a few strange machines off in the distance.

"What are those?" I ask.

"Oil wells! Big business down here," Mark exclaims. "That's about the only thing you're going to see until we get to my town; a bit longer and we'll be there."

"Here we are!" Mark proclaims, pulling into Spearman. In a second, we are at his house. Once we are out of the car, an overpowering heat slams into us. No wonder trees and plants don't grow here. We all take a minute to adjust; it feels like the sun is burning me right through my jumpsuit. Standing in Mark's little yard, I see that it represents Texas well—it is filled with the driest looking dirt I've ever seen.

Mark unlocks his door, and we all pile into his house. To describe it as a little house would be generous—teeny-tiny would be more accurate. The entire house fits in one room; the kitchen and bathroom are all the way to the back, and living/bedroom area is towards the front. As Mark gives us the ten-second tour, he informs us that what is now his house used to be a one-car garage.

"Good thing it's only you living here!" I say as Gloria starts to explore the music corner in the living area.

"Yep, just enough room for me, my amp, and my guitar!" Mark proclaims.

The radio station Mark works at is conveniently located right next door, and Mark takes us inside for a tour. The station is a little bigger than his house, and we get to see where he sits when he's on the air.

"Do you get to play rock and roll?" I ask.

"No, there's not a lot of call for music, unfortunately. Mostly I give out weather and crop reports, oil prices—that sort of thing. People down here are mostly into country music anyway."

"What IS the temperature today?" Mom asks as we head back outside. She looks as though she's been in an oven for a couple of hours.

"High today is ninety-five degrees!" Mark says. "It's a dry heat; it doesn't feel as bad as it would in Minnesota with all the humidity up there."

"I'm not so sure about that," Mom says. "I think I need to stay inside for a bit."

The next morning, we listen to Mark on the radio for a while, then head over to the station because he wants to interview Gloria on the air. My five-year-old sister, who also got a haircut before the trip, looks perfectly adorable sitting at Mark's side in the studio. She proudly tells the people of Spearman who she is and where she's from as if she's been an interviewee all her life. So, so cute!

"Okay, that's a wrap!" Mark says. "I'm done working for the day, thought we'd do a little sightseeing. Are you guys up for that?" We are, so we all climb into Mark's car, which is about as hot as the Towering Inferno, and head towards Amarillo.

"What are we going to see, Mark?" Gloria asks from the back seat. I, too, am curious. I'm ready to spend my fifty bucks on some souvenirs.

"We're going to this great national park—it's an area filled with this cool rock called Alibates. The Indians used it to make tools and arrowheads and stuff."

When we drive onto the property of Alibates National Park, I realize this is most likely not where I'm going to be spending my fifty bucks. We slowly climb out of the car—and, again, into the heat. "Not a speck of shade in this state, is there Mark?" Mom complains.

"Yeah, well. Nothing we can do about the heat! C'mon, let's find the Park Ranger," Mark says as he starts walking up a dust-filled incline. At the top of the slope, we come across a small trailer. Mark knocks on the door, and out pops our tour guide.

"Step right in!" The ranger is dressed in what looks like a Boy Scout uniform.

"Thanks! We're here to learn all about this place," Mark says, adding that he lives in Spearman and we live in Minnesota. And God bless America! The trailer has air conditioning! Whoever invented air conditioning should get the Nobel Prize for Science, in my opinion.

"This here is our Alibates Rock Collection," the man says, proudly. I'm guessing he's expecting us to ooh and ahh over it, but honestly, I'm not all that impressed. I guess it's pretty— the red, pink, and cream colors look kind of like marble—but let's face it: a rock is a rock. He ends his demonstration with an explanation of how the Indians would have carved arrowheads from the rock, and he gives each of us a small arrowhead to keep. Once he's done showing off the collection, we follow Mr. Ranger back outside.

"Head up that way a bit," he says, pointing in the direction of what I would call an old dusty trail. "You'll see a ton of the

Alibates in the quarry." Didn't we just see a ton in his little trailer? Whether it was or not, it was enough for me. But I guess Mark wants to see more, so Mom, Gloria, and I follow him up the trail.

I guess I understand what Mark meant by Texas having a dry heat. As hot as I am, I am not breaking a sweat, even while climbing up this rock infested hill. Though it feels like my jeans are melting right into the flesh of my legs, and the top of my head feels as hot as the surface of the sun, I am not sweating—but I am drying out. In biology, Mr. Gilmore told us that water makes up about sixty percent of our bodies. I think I'm down to about ten percent right now; my mouth is so dry it feels like it's lined with snakeskin.

"This quarry was dug by hand," Mark tells us, as we reach the top of the trail and look out over the valley. "The Indians discovered the Alibates rock, then realized there was a whole bunch of it in the earth. Once they learned how to carve the Alibates into arrowheads, they were able to hunt large animals. Probably saved their lives!" Mark sure is into this Alibates thing.

"That's cool," I say, not wanting to hurt my brother's feelings. There is a smattering of trees in the valley. They aren't tall like our ash tree at home, but at least there is some green amidst the brown. From our viewpoint, large chunks of Alibates glimmer in the sunlight—and I guess it is kind of pretty.

"Where are we going next?" Gloria asks as we all climb back in the car.

"Thought we'd go for a drive, and then I want to take you to this huge steakhouse for dinner," Mark tells us. "It's in Amarillo and is called The Country Barn. If there's one thing they do right in Texas, it's steak!"

When we get inside the restaurant, I feel like I've died and gone to heaven—it looks fantastic! This is no Ponderosa, or even McGuire's! It's enormous! There's a pool table right in the middle, a jukebox for us to play all our favorite songs, and pinball machines! Mom gives Gloria and me some quarters to play the games while she and Mark find us a place to sit. It's not the kind of place where every family has their own table—it's more like indoor picnic tables. Mark says we should all order a steak, because no one should leave Texas without having a steak, so we do.

"Wow!" Mom says, as her food is placed before her. "There is no way I'm going to be able to eat all of this!"

"Yeah, well, I'm here to accept all leftovers!" Mark says, laughing. As I eat my food, I notice how happy Mom looks. Her smile is different than it is at home—carefree, I guess. And as if she's reading my mind, Mom sums it all up.

"I'm so glad we're able to come and visit you, Mark! There's nothing more important to me than having my three kids together, all in one place. I love being on vacation! No worries, not a care in the world!"

Despite the heat and the weird Alibates rock place, this trip was a success! I got to ride in an airplane, see my brother at work, and eat some fantastic steak! I guess Texas isn't a good place to go if you want to spend money, though—I still have my fifty bucks!

MR. HOFFMAN

NINTH GRADE! SUPPOSEDLY ALL 320 of us are now the Kings and Queens of Johanna Junior High! I'm making an extra effort not to care about the Trio and the boys on the bus, but it's not as easy as I thought it would be.

Oh, and yes, I still must take good old gym class. What would happen to our poor bodies if they were denied torture every day? At least I don't have Miss Wiig again—this year the assigned tormentor is Miss Brunsell. I can't wait to find out what she has in store for me this year. Gym class falls into the same category as the Trio as far as I'm concerned—the I Don't Care category.

Because you know what? I rocked at track and field last spring. So far, it's the only good experience I've had in physical education. I loved the hurdles: I leaped over them like they weren't even there—and not only improved my time but also raised the height of the hurdles higher and higher. And each week of class I excelled—yes, excelled—at the long jump. My legs were about two inches longer than any other girl in my group, and I leaped farther than anyone else on the first day! And—I proved to be a good runner. My favorite? The relay race. My group always put me as the last runner, because they knew I would be able to make up any time that was lost in the beginning. Plus, I accomplished it all with my stupid tennis shoes from Connco. And what was the big reward for my effort in track and field? A big fat C. So I could care less about gym.

Walking through the halls on this first day of ninth grade, all I can think about is how glad I am that this is my last year at good old Johanna Junior High. I have absolutely no idea what high school will be like, but it has to be better than this place—it has to be. I ended up with math as my first hour class, torture to be specific. Glad that's over for today! My next class, creative writing, is all the way on the other side of the school.

As I enter through the open doorway, I'm greeted by the teacher, a haphazardly-dressed older man. His wrinkled white shirt and baggy slacks are a distinct departure from my math teacher's crisply-pressed outfit.

"Okay, okay," Mr. Hoffman, says, peering at us over his black-rimmed glasses, trying to get us to take our seats. He's not bald exactly, but I would say he's going to be very soon. Most teachers let us sit wherever we want and make the seating chart up accordingly. But Mr. Hoffman has created a seating chart before even meeting us—like we're back in sixth grade or something! Each kid has to stop to see him and look at the chart to find out where to sit. He didn't put me in the back corner where I like to be—I'm in the middle row, second desk in—visible to everyone in the class, including Mr. Hoffman. "Come on now—find your seat—the bell is about to ring!" I climb into my seat and slump down as far as I can. This old guy obviously doesn't have a clue how to treat ninth graders, and I plan to zone out as best I can.

Mr. Hoffman proceeds to welcome us to his class; he's truly glad we're here! And then he launches into a description of what creative writing class is all about.

"Creative writing is a class where you get t⁓ ⁓ress your thoughts, ideas, and emotions in the wri⁓   You'll be writing about people and experiences that have affected your life—but we'll also be doing a lot with imagination." Mr. Hoffman, sitting on a chair in the front of the classroom, clearly loves the idea of writing creatively. As he briefly describes the different forms of writing we will be doing—character profiles, short stories, poetry, drama, and something called an essay—I start to perk up a little bit. The energy that Mr. Hoffman puts forth is enticing—pulling me in a bit.

"The one thing you have to do for me is to write every single day. Writing on a daily basis is the only way that writers improve," Mr. Hoffman stands up to help make his point. His voice is strong and encouraging, and he's looking out across the room to make sure everyone is listening. "You will each start a writing notebook—you can write whatever you want in it, but you have to put something down in it every day." He goes on to tell us that basically, we have an A for the notebook assignment; the only way to drop it to a B is to miss a day of writing. He claims that even one sentence—even a word, or a drawing—on any given day counts; a blank page does not. "This is in addition to whatever writing assignment we're working on. Consider it an easy A."

"Like, what do we write about?" A kid in the back asks.

"Anything, anything at all. Write a ghost story. Write a poem. Write about your day. Write about your annoying little sister. The point is simply to write." He finalizes the plan by telling us we will turn in our notebooks every Monday—he will return them to us on Tuesdays.

❧

I must admit, the daily writing in the journal was easy. I decided to take Mr. Hoffman at his word—that something as short as one sentence written in my green notebook will ensure an A. When I got it back today, I was surprised at some of his responses—all written in blue ink. His comments are hard to read, because he has the scrunchiest, tiniest cursive I have ever seen.

Tuesday: I think I might like Creative Writing.

I'm so glad. I love teaching it!

Wednesday: I have an older brother who lives in Texas, and a younger sister, Gloria.

How old are your siblings? I don't remember having your brother in class.

Thursday: I have no idea what to write today.

This is called writer's block—it happens to even the best of writers.

Friday: I wish gym class wasn't mandatory.

What is it that bothers you about gym?

Saturday: I helped Mom clean the house and do laundry today.

Your mother is teaching you to be a good citizen! Hooray for her!

Sunday: We went to noon mass; we go to St. John the Baptist Catholic Church.

Do you go every Sunday?

Monday: I'll be turning this notebook in to you today.

Thank you for writing every day. I look forward to hearing more. D Hoffman.

I was expecting him to correct spelling and grammar like a regular English teacher would, but instead, it seems he's interested in what I wrote. I guess it couldn't hurt to write a little more than one sentence each day.

෨

It's already Tuesday, and I'm waiting with the utmost of anticipation to get my green notebook back. I can't wait to read Mr. Hoffman's comments. When he hands our notebooks back, he gives it straight to each student, no passing them down the row or anything like that. I like knowing that what I write is private—well, semi-private, anyway. Once again, Mr. Hoffman's comments surprise me. I'm starting to think the old fellow DOES have a clue.

Tuesday: Today in gym class, we got to go outside to play softball. Oh yeah! My all-time favorite thing to do. NOT! I swear that ball is going to hit me right in the head when the pitcher sends it my way. And catch it—couldn't do it in seventh or eighth, and apparently, I can't in ninth either. No one, absolutely no one, wants me on their team. This is why I wish gym class wasn't forced on us, it's more like punishment than a class.

Softball isn't for everyone and I can relate to being scared of the ball. I bet you'll find an activity someday that you really enjoy.

Wednesday: Today I picked my sister up from the babysitter (Bernice) after I finished my homework, because my mom had to work late. My sister, Gloria, is going to be six years old in December. She is the light of my life, I love her more than anything!

*There is nothing in this world better than a close sibling.
I'm glad you have your sister in your life—I love her name!
I'm proud of the way you care for her.*

Thursday: I haven't told many people this, but my parents
are divorced. You might think I would be sad about it, but my
dad has a problem with his temper, and can be pretty violent—
so I'm actually happy about it. I'm pretty sure I'm the only one
in this school that has divorced parents, so that's why I don't
talk about it.

*Wow, that's heavy stuff you're dealing with. I'm sure it's
been very difficult for you to deal with your dad's temper.
It sounds like he might be an aggressive person. I know
divorce is hard on kids, no matter why it happened. I hope
that you are safe.*

Friday: On Fridays, I pick Gloria up from Bernice's
right after school. I babysit until 8:30 p.m. or so, because my
mom works late on Fridays. Tonight, I made Kraft macaroni
and cheese for us for supper. Then we played outside for a
while, and then we watched *Planet of the Apes*. When I tuck
my sister in, I always sing her the "Goodnight Sleep Tight"
song from Lawrence Welk.

*You babysit every Friday night? You have a lot of
responsibility at home. I enjoy the Goodnight song as
well. Did you know that a lot of music writers got their
start in Creative Writing? Bob Dylan, for instance. A few
of his songs started out as writing pieces, then were put
to music to become the famous ballads they are today. At
least I think that's true!*

Saturday: Great night! Our neighbors, Bernice and Lawrence, had a fish fry party tonight! Bernice (same Bernice that babysits my sister) makes everything—and I mean everything—homemade. She hand-dips the walleye (that they caught up on Lake Mille Lacs) in her super secret flour mixture, then fries it in a big tub of oil—oooohh yum! Plus, she makes her own dinner rolls and the most scrumptious thousand island salad dressing. In addition to all that, everyone gets a baked potato. I love her fish fry dinners!

Ah, your description of Bernice's cooking makes me feel like I was right there! Good job!

Sunday: Boring! Boring! We went to mass as always. Here's the thing about our church—it's huge and we know almost no one. Oh, sure, I might see someone sitting almost a block away that I know, but no one that's anywhere near me. And even if we do see someone, we rarely talk to them. When my brother was my age, he got to stand at the back of the church with his friends and as soon as mass started, they were out of the church. I still can't figure out how Mom never knew that. But me? Nope, not allowed to stand at the back of the church. Mainly, what I do during the hour of religious enlightenment is keep Gloria entertained. We play I-Spy, look for babies, count pink dresses, black hats—that type of thing. On the rare occasion that I do listen to the priest—guess what he's talking about? How bad we are: we are all sinners, every single one of us. Oh, that, and the church needs money.

Every Sunday before we go to church, Mom puts a roast beef in her electric roaster thing. The meat sits in there until about 4:00 p.m., and then we have to eat it. It is the grossest meat you could EVER have. The only way I can get it down is to cover it in ketchup—and even then I can hardly chew it. I'd rather have her fried chicken or pork chops. Really anything else would do! Please don't tell my mom this!

Hmm . . . well, I'm not much of a cook, but five hours does seem like a long time to cook a roast. I'll hope for more pork chops and chicken in your future! And your secret is safe with me!

Monday: I might as well get this out in the open. There are a lot of kids in this school that hate me. The three main ones are girls, and I call them the Trio. It's pretty much all my fault, because on the first day of seventh grade I accidentally bumped into one of them. That, combined with me being kind of ugly and a little fat, makes them hate me—and they aren't shy about showing it, either! Truthfully, it's been awful. Now there are quite a few more kids, including boys, who hate me—so now I call the whole group the Trio Plus. I have to watch behind my back, in front of me, on the side of me (you get the picture) to try to prevent them from tripping, hitting, or shoving me. So if you happen to see someone bugging me, they are probably part of the Trio Plus.

It is heartbreaking for me to hear this. I believe that students should not be able to treat other students this way. If you ever need assistance with anything, please let me know. Otherwise, hold your head up high! You are better than them. There is no way with a smile like yours that anyone could consider you ugly, and I certainly don't see you as a fat person. I hope that someday they will learn to be as kind as you are. D Hoffman

ໜ

As I finish reading Mr. Hoffman's comments, I set my notebook down and try to process what he's saying. I re-read the scrunched-up comments that he wrote in the margins. Mr. Hoffman is not putting the blame for the Trio Plus' actions on me? He thinks they shouldn't be acting this way? Could that be true? And he thinks I have a nice smile? And I'm somehow better than them? I don't know about that one—I still only have two pairs of jeans. And of course, there is the shoe situation. But still.

I'm glad I wrote about the divorce, too. I thought it might freak Mr. Hoffman out to read about Dad's temper, but it feels like he understands something about it.

Setting my notebook aside, I sit up a little higher in my desk and try to pay closer attention to what old Mr. Hoffman has to say. This teacher man with his rumpled clothing and black plastic-rimmed glasses is impressive.

"Today, we're going to start on our character profiles. I want each of you to think of an important person in your lives—try to pick someone you don't know absolutely everything about. Interview them, find out some unique qualities or characteristics about them—and then write a profile using as many adjectives and adverbs as you can," Mr. Hoffman instructs. I know instantly who I want to do it on, and I can't wait to interview her.

❧

The character profile was due last Friday, and Mr. Hoffman said we would get it back with our notebooks today. I worked so hard on it! I used almost every adjective I've ever learned! We didn't have to type it, but I did, which was hard, because each time I made a mistake, I had to start over again. Mom showed me how to put the paper in the machine, how to set the margins and how to mark the paper with light pencil at the bottom so I wouldn't type off the end of the page. I can't wait to see what Mr. Hoffman thought of it. When he hands mine back—again, he gives it directly to us—I think I see a little smile on his face. Quickly, I peek at the back page—and there it is—an A+!

On the bus on the way home from school, even though I have practically memorized the whole thing, I read the paper again. Placing the written masterpiece back on my lap, I decide to pay the interviewee a visit. It seems like it takes forever to get home, but soon I'm off the bus and on my way.

"Bernice! Are you downstairs?" I yell, as I come through her door after school. I know she isn't expecting me quite this early, but I can't wait to show her my paper.

"Yep, down here doing some ironing!"

"Guess what? I got an A+ on the paper I wrote about you! Can you believe it? An A+!"

"Oh, that's great, Joan! Wonderful! I'd love to hear it! How about if you read it to me while I finish up this ironing?"

As I read *A Lady of Many Talents* to Bernice, we both giggle at a few parts—like the fact that she hunts deer with a .32 caliber gun. But when I get to the last few lines, I suddenly start to cry—and when I look up at Bernice, I see that she has stopped ironing and is also crying.

Through the radiant glow in her face and her bubbly manner, one can see that Bernice is deeply in love with her life. She shares the happiness in her life with everyone she knows, and her exuberant personality permeates all she comes in contact with.

Bernice was put in this world for one obvious reason—to make others happy and comfortable, which is exactly what she does.

THAT DAMN ICE

MOM AND I ARE in the backyard outside my bedroom window, gazing up at the roof. There's been a water leak in the far corner of my room—drip-drip-dripping its way through the outside construction of the house. It started out small, but over the last few days it has gotten worse—my ceiling is stained a kind of light gray. Standing in the snow, with our winter coats, boots, and gloves on, we stare at an incredibly thick piece of ice directly over where the leak is.

"There's water trapped under that ice," Mom declares as though she's been inspecting roofs in the middle of winter every year of her life. "We're going to have to get rid of that ice before there's more damage."

In the garage, I watch Mom search through Dad's haphazard collection of tools. "Okay, this will do the trick!" she announces, holding up a small hatchet. "Let's get the ladder set up."

I carry the ladder through the snow-filled backyard and set it precariously between the north side of the house and the neighbor's chain link fence. "I'll climb up and chop the ice while you hold the ladder," Mom directs.

In my mind, there are a multitude of problems with Mom's plan. Number one, the ladder (the same one we use for apple picking) doesn't reach the top of the house, so Mom is going to have to stand on the top step to reach the roof. Number two, there isn't enough room between the side of our house and the neighbor's chain-link fence for the ladder to stretch out— therefore, it can't be locked in place. Number three, the winter snowfall has caused a deep snowbank between the house and the fence, making the ladder crooked and unstable. Number four, it's totally and utterly freezing out here.

"Mom, I don't think this is such a good idea," I say. "Maybe we should call Lawrence or someone?"

"Bernice and Lawrence aren't home this weekend, and I don't have any money to hire someone." Mom reports.

"Well, how about Mr. H from up the street? Didn't he help Lawrence fix our walls and stuff? I bet he'd do it if we made his family a nice dinner or something—maybe some of your famous banana bread."

"They don't live there anymore. The whole family had to move, because people were throwing bricks through their front window. The only Negro family in New Brighton and they got chased right out of town. And to think it's 1976! Very sad."

"What? But their son still goes to Johanna—he's in my math class. He's a nice kid," I protest. This is quite possibly the saddest piece of news I've ever heard. A whole family run out of town? "Where did they move to?"

"Well, I guess they must not have gone far if their son is still at Johanna, but I don't know where they went. They had to keep it a secret, so the people running them out of town wouldn't know where they went. So you see, it's you and me, young lady. Now hang on to the ladder so we can get this over with."

I'm holding onto the ladder as tightly as I can while Mom climbs up. First, she takes the edge of the hatchet and cuts off all the icicles that are hanging down. I can remember that as a kid, I would get so excited to get an icicle. I'd treat it like a Popsicle, licking it while it stuck precariously to my mittens. Today, as I dodge the sharp points of ice falling towards my face, they look like darts, and I have absolutely no desire to pick any of them up. Once all the dangling ice darts are cleared, Mom starts chopping.

The repetitious "chnkk-chnkk-chnkk" sound is mesmerizing, and it puts me in a kind of trance. I worry about Mom up on the roof—nothing to hold onto. I know she used to walk five miles each way to school when she was a kid in Madelia, but this is different. Back then, her mom bundled her up in a warm winter coat and covered her hands in handmade woolen mittens. She even had special leg coverings to wear to protect her from the wintery elements. Though she has told me about the time when she and her brother made the walk to school, and probably shouldn't have because there was a blizzard starting up, that seems to be the only day there was actual danger. Today, I can tell Mom doesn't have the right kind of winter clothes for being outside for a long time, and certainly not for climbing an icy ladder. Her long wool coat doesn't button high enough to cover her neck, and flies apart at the bottom with the slightest wind, exposing her thin polyester pants to the fierce winter. Her boots are the kind all moms wear— an ankle boot with no traction on the bottom. Her gloves are ridiculously thin—I have a similar pair—and I know they aren't warm enough. She's got her see-through blue scarf on—tied under her chin—but I can't imagine it's keeping her ears warm.

My worst fear is that she will fall. If that happens, we're in trouble. Most likely she'll land on the top bar of the fence, where the chain links turn into twisted-triangular formations.

Even though Mom received a big raise when she was promoted to vice president of the bank, we don't have much money right now. As part of the divorce, the judge ordered that the money in Mom and Dad's bank account be split in half—Dad got $400.00 and so did Mom. It was what happened next that severely hurt Mom's pocketbook. Apparently, when Dad shopped at most of the businesses in New Brighton, he would say "Put it on my account!"—and they did. Mom said it's kind of like having a credit card without the card—the store keeps track of what you owe, and then you pay for it later. The only problem is that Dad never settled any of the accounts, and even though Mom didn't buy any of the stuff, it's her responsibility to pay them off. There is a whopper of a bill at Coast to Coast, where he seems that is where he bought the ice cream maker, the apple picker, and a lot of the stuff he needed to build the bathroom. There is also a large bill at the Municipal Liquor Store and Bar and a hefty bill at Clark Pharmacy. I wish my dad wouldn't have done that, because if he hadn't, maybe we'd be able to hire someone to fix our roof. It's a "melluvahess," Mom told me. That's what she says so she doesn't say "Hell" in front of me. But I say it the right way to myself: It's a hell of a mess. A HELL OF A MESS.

My arms are getting tired from holding the ladder, and I'm as cold as the icicles on the ground, but mostly, I'm worried about Mom. The wind is blowing like crazy now, and I can't imagine how she's keeping warm. Though she's been chopping for about a half hour, there is still a lot of ice up there.

"How are you doing, Mom?" I ask. "Do you want to trade places? Let me chop for a while?"

"UGGH! This damn ice! I can't get it to give way," Mom calls down from the top of the ladder. "My hands are frozen solid; I can hardly move my fingers."

"Mom, you need to take a break. Let's go in and warm up for a few minutes," I suggest. "I'll make us some hot chocolate."

In the house, she takes off her thin gloves and massages her right hand. "My God, it hurts. It feels like the hatchet is cutting right through my skin," Mom tells me as I hand her a cup of Swiss Miss. "I guess we'll have to take turns."

On my first turn, I'm astonished at how thick the ice is. It curves right over the edge of the house and smooths out over the gutter so that the entire surface is as slick as an ice rink. I reach my left hand up as far as I can, and finally find a ridge in the ice to rest that hand on—not as secure as I'd like, but at least it's something. I can see where Mom had been chopping, so I start my own up and down motions and get into the "chnkk-chnkk-chnkk" rhythm. Mom chopped down about a quarter of an inch, but I plan to do a lot more to save her from having to get up here too many more times.

As the sun begins to fade and I feel like my hand has been molded into the shape of the hatchet, I make a small break in the ice.

"I think I got through, Mom," I say, coming down the ladder. Mom heads up to check it out.

"Yep, there is a trickle of water coming out. Let's stop for today—you need to get ready to go babysitting anyway. We'll work on it again tomorrow."

ᘒᘎ

I've been hired by a family that lives near St. John's to babysit their kids tonight. I have no idea how they got my name, but I was overjoyed when the Mrs. called to see if I'd be interested.

"I'll be in bed long before you get home tonight," Mom tells me. "That ice-chopping almost did me in today. I'll take the brace off the door before I go to bed. When you come in, make sure you lock both doors and set the brace."

"Okay, no problem," I say, heading out to Mr. Husband's car.

The braces that Lawrence made for the doors are working great. Dad has been to the house a few times and, though he got the screen door open once, he hasn't been able to break through the inside door. The front door brace hasn't been tested yet because Dad never goes to the front door. On the nights he came, I listened from my room as Mom called the police, using the new phone in the hallway. Each time the police came and escorted Dad to his rat trap van and off he went.

There is one major problem that has resulted from Dad's pounding and knocking—anyone who knocks on the door is automatically suspected to be Dad. Mrs. Do-Gooder from down the street collecting for the March of Dimes; Mr./Mrs./Miss Religion, coming by to convert us; Mr. Handyman, coming by to see if our house could use new window or a paint job; Mr. New Car, stopping by to ask Mom about interest rates. All of them are suspect. Each and every knock on the door causes Mom and me to cringe and then immediately react. One of us grabs the phone, ready to dial the police, while the other tries to figure out if the person at the door is Dad. Once we figure out it's safe to answer the door, the cumbersome brace has to be taken down and set aside, the various locks unlocked. By the time the door opens, most visitors have started to turn away, thinking no one is home. And of course, Mom doesn't help matters much—by the time she opens the door, she has typically sunk into a foul mood, which possibly startles the poor guest more than the elaborate locking system they are witnessing.

"What can I help you with?" Mom will bark, sounding more like a guard dog than a woman.

"Mrs. Hicks—it's me, Mrs. Do-Gooder from down the street. I'm collecting donations for the March of Dimes/Diabetes Association/Easter Seals of America."

"I don't know why you even stop here!" Mom shouts. "I make all of my contributions through my church!" After slamming the door shut in their face, we proceed with refortifying the house. I watched for Mr.'s car out the front window to make sure he didn't have to see the creative locking system, or come in contact with my mom.

I feel incredibly lucky to have gotten this babysitting job, and I'm planning on making an outstanding impression, so they will want me to come back again.

Mr. Husband has a nice car, seems friendly enough. He's asking me a bunch of questions on the way to his house and telling me about their two kids. I guess he doesn't know that his wife has already told me all about them.

When we walk in the house, I immediately greet the children. "Hello, Kid One and Kid Two! How are you guys tonight? Are you ready to have some fun?" Once the Mr. and Mrs. say goodnight to their kids, they head off to their dinner party. "Have fun!" I tell them.

The kids are so good—almost as good as Gloria. We spend the evening coloring, making things with Play-Dough, and creating a cute design on their Lite-Brite. They didn't even argue with me at bedtime. Once they are all settled, I pick up everything I can, wash the dishes that are on the counter, and sweep up the kitchen floor. Finally, I settle myself on their couch to read until Mr. and Mrs. come home.

"Well, how did it go?" the Mrs. asks as they come through the back door, bringing in a whoosh of cold air. "I can't believe we stayed out until midnight!"

"My goodness, your kids are so good!" I proudly report. "I didn't have any trouble at all. They went to bed just fine and everything. They wanted me to leave the Lite-Brite plugged in, so you could see what we made."

While I get my coat and boots on, the Mrs. pays me, thanks me, and says she'll be sure to call again. I head out the door and get into Mr. Husband's car for the ride home. About the time we turn onto Old Highway Eight, I start to panic. I can't answer any more of Mr. Husband's questions. I must think—think fast.

I'm still getting used to the idea of needing to have my house keys with me whenever I leave the house. The few times that I've forgotten them have been after school. That's an easy thing to deal with because I can go over to Bernice's, Nancy's, or Sharon's and wait for Mom to get home from work. But forgetting them tonight is a whole different story.

"Is something wrong?" Mr. Husband asks as we turn onto Eleventh Avenue.

"Um, well, I forgot my house keys, and I'm pretty sure my mom is sleeping," I say, my voice wobbling in reply. I don't know how to proceed. If I knock on the door to try to wake Mom up, I know she will assume it's Dad and call the police. I could ask Mr. Husband to take me somewhere to call Mom, but I know she won't answer the phone, because she'll think it's Dad calling. Either way, Mom will wake up and be scared to death, and it will be all my fault.

"Well, I'll wait in the car until you wake your Mom up," my escort advises. "Once I see you're safe inside, I'll take off."

"Okay." Truthfully, I wish he would leave—that way I could stay on the step or something and wait until morning to get in the house. It's not that cold out, I could figure out some way to keep warm. But he's waiting, so I'm going to have to try to wake Mom up and hope she doesn't call the police. He will probably freak out if the police come screeching around the corner and park right behind his car.

Walking up the sidewalk, I decide to go to the front door. I'm hoping that if I knock there, Mom will get a sort of clue that it's not Dad, since he's never pounded on that door before. I'm so nervous to knock on the door my hands are shaking. I knock softly at first, hoping Mom is still awake and she will hear my light knocking and stay calm.

"Is everything okay?" I turn back and see that Mr. Husband has gotten out of his car.

"Yeah," I lie, my breath making a little white cloud in front of my face. "I'll try knocking a little harder." I don't know what to say to him, but I wish he would get back in his car. I'm predicting this isn't going to go well, and the less he sees and hears, the better.

The screen door is unlocked, so I open it and pound loudly on the inside door. The knocking fills my body; my heart continues pounding even after my fist is still. I wait a minute, then knock again. Almost instantly, the hallway light flicks on, but Mom does not come into view. She's calling the police.

"MOM!" I scream loudly, forgetting that anyone else is listening. "MOM! It's me! I forgot my keys! Don't call the police, Mom!" Moving to the far edge of the step, I try to look in the front window—maybe my shadow will show through the drape, and she'll realize it's me. "MOM! It's me, Joan!" I scream again, as I slide on the ice and fall into the flower bed. Damn that ice!

"Are you sure everything's alright?" Mr. Husband says worriedly. Picking myself up out of the flower bed, which in the dead of winter transforms into a snowbank, I turn and see that he's on the sidewalk, walking towards me. He's wearing one of those long black coats that men with important jobs wear, like my Uncle Earle. His hands are thrust into the deep pockets, trying to stay warm. His bewildered expression tells me he's not sure what is expected of him.

"Sorry," I say, trying to sound more like an adult than a kid. "My Mom gets scared sometimes and she calls the police when she's scared. She might be calling them right now."

"What?" he says, alarmed. "Oh, well. Hmm." The awkwardness of the situation is starting to dawn on him. My adult-sized voice did nothing to erase the bewilderment from his face. "Do you think she forgot you were coming home late? Maybe you should wait in my car?" This is turning into a fucking nightmare!

Finally, I decide to scream to Mom one more time. At that, Mom comes to the door and opens it about a half inch.

"Mom, it's me! I forgot my keys. I'm so sorry!"

"MY GOD! You scared me half to death!" Mom screams at me. "I almost called the police!"

"Thank you for waiting. Everything's okay now," I say, turning to Mr. Husband. I can see he doesn't believe me, but there's no use trying to save him from worrying now. "Sorry for all the confusion. I sure did enjoy your kids!"

I step into the house, lamenting the fact that another babysitting job has gone to hell in a big ol' handbasket. And of course, Mom is raging. Her anger roars at me as if she were a lioness trapped in a cage at a zoo.

"If I've told you once, I've told you a hundred times! You cannot forget your keys!" Mom yells. "What in the world were you thinking?"

"Sorry! It's hard for me to remember; I didn't think of grabbing them tonight. I didn't mean to scare you!"

"I probably won't be able to get back to sleep! This can't happen again! You're fourteen, almost fifteen years old and it's time for you to become more responsible! Now, make sure you lock up the doors and put the barricades up before you go to bed!" Mom admonishes as she slams her way back upstairs.

I'm shaking so hard. My breathing is crazy fast—I need to slow it down somehow. Sitting on the couch, I try to concentrate on my heart and my lungs. *Slow down, slow down.* After a few minutes, I'm breathing normally again, but my heart still feels like it's pattering a little too hard and fast.

The wood brace for the back door is kept in the stairwell when it isn't being used—I open the basement door to grab it. Placing it against the basement door frame, I give the wedge a good shove, try to jam it in under the doorknob, and almost scream out in pain. I look at the palm of my right hand and see there is a bruise on it from the hatchet. Finally, I push the damn thing into place with the side of my left hand. Moving to the front door, I reset the lock on the doorknob, then place that brace. Once all fortifications are secured, I turn out the lights and head to my bedroom.

I'm not calm enough to fall asleep. Can't relax. Can't read. Can't cry. It feels like I could throw up. My heart stopped pounding, but now my breathing is acting up again. Everything hurts—my legs, my arms, my shoulders.

Why are we—my mom, my sister and me—the ones being punished for Dad's behavior? Why do we have to live in fear every single second of our lives—wondering where Dad is, what he's up to? Why do we have to live in a house that is fortified like a king's castle? Why do we (well, Mom) have to pay off all of Dad's stupid bills? Shouldn't there be some way to make him be the one who has to pay—to pay and pay and pay? What is the right answer to this shitty situation, anyway?

I remember some dumb television show I watched, *Dr. Doolittle* or some crazy show, where they attach a note to a bird and then train it to deliver it to another person. If I could get my hands on one of those birds, maybe I could attach a hundred notes to its body and then train it to give one to Dad each time he makes a move. *Don't call your family. Don't go visit your family. Don't threaten your family.* Dad would never read the notes, and he'd probably hurt the bird or kill it. And then there'd be a dead bird that was all my fault. I wish I was a smart person so that I could think of something that's not a stupid idea to help us.

To be honest, what I really want is to know what it feels like to be a normal girl. I want to have a day where I'm not terrified of every living thing—looking around every corner for the next traumatic event, waiting on Dad's next showmanship. I want to raise my shoulders up, see how tall I truly am, and give up this hunched shoulder routine.

As I ponder this, I hear a drip-drip-drip. I look up at the corner of my ceiling—water is dripping in from the roof. And then, I realize I'm crying. Sobbing. Bawling.

How do I write about this in my creative writing notebook?

☙

Sunday: I had kind of a rough weekend—sorry I didn't write on Saturday. I had to help my mom chop into an ice dam on our roof—it was hard on our hands, but between the two of us we got through it, and I'm hoping it will stop the water from leaking through my ceiling. That isn't the worst of it, though . . . I hurt my mom's feelings really badly, because I forgot to take my house keys with when I went babysitting on Saturday night. When the Mr. found out he asked if I wanted to call my mom to let her know but I said no, because I knew that Mom wouldn't answer, because she would think it was my dad calling to torture her over the phone so then he brought me home and I didn't know what to do, because my mom was already asleep and I knew that if I knocked on the door she would get scared and think it was my dad trying to break in and then she would call the police and then the police would come and find out it is only me so what I finally decided was to knock on the front door, because my dad never knocks on that door so then maybe Mom wouldn't automatically call the police but then I couldn't see and I had to shout to her to let her know it was me and I started to cry which made it so I couldn't yell as loudly as I wanted to and I was so cold and then I fell off the step, because it had ice on it and I could tell the Mr. was getting super nervous behind me so I tried to tell him not to worry that everything would be okay and I was glad when Mom finally realized it was just me and she opened the door but then she started yelling at me right away for making her so scared and forgetting my keys and then she told me what a dumb kid I am and what a stupid thing it was to do and then she told me to put the barricades up against the doors and then she slammed her bedroom door and went back to bed so I made sure the doors were locked tight and I put up the barricades and went to bed and bawled my eyes out.

Joan—My heart is broken into a million pieces over what you have shared on these pages. I'm truly honored to know that you feel this is a safe place to write what is happening in your life, and how it makes you feel. What I will tell you is that you are a remarkable young woman, full of warmth, empathy, kindness and sincerity. Every day you are faced with unspeakable situations, both at home and at school, and yet you persevere, always trying your best to rise above it. I am filled with sadness to know that you, your sister and your mother have to constantly fear for your safety—for your lives. From what you have written so far, your dad is very ill and needs help and I hope with all my heart that that happens soon. Please know that I am thinking of you and your family, praying for your safety and security. On another note—it is not a crime to forget your keys—I forget mine all the time. I even locked my keys in my car the other day. Things like this will happen all throughout your life—they are typically called "little things" and normally should not result in so much stress and strife. I'm sure that your mom was reacting because of her fear, not because she truly thought you were dumb. Lastly, I want to encourage you to keep writing. You have a gift for writing, and if you allow it to, it may relieve a tiny bit of your sadness.

Monday: I'm sorry I wrote all that on Sunday—you're probably getting sick of reading about all my problems! Oh, and, I'm doubly sorry that Sunday's entry is one big run-on sentence. If I could, I would erase the whole thing. I'm failing at this notebook thing!

Joan—As I said before, keep writing. It doesn't matter if you write run-on sentences, print, use cursive, write in all capitals or in block letters—just write. D Hoffman

HIA

"JOAN, SIT DOWN AT the table for a minute, I've got something to show you," Mom instructs me as she sets a bag, labeled with the Radio Shack logo, on the kitchen table. I watch as, one by one, she reveals her purchases. A cassette recorder. A package of fifty cassette tapes. A wire with an earpiece similar to the one I have for my AM/FM Transistor radio. And finally, a black box with a cord coming out of each end.

"What's all this?" I ask, looking over the items.

"We're going to start recording your dad's phone calls," Mom says, in a tone that is both matter-of-fact and confident. "I've been talking to a bunch of people, and this is what they recommend."

"What? Like on the detective shows or something?" I ask, trying to fathom Mom and me becoming private eyes.

"*Barnaby Jones*, here we come! I went to Radio Shack today, and the guys there helped me get all the right stuff and taught me how to set it up. It's more like the CIA than *Barnaby Jones*, though." I'm a bit stunned: Mom's acting like this is something people do all the time.

"Is this something your lawyer suggested? For court or something?" I ask as she starts to set up the equipment.

Mom removes everything off the ledge that separates the kitchen from the family room, the one where we always keep a box of Kleenex and pen and paper so that I can write down important phone messages for her. All is whisked away to make room for the cassette recorder and tapes.

"Nope, not my lawyer. Okay, hand me that cord, the one with the twisty part on one end," Mom instructs, leaving me to wonder who these people are she's been talking to, who gave her this idea.

"Pay attention!" Mom shouts, catching me in wonderland. "You have to know how this works! Since he calls you every day, you're going to be the one doing the majority of the recording."

I still want to know who is behind this spy operation, but the topic has been brushed aside; question and answer time is over. As I listen and watch, I realize that, at the age of fifteen, I'm the chief operating officer of the HIA: the Hicks Intelligence Agency.

Mom proceeds to attach the various cords to the phone, recorder, and black box so that they are all interconnected. I know she's watched a lot of television, but I have to wonder how she has become so capable at being a spy. The earpiece has a suction cup on it, and I watch as Mom places it on the outside of the receiver, opposite where my ear will be when I'm on the phone. The other end of that cord has a jack on it, which Mom connects to the recording device.

"All set," Mom announces. "Always have the black box set to record—not playback." As Mom continues her final instructions, I decide that I will never let any of my friends inside this house ever again. How would I explain such a contraption, let alone the HIA, to Sharon? Nancy? Elise? No way.

"So now I just wait for him to call?" I ask. "It's all set to record?"

"Yes. Remember to push down on the record button when you answer. When the tape runs out, press eject and turn it over. Once both sides are full, pop a new tape in," Mom tells me, making it sound as if it's the easiest thing in the world.

☙

On the way home from school, I start to anticipate my first spy mission. Dad calls me almost every day now. I have no idea where he is; Mom says it's possible that he's homeless. That doesn't make sense to me, though. I don't think a homeless person would have a phone or a van. The only thing I do know is that when he's on the phone, he's not at our house.

As I unlock the doors, I hear the phone ringing—a sound that, even though I'm constantly anticipating it, sends a chill straight down my spine. I've heard girls at school talk about being on the phone with their friends for hours and hours discussing who knows what. That will never be me. I can hardly stand to touch the thing, for fear it will snap at me like one of the turtles in the creek at Hansen Park.

"Hello?" I answer, pushing down the record button on our new contraption. As Dad prattles on and on—today's rambling is about a large crack in a road, or sidewalk or something—I watch the little dials inside the cassette recorder wind the tape from one side to the other. Around and around it goes, as does Dad's rambling. No matter what he has to say, listening to him is a puzzle, but with practice, I've put some of the jigsaw pieces together. For instance, when he's talking louder than normal, or super fast, I know he's distressed about something. When he talks to The Others, people that aren't really there, I know he's unreachable, in a world created in his own brain. That's when I get horrible stomachaches, like the feeling I get when I'm super hungry mixed with the feeling I get when I have the stomach flu.

I've noticed Dad is having more and more of these one-sided

conversations. Sometimes he'll throw out a bizarre question to The Others, and, if they don't answer the way he wants, he will start to argue with them, increasing his agitation level dramatically. I guess it's like when a little kid has an imaginary friend—except that my dad is not a little kid. And on the other end of the phone is a real live person: me. Occasionally, he will try to draw me into his argument with The Others. I have learned that my response shouldn't go against his thoughts, but also shouldn't discredit The Others.

"You've seen it, I'm sure. Right, Joanie?" Dad asks.

It's difficult to determine how to answer, since I can't hear The Others. If I answer in a contradictory manner, Dad is faced with an imaginary dilemma: why doesn't his daughter believe The Others? While teasing out the quandary, he becomes more distraught. To prevent conflict amongst all of us, I've developed a standard response to most of his questions.

"Yeah, sure, Dad," I say.

He moves right along with his tale, the various places in his brain take me from the sidewalk story to something about the moon. I can't imagine anyone listening to this recording. What will they be able to make of it? I hear the recorder click off, as if it's heard enough of the rambling. I turn the cassette over and press record while Dad chatters away.

This HIA recording system is going to severely restrict my ability to get my homework done. We had a super long cord on the phone before, allowing me to stretch it over to my spot at the table, hook the phone between my ear and neck—and work away. Now, I must stand by the phone to talk.

"Okay, Joanie. Your dear old Dad has to get going now," Dad says. I glance at the clock and see that he's been on the line for over an hour. After I hang up the phone, I hit the stop button on the cassette recorder and set out to do my homework. Not bad for my first day with the HIA.

"Well, how did it go?" Mom asks, coming through the door after a long day at the bank.

"Fine, I guess. The tape is still in the recorder—I think there's only about five minutes left on the second side." I dutifully report.

"Wow, okay. He talked for a long time, then? What did he talk about?" I give Mom a brief recounting of the crack in the sidewalk and the moon.

☙

I've been with the HIA for about two months now. I don't know exactly what the purpose of my secret-agent lifestyle is—the recorded tapes are simply stacked inside the cabinet under the end table—right next to the phone books. Mom has labeled each tape with the date and whether the conversation was with me or her. I have a bittersweet feeling about recording my dad's calls. Despite the destructive, despicable things he has done to us, I'm not sure it's the right thing for me to be doing. It's not something I can explain—it just doesn't feel right. More than once I have thought about not pushing the record button; I try to reconcile my feelings by knowing that it may help Mom, and therefore the rest of us, in some way.

When Dad calls after school, it's up to me whether I want to answer or not—and most of the time, I do, because I don't want to listen to incessant ringing or the busy signal while I do my homework. Plus, it might be a super important call from Sharon or Nancy. In the evenings and on the weekend, Mom makes the decision whether to answer or not—and most of the time, she decides to let it ring, or take the phone off the hook for the day. So the tapes labeled with "Joan" greatly outnumber those labeled with "Lyla."

Today, though, I'm going with Mom's decision-making process, because I have a lot of homework. For some reason, they pile it on in ninth grade, and since I haven't been keeping up all quarter, I've got some work ahead of me. My goal for today is to get caught up in social studies.

As usual, the phone starts ringing soon after I walk through the door. I listen to it ring as I fix my snack and get settled at the table. There is a moment's pause—no ringing—but it starts back up almost immediately. After a half hour, I accept the fact that I can't concentrate and decide to answer the damn thing. So much for getting caught up in good old social studies.

"Hello?" I say, pressing down the record button, as always.

"Well, well! Where have you been? I was starting to think you were trying to ignore your dear old Dad!" Dad's voice is different today. He doesn't sound far away, and there is a lilting to his speech—cheerful, bouncy.

"I'm here, Dad. Doing some homework," I say.

"Ah, well. Much ado about nothing . . . " Dad begins his ramble of the day. Where most of the time Dad's voice fades in and out while he talks with The Others, today his speech is clear. Not making any sense, but clear. It seems like The Others have the day off or something; Dad is focused solely on me.

"So, homework?" Dad says suddenly. "How's school going anyway?" I can't believe what I'm hearing. Dad has never asked me a question about myself before. That Dad has asked me a normal question temporarily confuses me. I wonder—is it possible that whatever has been wrong with Dad is getting better? I tell him what my classes are, what I'm working on for social studies.

"I'm getting an A in creative writing," I say, somewhat proudly.

"Oh, an A, ha?" Dad says. The hair on the back of my neck bristles as I note a change in his voice. The cheerful lilt is gone and has been replaced by a fast-paced speech pattern. "You think you're just a little smarty-pants, don't you? Sitting over there bragging about your A's!"

"Dad, no, I—" I want to tell Dad that this is the only class I'm getting an A in, how I'm barely getting B's in most of my other ones, and have mastered a solid C- in gym.

"Well, well! What would you think if I came over there with a gun and blew those smart brains right out of your head?" Dad screams.

His words pass through the phone and enter my ear like a lightning bolt; it feels like my ear canal is on fire. Did he say what I think he said? And Dad has a gun?

"What would you think then? A quick blast right into your brain," Dad continues, and I feel my eardrum light up as though it is part of the phone—the wires and recording equipment now a part of my internal anatomy. The words and equipment are taking up a lot of room in my ear; it feels like a steak knife is being forced through my ear. I squint my eyes and try to push the severe pain back into the stupid phone. Who invented this cruel device anyway?

My mind is in a state of uproar. A tornadic storm is whirling around the hills and valleys of my brain, and I can't make it stop. I need to say something, do something, but the pain in my ear is taking up every single ounce of my energy. Suddenly, a *snap* sound causes me to jump. The tape in the recorder has reached its end. With trembling fingers, I change it and press record again. If there is a conversation that needs to be recorded, it's this one.

"What was that noise?" Dad's voice booms into my already ravaged ear. I can't believe it! Dad heard the click when I pressed the record button!

"Nothing, Dad—I just, um, I opened the fridge, that's all," I try, holding back tears. But Dad is apparently having a moment of insane clarity and is onto me. What is his best girl up to?

"My God! You're recording this call, aren't you?" Dad says, incredulously. How in the world did he make that leap from a simple clicking sound? I am stunned at how clearly he's talking; his speech is suddenly percussionistic, precise. "GODDAMN

YOU AND YOUR MOTHER!" Dad thunders.

Standing in the family room, I'm temporarily stopped in motion, like I'm in a freeze-frame cartoon or something. I hold the phone to my ear as Dad continues talking, screaming, yelling—but I'm no longer listening to his words. I want to pull the phone away from my ear, but I can't make my arm move. I stare at the recorder, winding the brown ribbon from one side to the other; the cruelty that defines my dad is being permanently recorded and will be filed away in the HIA archives.

And then sudden silence fills my burning ear canal. Dad has hung up the phone. I stand and stare at the recorder—the machine is still trying to put his voice on the tape.

My mind is whirling with questions. What the hell just happened? Did I dream it? Is Dad on his way over here, with a gun? Will I die today? But I have no answers and no emotion. I'm not crying: my tear ducts are empty. All I do is stand and stare.

The fire in my ear eases a little—my brain cells are activated again. What am I doing just standing here? I've got to get out of here, and fast! I have no way of knowing where Dad is. How long will it take him to get to 509? If he's in New Brighton, at the Municipal Bar or the Log Cabin, I'm down to only minutes to get to safety. I quickly hang up the phone, click off the recorder. At the side door, I remove the wood brace and fly out the back door, planning to run to Bernice's. Shit! I didn't lock the doors. I run back inside, grab my keys off the table, lock the door. I slam it, maybe a little too hard, but I can't help it. I've got to hurry. I try to lock the outside door with the little key, but I fumble, and my whole key ring drops to the ground. I pick it back up and try again. Finally! Success—the door is locked. I look around, figuring Dad is lurking nearby. Bernice has told me about deer hunting, about how she sits high up in a tree with her shotgun to shoot a deer, and as I run under our apple tree, I peek up to be sure Dad's not up there, snaked around a limb or something.

When I get to Bernice's, I skip knocking on the door and run right in. "Bernice!" I scream. Her basement door is open, and in a wink, she's flying up the stairs.

"What? What's going on?"

"Lock your doors!" I scream. "I don't know where he is, and he told me he has a gun! Where's my sister? Is she home from kindergarten yet?" Getting this out takes all my energy, and my legs suddenly wobble like a roly-poly Weeble toy. I fall, landing on the rough carpet in her kitchen. Bernice helps me up, gets me settled on one of her kitchen chairs, and proceeds to shut and lock both of her doors. Returning to the kitchen, she pulls her chair close to mine.

"Okay, what happened?" Bernice asks. "Don't worry about Gloria; she's downstairs watching television." My body is in full tremble now, and my ear hurts so bad I think there is hot lava forming inside of it. My ear, transformed into a volcano.

"I can't stop shaking, Bernice," I say, looking up into her steamy glasses.

"It's okay," she says, taking both of my hands into hers. "Tell me everything you can." And so I tell her the whole crazy story. By the time I finish, Bernice is on the phone to the bank.

"Would he do it, Bernice? Do you think he would shoot me?" I can't believe it—won't believe it. I should cry—why aren't I crying? A kid should cry over something like this, shouldn't they? What's wrong with me?

"Oh, sweetie. I just don't know. Right now, I need you to breathe. Take some nice deep breaths. Once you calm down, I'll fix you some milk and cookies—okay?"

Mom arrives on the scene quickly—she left work early, something she never does. I repeat my story for her benefit. Mom calls the police, who agree with her that Dad has gone against the restraining order—apparently. The order restricts him not only from coming to 509 but also from calling us. The problem? They have no way of knowing where he is. They offer to check the local establishments, but beyond that, there isn't anything they can do until he shows up again.

"I guess we'll head on home," Mom says, which is the last thing I want to do. If I had my way, we'd never go back to 509. "If he shows up, we'll call the police. I'm sure they'd take him in for this."

But Bernice overrules her and she insists we stay for dinner so that the whole thing can be discussed with Lawrence. Minutes later, Lawrence, home from work, tries to come in the kitchen door but finds it locked. Bernice hops up and lets him in, and I can see he has already sensed some sort of danger.

"What's going on here?" Lawrence says in his gruff voice, glancing at the three of us. I am mostly silent as Mom and Bernice talk—they are the storytellers now. Occasionally, I add a sentence for clarification or nod my head to let Lawrence know that what they are saying is true.

"Harrumph," Lawrence says once the full story is out. "I can't imagine he's got a gun. I mean, where would he get it from? But Lyla, I certainly think you and the girls should stay here tonight." Thankfully, Mom agrees, and I breathe a deep sigh of relief. And even though I've never so much as held Lawrence's hand, I feel an urge to jump up and hug him.

I wonder how it is that Bernice found a good husband and my mom found a bad one. I would like to be a wife someday, but I'm not sure I want to take a chance on getting married—what if I marry someone like Dad instead of someone like Lawrence? I think it would be better to stay away from the whole marriage thing altogether.

Once Bernice has supper ready, I fix a plate for Gloria and myself and head down the stairs.

"Hey, there," I greet my sister, who is engrossed in some little kids' show.

"Is it time to go home?" Gloria asks.

"Nope. Bernice made us some supper. Mom's here, too. We're going to stay here tonight," I say, trying to keep my voice as calm as possible.

Gloria looks up at me and, after we've stared into each other's eyes for a minute or two, I can see that she knows something bad happened. I wonder if she can sense my body shaking and the fire burning inside my ear.

"It'll be okay," I say—but since I can't even convince myself, I'm not sure how effective I am at reassuring her.

At bedtime, as we fall asleep, I wrap my arms around Gloria, hold her close to me. She is such a beautiful little girl. When her breathing quiets, I slowly remove my arms from around her and roll over onto my right side. I'm hoping that if I press my ear into the pillow, it will stop burning, hurting. Maybe the pillow will somehow take in the words Dad said to me, so I won't have to think about them again. Instead, the pillow acts like it's hollow, a weird type of echo chamber—popping the words back into my ear over and over. The pillow does not absorb the words or the pain like I want it to. Instead, it seems to increase the internal pressure, causing me to wince. I don't know what to do, so I roll back over to my left side and let the pain and words float up into the air—up into Bernice's basement ceiling.

When I finally close my eyes, my mind once again ponders the paradox that is my dad. Was he ever capable of feeling love, joy? Was he ever the kind man my Aunt Sharon claimed he was? Why is he like this? How did he become our enemy? My enemy? Why does he become more and more hurtful, more intent on causing us harm? How will we stay alive and out of harm's way?

I know one thing for sure: my days with the HIA are over.

ॐ

Thursday: Have you ever had something happen that was too scary, or too bad, to write about? Something like that happened to me last night. It's something I can't tell anyone. The only people that know about it are my mom and dad, Bernice and Lawrence, and the New Brighton police. If you can, will you say a prayer for me?

> *Joan—I am sorry to hear this. It seems like you have had enough scary things happen to you to last a lifetime. I wonder if you could find a way to write about it, because I think it may help to get it out on paper. Maybe you could use a different notebook and keep it private, something only for you to read. Think about it, anyway. In my own way, I pray, and I have been, and will continue to, pray for you. D. Hoffman*

MAVERICK VS. DAD

MY GOD, WHO'S KNOCKING on the front door? I finally have some time to do homework and now some idiot is at the door! Probably a stupid salesperson. UUGGH! Good thing Mom isn't home—these salespeople always put her in a bad mood.

"Well, hello there, Joanie!" Dad says, grinning happily as I open the front door. Not a salesperson after all. Why did I answer the door? How could I be so stupid?

"Hi," I say, cautiously. I want to reach out and make sure the screen door is locked, but I'm afraid to make any quick movements. "What're you doing here, Dad?"

"What do you mean? Can't your dear old Dad come and visit once in a while? I haven't seen you in an extraordinarily goddamn long time!" He's standing on the step, arms folded, rocking back and forth on his feet. No cheery voice today, but sinister, evil. He tries to look past me, see into the house. I reach out and check the latch on the door—it's locked. What does it matter anyway? All that separates Dad from me is a flimsy screen. "Ah, yes, lock up that door, Joanie! Protect yourself from your mean old man." Dad's sly voice worries me. I'm sure he has something sinister planned, but what?

I look over to the Kewatts' house to see if Nancy or her sister are outside. Maybe they will notice Dad is here and call the police. But as far as I can tell, all is quiet in the Kewatt household.

"Nothing wrong with stopping by to shoot the breeze with my best girl, is there, Joanie?" Dad stares at me through the screen. His blue eyes seem to be sparking, like a bit of electricity is flowing through them.

"I guess."

Dad starts to ramble on and on . . . I'm not listening and listening at the same time. I keep an eye out, hoping to see anyone, anyone at all that might be enlisted to help me. What if I slammed the door, could I get the brace on fast enough? No, Dad would be quicker than me, and he'd be in here in a flash. I need a plan.

Dad is way stronger than I am, but I'm guessing he can't run too fast. Granted, I can't run long distances, anything over a mile, and my side starts to hurt like crazy and I can't breathe, but short distances are somewhat easy. Finally, I decide that at the first sign Dad's coming in, I'll fling open the screen door and kick him, hopefully hard enough so that he loses his balance and falls backwards off the step. Then I will take off. He can have the house all to himself. Maybe he will burn the place down and finally get arrested. But in case he does give chase, I need to have a place to go. Where? Finally, I decide to run to the cemetery. I'll tuck myself behind the tree by Cecelia's grave. Dad would never think to look for me there. I repeat my plan over and over in my mind while Dad prattles on.

"I saw a bird the other day, don't you know. It had the coloring of a cat, though. It was kind of psychedelic; you know what I mean? Like a tie-dye shirt. Imagine that, a bird looking like a cat and a shirt!" I have no answer to this, I can't imagine what he's even talking about, so I stay silent. Dad's arms are crossed, hands hidden under his armpits. Is he holding something in one of his hands? Standing on the step, he rocks back and forth, back and forth while he rambles. Occasionally, his eyes dart away from me, and he looks out towards the corner of the street—then he turns and locks his eyes back on me. My insides are shaking like a baby's rattle—shake, shake, shake. I hope Dad can't tell; I don't want him to know I'm petrified. In the middle of one of his long-winded edicts, the phone rings.

"Better get that, Dad. Hang on a second," I say, racing to the phone in the hallway. Please let it be someone who can help me! I grab the phone and pull it into the living room, keeping my eye on Dad. "Hello?"

"Well, hello, love bug! I was afraid you weren't going to answer! I'm calling to find out if you guys can stay for supper tonight. I made enough spaghetti for an army!" I want to cry at hearing Bernice's voice, but know I must play it cool, can't let Dad know who is on the line.

"Sorry, we don't want the Pioneer Press," I say, hoping this will alert her somehow. "I'm pretty sure my mom told you to never call here!"

"Joan, is something wrong?" It worked—Bernice's intuition is kicking in!

"I told you! We already get a newspaper and we don't want another one!" Dad is watching me through the screen, rocking gently back and forth on his feet, arms still folded. I hope he's not figuring out that I'm talking to Bernice.

"Is your dad there?" Bernice asks, calmly but firmly.

"Yes! Fine! Do what you want! Call my mom later for all I care—she'll tell you the same thing!" My voice is cracking a little. *Don't cry, for God's sake!*

"I'm calling the police," Bernice announces, and she hangs up the phone. At that, I slam down the phone, trying to indicate to Dad my fury with the Pioneer Press.

"I suppose your lovely motherstill reads the StarTibune

Newspaper every day,'"' Dad says, seeming to buy my cover story.

"Yes she does, no Pioneer Press for her! She still does the crossword each morning before work." Mom is due home any minute, so I continue to try to get Dad to watch me instead of the street. I don't want him to see her car approach. "So, Dad, I still don't know where you live," I say, trying to engage him. "Are you downtown now, or what?"

As I finish my question, Mom drives by. She's on Fifth Street, and at first, it looks like she's going to turn onto Eleventh. At the last second, she changes her mind, stays on Fifth. I'm guessing she saw Dad on the step and decided to head to Bernice's. "I mean, a girl should know where her dad lives, right?"

"Oh, I live here, there, everywhere. And nowhere, of course!" Dad's agitated now, his arms are uncrossed, and he's moved a little closer to the screen door. He didn't like my question, I guess. "How about if you let your dear old Dad in for a while? Ha, Joanie? How about it?"

After I tell Dad that he cannot come in, he starts to pace—takes tiny steps around and around on the top step; he's winding up. When are the police going to get here? I prepare myself to kick and run.

"Dad, I've got kind of a lot of homework to do," I try. "Maybe you should leave now."

"Oh, homework, right. There's always homework, I suppose. Yeah, I guess you're right, I should leave. Isn't it exceptionally sad that my best girl, my own daughter, won't even let me in my own house. At least it used to be my own house."

I try to think of something else to say, but my mind is a blank. Where are those damn policemen? And then, suddenly, without saying another word, Dad turns and heads down the sidewalk to his rat-trap van. He's leaving! Oh, my God, I'm safe! As soon as Dad drives away in his van, I close the door, lock it and put the barricade up.

Sitting in here with the doors barricaded, I feel like I'm a prisoner. What am I supposed to do now? Wait here for the police to come? Go over to Bernice's? What if Dad comes back? I pace through the house, peek out of the curtains to see if there is any sign of the police or Dad. Finally, I decide it's been long enough and head out the back door, over to Bernice's.

"Are you okay?" Mom says as I walk in the door.

"Yeah, I guess. He stood there for I don't know how long—talking and talking—and then, abruptly, he walked to his rat-trap van and drove away," I say, trying to catch my breath. "You drove straight here then? I thought the police were going to show up, but they never did."

Over supper, the adults discuss what to do while Gloria and I eat downstairs. Eventually, Mom, Bernice, and Lawrence come down to have a drink at the bar.

"Why don't you and Gloria play a game or something while we have a drink, and then we'll head home," Mom suggests. I guess we're not staying overnight this time.

Gloria and I play a few rounds of Rock 'Em Sock 'Em Robots and then head into the bar area to join the adults. Mom finishes up her beer, and then we head up the stairs.

"Have a good trip home!" Bernice says, jokingly, as we make our way out her side door to our car.

"Seems funny to be driving home from Bernice's house, doesn't it?" Mom says as we all climb in. "It'll be a short ride, that's for sure!"

We have a new car now, due to a bad car accident that happened on our way to Madelia last Easter. Our green Chevy Impala has been replaced with a shimmering-brown Ford Maverick. It's an okay car, but it doesn't always want to start, especially if it was shut off a short time ago. It's happened a bunch of times in the driveway; Mom will turn the car off to get out and unlock the garage door, and then when she gets back in the car, it won't start. It also has a habit of dying at stop signs, which can be annoying if another car is behind us.

Yeah! The car starts right up. As Mom starts driving down Tenth Avenue I see what looks like Dad's van parked on the other side of the street. It's down a few houses, but I'm sure it's his van.

At the same moment I'm about to say something, Dad takes off from his spot and starts driving at what seems like the speed of light. I watch his van cross over to our side of the street: he's headed directly for us. Before we even know what's happening, Dad's rat-trap van is eye-to-eye with our Maverick.

"Gloria! Lay down on the floor!" I shout, turning to the back to make sure she complies with my order. She's already crying, but there's no way to comfort her right now. "I know you're scared. I need you to stay down," I say, trying to use a calm voice.

Mom tries to go around Dad, steers quickly and starts driving on the wrong side of the road. But Dad apparently anticipated this and matches her move, maintaining a short distance between the two vehicles. He's driving with the skill of the race car drivers on television. Mom decides to stop the Maverick; her foot presses forcefully on the brake pedal. Dad, however, keeps driving forward. "MOM!" I shriek as Dad's van inches closer and closer to our car.

"My God! I don't know what to do!" Mom yells. And then, an idea comes to her. I watch as she moves the shifter into reverse and presses her foot on the gas. We start to move backward as Dad continues to drive forward. She speeds up a little; Dad speeds up accordingly. It's hard for Mom to drive straight—we are in a backwards weave of sorts—and Dad weaves right along with us. If the Maverick's engine cuts out, we're doomed. The two vehicles are so close to each other they are almost touching. About the time that I realize we are in front of Bernice's house again, Mom starts honking the horn. Not like a honk-honk kind of thing—she depresses the horn with her hand so that it continuously blares out into the atmosphere.

I clench my teeth and stare through the windshield at Dad. He is not looking at me, though. Dad is watching Mom's every move—looking through his dirty, grimy windshield and into hers. His face tells all: he wants her. The hair on the back of my neck bristles and the wobbliness of my insides returns as I realize this is what he wanted all along. He didn't stop by to shoot the breeze with his best girl—he stopped by to do what he always does: torture Mom.

As the sound of the horn pierces the air in the neighborhood, Lawrence and Bernice come flying out of their house. Bernice turns back immediately—to call the police, I hope. As Lawrence approaches the street, another neighbor guy joins him. They are both shouting at Dad, tracing the path of our vehicles with their quick feet. Out of the corner of my eye, I see other neighbors come out; they start to gather in a small group in one of the yards.

"John, I mean it. Stop! You're scaring the children! John, can you understand that? Stop right now!" Lawrence is shouting, but Dad does not halt—refuses to end this nightmare he has dreamt up. He does not say a word, does not take his eyes off Mom, not even for a second. It's like he can't see or hear anyone but Mom. The back of our car is almost to the corner, almost in the intersection, when the police finally arrive. Two cars pull up right behind Dad's van, and, as the officers approach the driver's side of his van, Dad puts on the brakes. And so does Mom.

One of the officers approaches our car and opens the front and back doors. As soon as we are outside, I scoop up Gloria and run into Bernice's house. "It's okay. I've got you. It's okay," I say into her ear.

"Downstairs! Everyone downstairs!" Bernice instructs. I run down the stairs with Gloria and breathe a sigh of safety. As I settle Gloria on the couch, I realize Mom and Bernice are not with us.

"Mom? Bernice?" I call up the stairs. "What's going on?" It doesn't seem safe to go upstairs—what if everyone is dead or something? Finally, Bernice appears at the top of the stairs. When she appears, my legs become weak, the strength in them is leaving, my muscles wasting away, melting like a snowman into the tile floor of Bernice's basement.

"Don't worry," she says. "The police are still in the street with your dad. They want to talk to your mom, too, so it may be a while before we come down. There's ice cream in the deep freeze—why don't you fix some for you and Gloria?"

Don't worry? Is that what she said? Don't worry? How is that even possible? Worry is all I do now—the word defines me; it might as well be my name. UGGH! Slowly, I head back to Gloria, still sitting on the couch right where I left her.

"Guess what, sweetheart?" I say, sitting down next to her. I reach my hand up to her hair, smooth it out a little. "Bernice told me we could have some ice cream. Do you want some?"

Gloria smiles through her thumb—I'm not going to pull it out tonight, she needs it. Gloria nods her head, letting me know that, yes, she is up for some ice cream.

"How about if you go in the fridge behind the bar and see if there is some Hershey's syrup while I grab the ice cream?" I suggest. But as we get up off the couch, I change my mind. I don't want us to go our separate ways. "Scratch that idea! Let's do everything together!" I say, trying to muster up a cheerful voice. We hold hands as we head to the laundry room and open Bernice's large deep freeze to get the ice cream—we hold hands as we head to the bar refrigerator to get the chocolate syrup— we hold hands as I scoop out the ice cream and pour the syrup on—we hold hands while we put the ice cream away—we hold hands as we sit on the barstools and polish off what should feel like a treat, but doesn't. And we hold hands as we head back to the couch, where we lie down together and snuggle up like two peas in a pod.

My sister has not said one word all night. I know she's scared and she knows I'm scared. I should say something to her, but what? I used to be able to reassure Gloria. But tonight, whatever I said would be an outright lie. The words would be as weightless as the clouds in the sky. And so, I say nothing, just wrap my arms around her and hold her as close to me as I can.

"Joan—it's time to head home," I hear Mom saying. Somewhere along the way, Gloria and I fell asleep. I have no idea what time it is or anything.

"What? Oh, okay. What happened? Did they let Dad go?" I ask as I pick Gloria up and wrap her around my body.

"They took him away—not sure where, or for how long—but we are good for tonight anyway," Mom says, tiredly. "They took his van somewhere, too. Not sure if he'll get that back. I'm going to drive the Maverick home—no sense all of us getting into the car right now. After I get the car in the garage, you and Gloria can walk home. Bernice and Lawrence will watch you walk down the sidewalk," Mom continues. "Come on, let's get home and get to bed."

Once in the house, I tell Gloria to go potty, brush her teeth and get her pajamas on. After I get her tucked in, I head back out to the kitchen where Mom is cracking open a beer. I watch as she turns on the television, settles herself at her spot on the couch, lights a cigarette.

"Mom?" I say, tentatively. I can't quite read her mood.

"What is it?" she asks. She sounds irritated, exasperated.

"Well, I was wondering if you know why the police never came here this afternoon? I pretended like Bernice was the Pioneer Press and I was sure she figured out what was going on. She told me she was going to call the police. But they never showed up."

"That's because they went to Bernice's house. She's the one that called them, so they went there," Mom says, seemingly satisfied with her answer.

"Okay, I guess that makes sense. But then why didn't they come here, too?" My voice is cracking a little bit; I'm afraid my questions are going to push the wrong button and Mom is going to erupt. "I was waiting for them to show up, to tell Dad to take off or whatever. Because I was here alone with him and he's not supposed to be here. Ever. Right?"

"Well, once I arrived at Bernice's, it was decided that everything was okay," Mom says. "I was safe. You understand that, right? I was most certainly his target, and your dad obviously knew I wasn't home, so there wasn't anything for the police to do. So they left."

What the hell? Standing next to Mom, I try to take this in, try to reconcile Mom's and everyone else's logic with the reality of what happened. I'm glad Mom wasn't home, yes, and glad she wasn't hurt. But the police left? Didn't drive by our house to see what was going on? How did anyone know whether I was or wasn't okay?

"Okay. Yeah, I guess I understand. It's just that . . . "

"Time for you to get to bed, don't you think? We should sleep good tonight since we know the police took your dad away," Mom says. "Can you put the brace against the door on your way to bed? I'm going to sit here and watch television a little longer."

If we're so safe, then why do we still need to fortify the door with this damn brace?

❧

Thursday, Friday, Saturday and Sunday: Please see Monday.

Monday: Dear Mr. Hoffman—So sorry I didn't write in my notebook for so long. I know I won't get an A, but I hope it won't drop all the way to a B. Maybe an A-? I had kind of a bad week—again.

On Wednesday night my dad came over when my mom was still at work (I'm sure you know her, because she works at The First State Bank of New Brighton). I was just getting ready to start my homework when someone knocked on the front door. I never thought it would be my dad, so I opened the door. What an idiot, right? I was so afraid he was going to break through the screen and come in and get me, but he just kept standing there on the front step. Then, Bernice called to see if we could stay for supper—I pretended she was The Pioneer Press calling and told her we didn't want a subscription. And guess what? She figured out my dad was there and told me before she hung up that she was going to call the police. But the police never came. And then suddenly, Dad left. I waited for the police a little while, but it was too scary to stay in the house all by myself, so finally I decided to head over to Bernice's.

But anyway, what happened after that was pretty unreal. We were going to drive home from Bernice's, but when we started driving down her street, there was my dad in his van! He was parked on the side of the street waiting for us. Once he saw Mom driving, he started driving, too—headed right for us. His van and Mom's car were about an inch apart, and he wasn't going to stop. So then Mom drove in reverse while Dad drove forward. I thought for sure Dad would ram Mom's car with his van. He was staring right at her and I could tell he meant business. When Mom saw she had backed up all the way to Bernice's house—she laid on the horn and Bernice and her husband came out. Bernice ran back in and called the police (again). The police got Dad to stop his van, and then I guess they took him away somewhere.

Dearest Joan—I'm so sorry to hear about what happened to you and your family. I know how hard it must've been for you to share this with me. What occurred would have scared anyone, and I can't imagine how it affects a fifteen-year-old. I truly hope that your dad is in jail, maybe he will finally get some help. I am so glad that Bernice and her husband were able to assist you in your time of need. I am very impressed by your bravery, and by how well you handled the whole situation. I have seen a lot of kids in my career, and I will tell you that none of them measure up to you! I sincerely mean that. Oh, and, your abiding love for your mom and sister is just remarkable. Your mother must love you very much, and must be proud of you, as am I.

The last thing you need to worry about is achieving an A on your journal. If you write nothing else for the rest of the quarter, you will have an A. Because to me, you are an A.

D. Hoffman

TURNING

MONDAY: WELL, I GUESS this is our last notebook entry, which means that ninth grade is over! Did I tell you that they changed the school boundaries AGAIN? I will be going to Irondale High school instead of Mounds View, which is where my brother and practically everyone I know went. But here's the good news: the Trio and all associates are going to Mounds View! Though I know there could be a whole new group to take their place, I'm so relieved that this crew will not be at Irondale.

I'm trying to come up with a brand-new plan for myself. I want to do something different. You know how leaves change colors in the fall? Well, I've been thinking about that a lot, and I feel like I've always related to the leaves that turn yellow—those leaves still have a little bit of green—retain just a touch of chlorophyll in their veins, I suppose—on their backs when they break away from the tree. The leaves on the ash tree in our front yard turn that color. But here's the thing: I think I'm done with that boring color. There are a ton of maple trees in our neighborhood and the leaves on those trees change from green to the most beautiful red color—kind of a combination of a deep scarlet sunset with just a hint of burnt orange mixed in. Can you picture that color? The pigment goes all the way through—they are the same color on their underside as on the top. I think of them as being completely transformed. I've also noticed that the maple leaves turn later than other trees—our ash is almost bald before the maples even start to change color. But then, in mid to late October, the color change occurs, and the vibrant color is revealed. It takes my breath away.

So anyway, when school starts in the fall, I'm thinking I want to try out that red color and let the yellow color go. I don't have any money, so I know I can't buy cool clothes and makeup like the other girls, so I figure this is something I CAN do, because it is free. I suppose that's one of the basic freedoms of life. But here's the problem: I want to, but can I? I'm not sure I'm brave enough to be vibrant. What if no one likes me when I start to try new things, try to hold my head higher, stop rolling my shoulders? I don't want to be a completely different person exactly, I know I'll always have some of that yellow-green color in me. But I just want to be more of who I already am. Does that make sense?

I don't know how I will get through high school. I want to graduate like my brother did, but he was so smart, and since I'm kind of dumb I realize I might not make it. But then again, maybe with my new coat of color I will become a little smarter! Maybe I will get A's and B's instead of B's and C's!

Speaking of A's: I still can't believe you are giving me an A on my journal when I missed writing in it a whole bunch of days. I haven't told anyone else, because they'd probably be jealous!

I want to thank you, Mr. Hoffman, for all that you have done for me this year. I have written about so many things in this notebook—mostly bad things, I know. Sorry I was your bummer student! But it's YOUR words, what you wrote in this notebook that mattered. You helped me see life for what it is, and your advice has been precious. I plan to save this notebook forever and ever.

Joan—You can, and you will! You are already a wonderful, young person with so much talent and intelligence (yes, you are smart!) and I have no doubt that high school (and beyond) will be a successful venture for you. I can picture the color you describe, and I just <u>know</u> it will look great on you! D Hoffman

AUTHOR'S REFLECTION

THE WRITING OF *THE BEST Girl* required a bit of research. Though I had the names of Dad's six brothers and four sisters, I didn't have much else to go on. In the process of mapping out his family, I learned that two of his paternal uncles and three of his siblings (two of his brothers and one sister) committed suicide. At least four of Dad's brothers were alcoholics.

My brother, sister, and I had quite a few discussions as well—trying to piece together the memories that I had with what they knew, etc. Mark told me that after he moved to Texas, Mom never informed him of what was happening at home. During the Frozen incident, Gloria remembers standing in the kitchen and thinking that if she could get Dad's glasses off, he wouldn't be able to see, and therefore would stop hurting Mom. She remembers trying to find me, getting more scared when she couldn't, feeling safer when I came through the door and scooped her up.

It's amazing for me to see, through my writing, how many times Dad slipped through the cracks of law enforcement, how the decisions made by the legal system seemed to favor him. That I know of, there was only one time that Dad spent any time in a facility—and that was after the incident at the bank, for which Dad spent thirty days at the Ramsey County Workhouse. I don't know at what point he became homeless, but by the time I entered high school, we knew he was living on the streets of downtown Minneapolis.

One of the most difficult things I have ever done was to forgive Dad for all the heinous acts he committed, and particularly for his threat to shoot my brains out. A phone would ring, or someone would discuss a shooting, and the memory of that phone call would come to the front of my mind and then activate my old coping skill of wanting to run, to flee, to get away—even though in reality there was absolutely no sign of danger. I came to a point, when I was about thirty years old, that I knew I would have to forgive Dad if I wanted to be free of these episodes. Dad had passed away by this time, and I was at a loss as to how to go about forgiving him. I was also experiencing severe neck pain, to the point it was hard to turn my head from side to side. My health care provider had an idea for this—a clinician by the name of Keith Sullivan who was studying myofascial release therapy.

After some discussion, Keith told me that you don't have to see someone face to face to forgive them—that the idea of forgiveness is to let go of the past on your own terms. On about the third session, he thought I was ready to try out his method. I lay on my back on the cot, and Keith sat behind me at the head of the table.

"Okay, Joan, I'm ready. I want you to close your eyes, okay?" he instructed. Once I had my eyes closed, I could feel his hands on my neck and shoulder area. "I'm going to work on what are called trigger points. As I find one, I'll apply pressure to it for thirty seconds or so, then move my finger slightly and again apply pressure. The idea is to reduce the inflammation in these areas. Okay, here's the first one—can you feel that?"

"Yes," I said, wincing. The amount of pain associated with each pebble-sized pressure point was excruciating and occasionally radiated to other areas of my body—down my arm, into my back, my eyes or forehead. As he pressed his finger or thumb into the various trigger points in my neck and shoulder area, he started asking me to try to visualize the reason for the pain.

During a subsequent session, again with my eyes closed, Keith's pressure on a trigger point elicited a red color. "Do you see anything else?" he asked. Soon after, a white letter Y appeared within the red.

"I think the letter represents all of my 'Why' questions," I said. "Why did Dad do the thing he did? Why was he so violent? Why was it so hard to get someone to help us? Why did we have to endure this?"

"Is there anything else in the red area, any other colors, letters—anything at all?"

"Yes," I said. "But I'm too scared to keep going."

"Okay, let's slow down a little. I am going to ease up on the pressure a bit. Can you look at it now?" he asked, gently.

"It's Dad," I answered. "It's him. His blue eyes are looking right at me."

"It's your decision. You can either hear what he has to say now or wait until the next session."

In my trance-like state, trying to hold back tears, I decided that I did want to hear what Dad had to say.

"He told me he's sorry. Sorry for everything, but that he has no answers of his own. 'I can't answer your questions, Joanie. I can only tell you I'm sorry.' That's what he said." At that, I broke down in sobs. Keith then eased up completely on the trigger points.

Though the experience left me quite shaken, I agreed to come back. With each session, I learned something new about myself or my family. And with each session, my neck pain seemed to dissipate a little. It was then that I could make my own mind-body connection and see how the emotional pain that I had suffered through as a child was still a part of me. I had worked so hard to hide and bury all the memories, and to me, they were stored away to be forgotten, but my body remembered them all.

Despite everything, the ear pain that started after Dad told me he was going to shoot me has continued. Sometimes it's a mild, trivial type of pain—I hardly know it's there. Other times it sears all the way through to my eardrum. If I become stressed or angry about something, it ratchets up a degree or two. Every year, when I have my annual physical, I ask the doctor for a full report on the status of my right ear. Normal as can be, is always the answer.

I don't know who gave Mom the idea to record the phone calls. That I know of, none of the tapes were ever listened to by anyone in a position of authority. It was a very difficult decision for me to stop being a part of the HIA, because the one thing I sought above all was my mom's approval—and it was only on the rarest of occasions that I went against her wishes. I agreed to be a part of the HIA because I wanted her to think I was up to the task, able to be a part of her team. Ultimately, if there was something I could do that would decrease her/our misery, I did it. When I stopped recording Dad's calls, I felt like I was letting Mom down.

Though I've always known how much Bernice and Lawrence did for us, the writing of the book helped me to see it in a way I had not before. The two of them stepped up, stepped right into the mud and murk. Bernice carefully crafted a relationship with Mom that preserved their friendship, but provided a safety net for Gloria and me. The first time they sheltered us was the first time I slept without a feeling of dread looming over me. But now, I wonder if Bernice and Lawrence slept at all—possibly every time they sheltered us, Lawrence stayed up all night, shotgun loaded and at the ready, in case my dad showed up looking for us. I see now how they put their own lives at risk for ours. The moment when Lawrence teaches me how to place the braces on our doors is as important to me as my wedding day and the births of my children.

I have yet to come to terms with Mom's harsh treatment of me. Her criticisms about my face and body have stayed with me. It is very difficult for me to accept a compliment where my appearance is concerned and almost every time I was with her, I felt like I was being inspected. I'm hyperconscious of my face—feeling my cheeks, chin almost constantly to make sure I don't have any acne, picking at anything I find to try to make it disappear. Assembling the photos for *The Best Girl*, I tried to find one of the Joanie she described—an overweight girl with huge thighs and a face marred by acne. Standing at my dining room table, looking over the photos from my adolescence, I started to cry. There weren't any photos that reflected her words—what I saw, for possibly the first time, was a tall, young girl of average weight with clear skin.

Though I knew that Mom was emotionally absent from our lives, I didn't realize the extent until writing this book. Scene after scene revealed to me how hard I tried, even as a young child, to connect with her on an emotional level. I continuously tried to reassure her, tried to get her to smile. Mom was a respected woman, as she should have been. I have the utmost respect for her as well, which is what makes it even harder to admit the other feelings I have surrounding her role as my mom.

Mr. Hoffman came into my life at a time when I was running out of options—out of ideas of how to keep going, how to move myself from one moment to the next. I was emotionally and socially behind my classmates. My number one priority was the safety and security of my mom and my sister. Mr. Hoffman was the first person who recognized the dire situation we were in and named it for what it was: wrong. I felt vindicated—finally, someone agreed with me! Our back-and-forth journaling taught me the value and the power of the written word. On more than one occasion, his writing let me know he cared about what was happening in my life—whether at home or at school. And yet, he didn't want me to linger in his empathy. His messages—*you are a good person, you will go far in this world*—gave me hope.

In the spring of 1982, as I was completing my sophomore year of college, I received a letter from the principal of Johanna Junior High. Mr. Hoffman had been selected as a candidate for the Excellence in Education award, then sponsored by the Minnesota Business Foundation. The principal wondered if I could take time out of my busy schedule to write a letter of nomination in support of Mr. Hoffman. To this day, it is one of the most important documents I have ever signed.

Upon completion of the manuscript, I was encouraged by my close circle of readers to contact Mr. Hoffman to let him know about the book, and of his vital role in my life. Though I agreed it was a good idea, it took me a while to act. I had not seen him since junior high, and I wasn't sure he would remember me. When I finally decided to look him up in the White Pages, I found over twenty listings for Donald Hoffman in Minnesota. At that point, I posted a query on the "If You Grew Up in New Brighton" Facebook page, which led to me obtaining his phone number.

But even after I had his phone number, I hesitated. Then one day, I set a goal that by the end of that day I was going to make the call—and I did. When his wife answered the phone and I started to explain who I was, she handed the phone to her husband and, just like that, Mr. Hoffman's voice was on the other end.

"Mr. Hoffman," I started. "It's so good to hear your voice. My name is Joan Hicks—you were my Creative Writing teacher at Johanna in 1976. That was a long time ago, so I'm not sure if you remember me."

"Well, sure! I remember a Joan Hicks," he answered. I knew that it was still possible he didn't, but I secretly hoped it was true.

"I'm calling to let you know I've written a book called *The Best Girl*. It's a memoir and covers my life from age four to fifteen," I said. "You're a prominent person in the book, and I would be honored if you would consider reading the manuscript."

"Well now," he responded. "I'm an important person in the book? I'm intrigued, and would be honored to read it."

At that point, we set a date and time to meet for lunch, at which time I would give him a copy of the manuscript. I encouraged him to check out my author website in the meantime so that he would have an idea of what the book was about. And then, a week later, on January 19th, 2017, we met for lunch.

As I gave him a recap of my life experiences, it was hard for me to hold back tears, and, though I would never speak for him, I think it was for him as well. As I finished recounting my home situation and a summary of my years at Johanna, including the bullying incidents and my extreme difficulties in gym class, he reached into a bag and pulled out a copy of his yearbook. He turned to the page where I had written a note to him and read two of the lines out loud: "I'm so glad to be done with gym class!"—which we both chuckled over, and "I'm impressed you got my mom to like you"—which surprised me, because I have no recollection of them interacting with each other.

"I remember your mother, oh yes. And I remember she worked at the bank," he said. There are moments in life where you know you should push forward, and instead, you pull back, and this was one of those. On some level I wanted to know more—what did they talk about? Did he call to tell her about what I was writing, or that he was concerned for my wellbeing? But in the end, I let the moment pass. Possibly we will see each other again, possibly after he has read the manuscript, and perhaps then I will feel brave enough to ask.

Before we knew it, three hours had passed. Our waitress was afraid we hated our food, because once I started talking, we both stopped eating (we each ate exactly one bite of our food).

As I concluded my story and outlined my goals and ambitions for *The Best Girl,* he attempted to apologize for not being able to remember the details of my journal, of my experience.

"That's okay," I said. "I know you taught a lot of kids in your career, and I didn't expect you to remember everything. But what I want you to know is that your words, written in that small half-printed half-cursive penmanship, came to me at a time when I desperately needed them, and, whether you knew it or not at the time, made a tremendous difference in my life. And I want to thank you for that."

"Joan, what you've gone through. I can't imagine. For you to share your story, in the hopes of the betterment of society—well, that's just simply remarkable."

As we concluded our lunch, I handed him my copy of my yearbook, so that he could read what he wrote.

Joan—It has been my very good fortune to get to know you this year. It is people like you who make my job so rewarding. Thanks for being a good friend. You have so many fine qualities—if only more people could be the way you are the world would be a better place. The best to you always, and in all ways. You deserve nothing less. TAKE CARE. D Hoffman

ACKNOWLEDGMENTS

The writing of *The Best Girl* would not have happened without the dedication and commitment of Patricia Hoolihan. Patricia is a professor at Metro State University and The Loft Literary Center in Minneapolis. Her astute attention to the detail, the flow, and the structure of the book helped me produce what I know is a quality piece of art. Patricia's belief in the social impact of *The Best Girl* kept both of us continually focused on the bigger picture.

Early on, I learned about the value of beta readers. These are people of the author's choosing that read the manuscript while it is being written. I chose three women, from different walks of my life. Each of them repeatedly interrogated the manuscript for clarity, conciseness, and typographical errors. These women: Melissa Driggers, Kate Fitzgerald and Lisa Gruentzel Thompson, became my cheerleaders, fortune tellers, and confidants. They know *The Best Girl* almost as well as I, and I will forever be in a debt of gratitude to them.

A special thank you to those who promoted the implementation of the 9-1-1 Emergency Response System: The National Association of Fire Chiefs, the Federal Communication Commission, The President's Commission on Law Enforcement & Administration of Justice, and AT&T Communications. Your hard work enabled people in all walks of life, in all types of crises, to immediately access assistance, saving countless lives.

DOMESTIC VIOLENCE RESOURCES

If you are in immediate danger, call or text 9-1-1.

The National Domestic Violence Hotline, 1-800-799-7233 or www.thehotline.org, offers education and assists victims in connecting with local resource organizations, including immediate placement in a secure shelter.

REFERENCES

Ackerman, Diane. *I Praise My Destroyer: Poems by Diane Ackerman*. New York, New York: Vintage Books of Random House, 1998.

Groves, Betsy McAlister. *Children Who See Too Much*. Boston, MA: Beacon Press, 2002.

Kolk, Bessel van der. *The Body Keeps the Score: Brain, Mind, and Body in the Healing of Trauma*. New York, New York: Penguin Books of Random House, 2014.

McGee, Caroline. *Childhood Experiences of Domestic Violence*. London, UK: Jessica Kingsley Publishers, 2000.

Renzetti, Claire, et al. *Sourcebook on Violence Against Women, Third Edition*. Thousand Oaks, CA: Sage Publications, 2018.

CPSIA information can be obtained
at www.ICGtesting.com
Printed in the USA
LVOW11s0045200418
574121LV00005B/872/P